Comic Crime

Comic Crime

Earl F. Bargainnier
Editor

Bowling Green State University Popular Press
Bowling Green, Ohio 43403

Library of Congress Catalogue Card No: 87-71031

Copyright © 1987 by the Bowling Green University Popular Press

ISBN: 0-87972-383-1 Clothbound
      0-87972-384-X Paperback

Cover design by Gary Dumm

Contents

Preface 1

Comedy and the British Crime Novel 7
  H.R.F. Keating

Laughing With the Corpses:
  Hard-Boiled Humor 23
  Frederick Isaac

"What Fun!": Detection as Diversion 44
  Elaine Bander

Farcical Worlds of Crime 55
  Earl F. Bargainnier

The Comic Village 75
  Mary Jean DeMarr

Crime and Comedy on Campus 92
  Wister Cook

Guises and Disguises of the
  Eccentric Amateur Detective 111
  Jane S. Bakerman

The Little Old Ladies 128
  Neysa Chouteau & Martha Alderson

The Comic in the Canon:
  What's Funny about Sherlock Holmes? 145
  Barrie Hayne

The Comic Capers of Donald Westlake 168
  Michael Dunne

Is It or Isn't It?:
  The Duality of Parodic Detective Fiction 181
  Lizabeth Paravisini & Carlos Yorio

Contributors 194

Preface

Earl F. Bargainnier

First on the bestseller list for months during 1983 was Umberto Eco's *The Name of the Rose*, a work which used formulas of crime fiction for many things. One of these was to discuss the propriety—even the Christianity—of laughter. The central mystery of Eco's novel is a secret book in a labyrinthine abbey library; that book happens to be Aristotle's lost treatise on comedy—alas, still lost. *The Name of the Rose* is only one of the latest works to succeed in conjoining mystery or crime and the comic. Though few have had its sudden and massive popularity, its predecessors are many.

At first glance, the idea of combining the comic with the criminal may seem tasteless, if not worse. Certainly, in the actual world crime is not a subject for laughter, but rather for anger or tears. If laughter is heard in the midst of a real crime, it is either hysterical or sadistic. The world of fiction, however, is a different matter. Most crime fiction, especially that called "classical," is much nearer the comic than the tragic. Indeed, in his influential *Anatomy of Criticism*, Northrop Frye places the entire genre of detective fiction among the Comic Fictional Modes, and in the oldest sense of the term *comedy*—that no matter the difficulties, misunderstandings, or even deaths, the evil are thwarted and the good rewarded—crime fiction is essentially comic, though admittedly there have been major exceptions since the 1920s. One evidence of that comic nature is the renewal of harmony in society at the end of crime novels, as in comedy, signified by engagements, marriages, births or the announcement of forthcoming ones, dinners (the traditional feast of thanks), and other such symbolic acts.

Nevertheless, there is still an uneasy relationship between mirth and murder, even in fiction. Characters making jokes over and about a corpse can repulse, rather than entertain, a reader. Gallows humor does appear, but it is probably the least effective form of comedy in crime fiction, and rare is the novel based solely upon it. More often the wisecracks, quips, and running gags are aimed at those still living and generally do not refer to the crime itself, unless deliberately facetiously so. Sardonic

1

they may be, but almost never gruesome. One method of solving the uneasy relationship is most evident in British classical detective fiction and is indicated by the epithet "cosy." This cosiness prevents a clash between crime and comic action. It owes a great deal to the novels of P.G. Wodehouse and the early ones of Evelyn Waugh, especially as to characterization. One can be comfortable at houseparties with silly-ass young men and bubble-headed, though titled, damsels. Murder becomes simply a lark: a game hardly more threatening than croquet on the manor lawn. There is less American cosy crime fiction than British, yet when it appears, it functions in the same way. Its one major addition is the homespun philosopher, male or female: purveyor of common sense, practical advice, and pithy comments on the events and other characters. Two recent examples are Lucille Kallen's C.B. Greenfield and Charlotte MacLeod's Martha Lomax. Whatever the technique used, writers in both countries have been able to overcome the seemingly innate incompatibility of crime and comedy to create novels blending the two. (It is not surprising that a number of crime novelists—from Carolyn Wells and A.A. Milne to Gore Vidal, as Edgar Box, and Tom Sharpe—have also written purely comic works.)

The simplest ways of incorporating comedy into crime fiction are parody, descriptive or scenic set pieces, and characters, major or, more often, minor. Parody of specific works and detectives and burlesques of types of crime fiction have a long history, for formula fiction lends itself to them, but that is not the concern here. (For *unintentional* comedy in crime fiction, see Bill Pronzini's *Gun in Cheek* [1982]—and be prepared to laugh.) Instead, the use of these within crime fiction itself is. Writers have not hesitated to use parodic elements within their fiction, lampooning the very form they are writing. For example, Agatha Christie's *Partners in Crime*, Leo Bruce's *Case for Three Detectives*, James Anderson's *The Affair of the Blood-Stained Egg Cosy*, and all of Ross H. Spencer's *Caper* novels are totally based upon such parody or burlesque. Even more prevalent is the introduction of parodic scenes, characters, or actions for short periods in a novel, as well as brief parodic comments upon the action. Dozens of novels in the genre have employed these to create laughter of recognition, to enliven repetitive questioning of witnesses, or to provide "comic relief" from more "serious" action. (For much more on parody, see the essay by Lizabeth Paravisini and Carlos Yorio.)

Another form of comic relief is the set piece, a descriptive passage or a scene which is included as much—or more—for its comedy as for its contribution to plot. The best of such set pieces, however, provide both. A superb example is the recital of the Leopold String Quartet in Matthew Head's *The Congo Venus*, which is both hilarious and absolutely integral to the plot. When such scenes do not advance the action, they may develop character in a surprising way, as with antique dealer-detective Lovejoy's baby-sitting episode in Jonathan Gash's *Gold by Gemini*. Even if such scenes add nothing but comedy yet are incorporated with care, they can serve to release built-up tension, one instance being Nigel Strangeways' nonsense questions on his first appearance in Nicholas Blake's rather grim *The Beast Must Die*. Whether employed skillfully or clumsily, the comic set piece is a staple of the crime novelist.

Comic characters are so numerous and so varied in crime fiction that their nature will be a major subject of the following essays; therefore, only a few general remarks will be made here. In an article entitled "Murder Makes Merry" in Howard Haycraft's *The Art of the Mystery Story*, Craig Rice, herself an author of screwball crime novels, comments on "that unbeatable vaudeville team of the shrewd detective and the comic cop." Certainly, conflict between amateur sleuth and professional— particularly if bumbling—policeman has been used again and again for comedy, as has that between sleuth and Watson—and even between policemen, as evidenced by, among others, Reginald Hill's Superintendent Dalziel and Inspector Pascoe. Hercule Poirot and Inspector Japp, Hildegarde Withers and Inspector Piper, Dr. Mary Finney and Hooper Taliaferro, Sergeant Beef and Lionel Townsend—a complete list would require pages, for comic conflicts between amateur and professional and sleuth and Watson are pervasive; the reason is that such pairings offer authors continuous opportunities for comedy. Authors may also make their detective eccentric in almost any way possible, but since he must represent truth, reason, and justice, he can never be completely laughable. Thus comic minor characters, from anthropomorphic animals and precocious children to quaint bucolics and dizzy dowagers, supply most of the comedy. They may be stereotypes, reversed stereotypes, caricatures, bizarre, gently satiric, or absurdly silly, but one of their functions as suspects and witnesses is to form the comic environment of their novels. When they reappear in series novels, the reader is prepared on their entrance for laughs. Without them, crime fiction might be more "realistic," but it would unquestionably be less fun. Who would want Martha Grimes to omit Lady Agatha Ardry from her Inspector Richard Jury novels?

These three methods of combining the comic and the criminal are only the most obvious of many, but the one essential for a successful combination is the author's management of tone. Tone is intangible; one cannot point to a particular item in a work and say that it is that work's tone. Rather, tone is the attitude the author takes toward his subject: tragic, comic, or otherwise. Comic tone is most often associated with the author's being detached from his characters and the situations in which they find themselves, and this is true of comic crime fiction. One does not really care about the victim, for neither the author nor the other characters do. But the author must establish a comic tone quickly or risk confusing the reader. Allusive, facetious, or punning titles often indicate the tone even before the reader opens the book: *A Clubbable Woman*, *Abracadaver*, *A Healthy Way to Die*, *Kissing Covens*, *Accounting for Murder*, *There's Trouble Brewing*, *Rest You Merry*, and many more.

Authors may be wry, ebullient, daffy, or irreverent, but if they are to write of comic crime, readers must know that it is comic—and quickly. A British example of immediately setting such a tone is the first few paragraphs of *One-Man Show* by Michael Innes, a master of comic crime:

> Lady Appleby finished her coffee, drew on her gloves and glanced round the restaurant. "John," she asked her husband, "did you say you needn't be back at the Yard till three o'clock?"
>
> "I believe I did." Sir John Appleby called for his bill. "Was it rash of me? Are you going to take me for an hour's quick shopping?"
>
> "Of course not. All men hate shopping. But it means we've just time to go to the Da Vinci. There's a new show."
>
> "Has it ever occurred to you that perhaps all men hate new shows? And with you, Judith, new shows *are* shopping, as often as not. The number of paintings you've bought in the course of the last year—"
>
> "You know that all my carvings now *need* paintings as backgrounds." Judith Appleby was a sculptress by profession. "And at the moment I very much want something abstract, with strong diagonals, and plenty of acid greens."

An American instance is the beginning of Edgar Box's *Death Likes It Hot*:

> The death of Peaches Sandoe, the midget, at the hands, or rather feet, of a maddened elephant in the sideshow of the circus at Madison Square Garden was at first thought to be an accident, the sort of tragedy you're bound to run into from time to time if you run a circus with both elephants and midgets in it. A few days later, though, there was talk of foul play.
>
> I read with a good deal of interest the *Daily News'* account. A threatening conversation had been overheard; someone (unrevealed) had gone to the police with a startling story (unrevealed) and an accusation against an unnamed party. It was very peculiar.

No one reading either of these opening passages could possibly assume that he will be confronted with deeply tragic events. The tone of comedy is set. To keep the tone comedic, a favorite device is to compare the happenings to those of other crime novels. Since the majority of these comments imply that crime fiction is not to be taken seriously—but these events are—the reader makes the automatic transferal to the book at hand and remains reassured that nothing tragic will happen. Leo Bruce and Edmund Crispin go so far as to let Sergeant Beef and Gervase Fen, their respective detectives, realize that they are fictional and comment on the narrator's or author's style in presenting them. Such comic ploys keep cases moving merrily along, if admittedly sometimes artificially. Crime fiction has time and again been described as "light fiction." If it is, the "light" tone of comedy is a principal reason.

Yet the element of comedy in crime fiction has received relatively slight critical examination. In his magisterial *Adverture, Mystery, and Romance* (1978), John Cawelti offers the most extended discussion of its nature. Though oversimplifying his argument, I would like to cite a few of his statements which are basic to any study of the relationship. He says that "the mystery presents the assertion of rational order over secrecy, chaos, and irrationality." To accomplish this assertion, it presents a "basically comic universe," and such a universe "in which characters and action are constructed as to continually reassure us that things will ultimately work out happily can encompass a considerable degree of disorder and danger." Authors in the classical mode particularly have "to achieve the appropriate relation between comedy and seriousness, between rational order and the threat of disruption of either a comic or tragic sort," for the development of "additional narrative interests without dissipating the central line of the action" is "the major artistic problem of the genre" (45, 108, 109, 110). (The value of these comments, and ways in which their ideas can be accomplished, may be seen by applying them to two successful television programs: *Barney Miller*, a comic police procedural, and *Murder She Wrote*, with Angela Lansbury as an Americanized Agatha Christie/Miss Marple amateur sleuth.) Only two other notable works are solely on detective fiction and comedy: George Grella's "The Formula Detective Novel" (*Novel*, 1970), which has been reprinted several times and is frequently quoted by other critics, and Hanna Charney's *The Detective Novel of Manners* (1981). Both of these studies discuss admirably the crime novel's relationship to the comedy of manners.

However, other forms and types of the comic—farce, satire, wit, black comedy, romantic comedy, and parody and burlesque—as they appear in crime fiction have yet to be examined in any detail. The purpose of this volume is at least to begin that examination by studying some specific instances of comic crime. No attempt has been made to be exhaustive as to authors or forms, and if some authors are mentioned in more than one essay, the reason is that as there are a number of approaches to crime fiction, there are even more to the comic. The following eleven original essays, nevertheless, cover a wide range in time, authors, forms of crime fiction, and types of comedy. I thank all of the contributors for their breadth of knowledge, their suggestions for subjects to be covered, and, perhaps most important in this context, their senses of humor. I hope readers will be both informed and entertained by this excursion into British and American humor and homicide, comedy and crime.

Earl F. Bargainnier

Comedy and the British Crime Novel

H.R.F. Keating

Crime and comedy; they might at first blush seem to be as far removed one from the other as it is possible to be. Yet in much British crime writing comedy is almost as important as the crime which is the raison d'etre of this whole area of fiction.

Of course ever since the scene of the discovery of the murder in Shakespeare's *Macbeth*, and probably before that, writers have known that suspense can be greatly stepped up if it is preceded by a passage of humorous by-play. Wilkie Collins, whose *The Moonstone* was called by T.S. Eliot "the first, the longest and the best" classical English detective novel, once gave as his formula for success the simple advice "Make 'em laugh, make 'em weep, make 'em wait." So numerous crime fiction writers have larded their works with patches of humour, and very properly so.

But there are many British writers in the genre who have gone further than this and have produced, in varying forms, books that are combinations of comedy and crime. Though there are writers in other national crime literatures who have embarked on the same mixture of modes (Americans from Phoebe Atwood Taylor to Donald E. Westlake, Frenchmen like Jypé Carraud, a German like H.H. Kirst) this is probably a particularly British characteristic.

It arises, I suspect, from the prevalence among British practitioners of the crime novel designed to establish a feeling of cosiness rather than of the crime novel designed to establish an atmosphere of unease. Agatha Christie, most British of writers, is, of course, in most of her output the archetype of the cosy crime novelist. Although she seldom attempted the combination of crime and humour, her stories almost all embody the happy ending of the unmasking of a murderer.

In the cosy crime story humour can take naturally an important share, though of course not a necessary one. Examining, then, some typical British crime novels I have detected five types of humour in general use, with as a sixth the borrowing from the American school of the wisecrack humour of a Gavin Lyall or of the imitators in British settings of the private-eye novel, a phenomenon parallel to the borrowings from Britain of S.S. Van Dyne, of the early Ellery Queen, of Elizabeth Daly (Agatha Christie's favourite) and of writers as recent as Amanda Cross. My five types I label as: the Traditional, the Witty, the Donnish, the Farcical and the humour of Social Comment (This last often to be found in the rather more rare British form of the novel of unease).

Let us examine these categories one by one, noting only that since life is not exactly as neat as literary criticism some of the books I mark out for attention will fall into more than one of my arbitrary divisions.

The Traditional

Traditional British humour, at least as seen in crime fiction, appears to me to have an essential gentleness. Its jokes are not crude. Nor are they, by and large, sharply pointed, however well they are timed. Let me give an instance from one of the comparatively rare ventures into comedy of Agatha Christie. It is some words she puts into the mouth of Ariadne Oliver, the detective novelist who appears in several of her novels as a pleasingly mild parody of Dame Agatha herself. Ariadne Oliver in talking about her detective, Sven Hjerson, is made to say: "If I ever met that bony, gangling, vegetable-eating Finn in real life, I'd do a better murder than any I've ever invented." The inverted reflection of the short, plump, gourmet Belgian, Hercule Poirot, whom Dame Agatha more than once declared herself to be thoroughly sick of, is plain to see. But the joke is gently made. Imagine how, for instance, Emma Lathen, were that writing team ever to tire of John Putnam Thatcher, might make the same point.

In Dame Agatha's treatment of the idea there is a sort of innocent simplicity. This, it seems to me, is another quality to be found in the humour of the British crime novel. You will see it even in a writer as seemingly sophisticated as Edmund Crispin, that arch-donnish exponent whom we shall be looking at more fully later. Take a passing reference in his *Swan Song*, the description of an opera rehearsal-room. "Its sole concession to aesthetic decorum was a lopsided photograph of Puccini, markedly resembling the proprietor of an Edwardian ice-cream stall." A nice, little joke. But not really a very funny one. You could call it a mild sally. And it seems to me as such to be typically British.

Conceivably an American might, in describing a similar setting, have invented the photo. But I venture to think it would not have been seen as lopsided. That is a touch of whimsy I would put down as sheerly English, were it not that that sort of humour is shared by the Irish though their whimsy tends to be more strongly fantastical.

Only as I set down this small example of British whimsy do I realise that in a crime novel of my own yet to be published at the time of writing, *Under A Monsoon Cloud*, I have played almost exactly the same trick. In taking my Inspector Ghote along to a room where he is to face serious charges of professional misconduct I decorated the walls of the corridor down which he walks with photographs, of past Inspectors-General of the Maharashtra Police. And I made some of them hang crookedly.

But there is another tiny point to notice about Edmund Crispin's small joke. I have imagined an American author making a similar light descriptive flourish, and it seems to me also that this imaginary author would never have written of Puccini as "markedly resembling" anybody. Instead, surely, an American would have said 'looking like'. The circumlocution gives the English joke its softening of gentleness.

Perhaps I can further illustrate the quality of innocent simplicity I have noted as typical of much British humorous crime fiction by pointing to what amounts almost to an obsession, certainly in the products of the so-called Golden Age (?1925-1940) of British detective fiction. It is an obsession with the humour of the natural functions. Again you find this mildly salacious subject in Edmund Crispin, the learned. In *Swan Song* the aged don, Wilkes, is speaking: "They made off. In pursuance, I imagined, of some bodily necessity." And, adds Crispin, "he lingered over the delicate obliquity of this statement," another example of mild humour generated by the unusual long word. And only a few pages later Crispin has his sleuth, Professor Fen, while searching a hotel bedroom for a possible murderous intruder, standing up from a look under the bed and saying thoughtfully "A friend of mine has his chamber-pots fitted with musical boxes which come into operation when they're lifted from the floor. It embarrasses his guests greatly."

Chamber-pots, indeed, are seen by many British writers of the first half of the twentieth century as automatically humorous. I could multiply instances. But let me cite just two others from very English writers of the Golden Age. Ronald Knox, Roman Catholic priest and law-giver for a famous Ten Commandments for detective story writers, heads a chapter in *The Body in the Silo* (1935) 'How Celebrities Undress', though its contents are limited to a description of what objects and in what order one of his characters, a celebrity, takes out of his pockets as he prepares for bed. And Gladys Mitchell, an author significantly much more enjoyed and praised (e.g. by Philip Larkin, the poet) in Britain than in the States, heads one of the chapters in her *Laurels Are Poison* (1942) 'Multiplicity of Promiscuous Vessels' and chamber-pots, those objects of innocent mirth, duly figure in the ensuing pages.

Multiplicity of promiscuous vessels. The words lead us back to that other characteristic of British humour particularly prevalent in crime novels, the love of word-play of all sorts especially that rather simple kind that comes from the mere use of lengthy expressions.

E.C. Bentley, another very English writer, actually comments on this in his seminal detective novel *Trent's Last Case* (1913). "Let me explain," Trent is made to say. "A people like our own, not very fond of using its mind, gets on in the ordinary way with a very small and simple vocabulary. Long words are abnormal, and like everything else that is abnormal, they are either very funny or tremendously solemn.... There's 'terminological inexactitude'. How we all roared, and are still roaring at that! And the whole of the joke is that the words are long." And Trent goes on to say that even Parisian cabmen have much larger vocabularies than most Englishmen. "I'm not saying that cabmen ought to be intellectuals. I don't think so; I agree with Keats—happy is England, sweet her artless cabmen." (Some typical whimsy here, note).

Allied to this humour of long words is, again pretty innocent and simple, the humour of funny names. They abound in British crime fiction, from the Magersfontein Lugg of Margery Allingham, another echt English writer, to their prolific use by those two supposedly scholarly crime novelists, Edmund Crispin (Furbelow, Rashmole in *Swan Song*) and Michael Innes (Ffolliot Petticate, Wedge, Alspach and Gotlop all from the first few chapters of *The New Sonia Wayward*).

Akin to this simple delight in funny names is a simple delight in funny foreigners. Or, rather, a delight in finding foreigners funny. Examples are legion. Agatha Christie's Hercule Poirot must be seen as leading them all. From her own account in *An Autobiography* (1977) she did not at first see Poirot as a figure of comedy. She wanted a detective. She decided he ought to be someone notably different from the great and much admired Sherlock Holmes. She toyed for a little with the notion of a schoolboy sleuth. Then she remembered the Belgian refugees living at the time of World War I near her home in Torquay, and she fixed on a Belgian, that and no more. Yet soon a hint of the ridiculous began to emerge. When she came to look for a name, having by then seen her putative hero as a short-statured, rather meticulous individual, she at once decided that he must have a resounding name and hit on Hercules, later modified to Hercule.

And as soon as the young Agatha Miller, as she then was, began to write, the funniness of her foreigner manifested itself to the full. Because Poirot was short and altogether unsoldierly in appearance (The average Englishman, certainly in World War I days, thought of himself automatically as having a soldierly bearing, and the average middle-class Englishwoman thought of all eligible males in these terms equally as naturally), he at once became endowed with an excessive pair of the most military moustaches, and the neatness of his attire, potential readers were told, was "almost incredible." Englishmen were, of course, not sloppy in appearance, but decently tidy and no more.

In the course of time, too, Poirot acquired more and more somewhat arbitrarily assigned marks of the comical foreigner, his inability to master simple English (except when he had complicated ideas to put over), his addiction to unsuitable clothes such as patent leather shoes and an overcoat and muffler if the weather was anything other than scorching, his addiction to appalling foreign drinks such as tisane in place of your decent Englishman's cup of tea and sticky liqueurs in place of proper port.

And all this was seen as being funny, simply funny. Not that Mrs. Christie, wonderfully adroit writer as she proved to be, did not quickly enough take advantage of the stock responses which this funny picture would give rise to in the minds of almost all her readers. She used them to allow Poirot to do things no Englishman would ever do, such as boasting (and thereby conveying useful information), listening at keyholes and opening other people's letters. Further, the comicality of her Great Detective provided Mrs. Christie with that necessary endearing weakness in him making him acceptable despite his omniscience to a wide readership, much as the vanity Conan Doyle gave to Sherlock Holmes had done earlier.

The funny foreigners that have come trailing after Poirot are too numerous to name. I should perhaps only add that my own Inspector Ghote must be numbered among them, however much I strive not to make use too often of this dreadfully simple device.

Whenever any high-spiritedness is called for in the British crime novel, it is apt to take the form of playing with words. Persiflage is the mark of a whole succession of the celebrated detectives of the Golden Age, Trent, Knox's Miles Bredon, Innes's Appleby, Crispin's Fen, Margery Allingham's Mr. Campion, Nicholas Blake's Nigel Strangeways, Dorothy L. Sayers's Lord Peter, even the great Sherlock Holmes himself from time to time. While Agatha Christie's occasional ventures into the humorous novel include the cheerful chatter of the dual heroes, Tommy and Tuppence.

Perhaps the use of extended passages of simple persiflage is the mark of a certain amateur quality in much British crime fiction. The amateur writer—and, since the financial rewards of much crime fiction have never been large, the majority of British writers in the genre have had other main occupations—is apt to launch into happy, inconsequential passages which do little or nothing to forward the main purpose of a particular work. The extended remarks about the use of long words that I have quoted from E.C. Bentley, full-time journalist, are an example.

I do not mean to denigrate those British writers who can clearly be labelled as amateurs. The amateur writer can hit on inventions, whether of comedy, plot or characterization, that are every bit as attractive to the reader as anything a more professional approach might produce, and often more so. But such inventions frequently fail to contribute to the business in hand.

Let me hark back, as an example of this, to my reference to Edmund Crispin (who wrote his first book while still an undergraduate at Oxford and devoted his life to professional music composition under his own name of Bruce Montgomery) and his whimsical use of a lopsided photo of Puccini in describing, by no means necessarily for his plot, an opera rehearsal-room. I mentioned that I also by chance use practically the same trick in my *Under A Monsoon Cloud*. But, thinking of how I used it, I see that whereas Crispin refers just once to the lopsided photo and then forgets about it, I use the crooked photographs of the police Inspectors-General more than once in the course of the book so that they come to have a rhythmical effect, each time reinforcing a contrast between Inspector Ghote's grim predicament and the happy-go-luckiness of life in general.

Let me repeat that I do not mean to use the word "amateur" in any pejorative sense. Many of the best British exponents have been amateurs, from Ronald Knox and E.C. Bentley of the earliest times to the journalist Tim Heald and the antiquarian bookseller George Sims (both of whom I have remarked on in reviews as being in a sense amateurs of fiction) of today. But a certain amateur quality is clearly a mark of British humorous crime writing.

It is unserious often. One might expect comedy to be unserious. But such, in fact, is not the case. The effect must be unserious, but the means should be as serious as need be. The craftsman should be at work. Instead, often the dilettante is enjoying himself. But this unseriousness is both cause and effect. Even with a writer as professional as Margery Allingham, who once said that she had begun to write as soon as she had learnt to put the marks on the paper and who continued to be nothing but a writer all her life, you find this quality in her humour. Erik Routley in *The Puritan Pleasures of the Detective Story* (1972) has well characterized this aspect of Margery Allingham's Mr. Campion as "measured casualness." The example he cites is Campion returning from mysterious war service, seeing his first-born child for the first time, and being greeted by his wife with the laconic words "Meet my war work."

This is deflationary humour, and deflationary humour of the gentle sort is what British crime humorists excel at. It lies at the root of the paradoxical world of G.K. Chesterton; it was used by Agatha Christie; it is the mainstay of the donnish Crispin and Innes. You get it occasionally, but superbly, in the greatest of all British crime writers, Conan Doyle. Watson speaking: "The most famous scientific criminal, as famous among crooks as-" "Spare my blushes, Watson." "I was about to say 'as he is unknown to the public'."

The unseriousness of gently deflationary humour is linked, too, with the whimsy I have briefly alluded to. Whimsy, the final component I find in traditional British humour, may need some further consideration. It is certainly a major factor, beguiling for its essential gentleness.

Plainly its most notable manifestation must be seen in the work of Dorothy L. Sayers, though Lord Peter Wimsey—name carefully chosen—in fact progressively lost the quality as his career was chronicled and as his creator found more and more that she could use the form of the detective novel to say as much, or nearly as much, as the mainstream novel. In his earliest appearances Wimsey is in large part one of the silly-ass young men that P.G. Wodehouse, perhaps the best British humorous writer, brought to life so expertly. To Wodehouse man, to make successes in detection credible, Dorothy Sayers at first added a dose of Baroness Orczy's Scarlet Pimpernel. But towards the end, in Lord Peter's tortuous courtship of Harriet Vane over several books, he becomes almost wholly a different, altogether more lifelike a figure, "an eighteenth century Whig gentleman born a little out of his time" as his creator once described him.

The silly-ass young man is a fanciful notion endowed with fictional life. And, again, Wodehouse never stated this notion of his too boldly, though it is always presented with magnificent timing. The conceit is a gentle one. If the silly ass were simply and boldly stupid he would not fit the pattern of British humour, but willing and too lazy to think or too lazy to pursue subjects that do not interest him, he fits very well. Only as Dorothy Sayers needed to make her version of this figure succeed more and more often in solving criminal mysteries of the utmost complexity did Lord Peter have to lose more and more of this endearing quality.

Appended to the original whimsical creation of Lord Peter comes the equally fanciful figure of the perfect manservant, the Jeeves. With Dorothy Sayers this was Bunter, early on murmuring "Very gratifying" at the news of a man mysteriously murdered, later proving himself a dull and worthy expert with the camera and developing tank. He is character as whimsy. Equally so, but playing as it were the backhand stroke, is the manservant Margery Allingham created for Mr. Campion, the lugubrious, class-conscious, ex-convict Magersfontein Lugg, "a hillock of a man." Yet, crude though he ought to be as a deflator of his master's fanciful notions, he is not ever so devastatingly crude as to wreck the tone of mild humour that pervades the comic passages of the Allingham books.

We have looked at whimsicality of speech and at whimsicality of character creation. But it is worth pointing out that the quality can be extended to the whole mise-en-scene of a crime novel. As it is, magnificently, in much of the work of Peter Dickinson. Peter Dickinson is certainly a very English writer, the British eccentric on the page. Look at the settings of each of his first four books, a New Guinea tribe living in the attics of a row of London houses (*The Glass-sided Ants' Nest*), aged protagonists of past battles embalmed alive in a gamey old mansion (*A Pride of Heroes*), a community of highly flavoured spiritual nuts on a remote Scottish island (*The Seals*) and a clinic-full of charming, sleepy child victims of an obscure (and invented) disease which endows them with extra-sensory perception (*Sleep and His Brother*). Each book bestows on its main characters, whether the whole primitive tribe or the mass of child sensitives, undeniable charm. And charm, perhaps, sums up the bundle of qualities that go to make up traditional British humour.

The Witty

However, there is another and quite different strain of comedy to be found in British crime writing. This is the elegantly witty. It is less complex to analyse than the bundle of qualities that make up traditional humour, but it is nonetheless typical, if less frequently to be found.

It is to be seen first in point of time, probably, in the Sherlock Holmes stories. We are perhaps accustomed to think of Conan Doyle as a writer somewhat in the stolid Victorian mould, and indeed the tone of those stories of crime and justice in the world of hansoms and gaslight is marvellously solid and bourgeois. But there is in them as well a strain of the more hectic world that began coming into existence in the last decade of the nineteenth century, the world of the decadents and the wits, the world of Oscar Wilde. Conan Doyle, upholder of stern morality that he was, the man who rebuked his brother-in-law E.W. Hornung for creating in Raffles a sympathetic burgling gentleman, could nevertheless on occasion hit that note of wittiness fair and square.

"There is nothing in which deduction is so necessary as in religion." Or " 'I saw no one' 'That is what you may expect to see when I follow you'." Or "The idea of a vampire was to me absurd. Such things do not happen in criminal practice." Or "singularity is almost invariably a clue. The more featureless and commonplace a crime is, the more difficult it is to being home." Or "There is a spirituality about the face, however, . . . which the typewriter does not generate." Or "The vocabulary of 'Bradshaw' is nervous and terse, but limited." The examples are there.

Less easy to pick out are examples from writers of a later date. A line that seems as one reads to be brilliantly witty will very often, taken out of context, seem almost totally unfunny. But I have been able to find a reasonable example of the witty British crime novel from a time just past the Golden Age as an example. It is Guy Cullingford's *Post Mortem*.

The whole conception of this murder puzzle can be seen, in fact, as witty. The detective is none other than the ghost of the murdered victim. Guy Cullingford plays with this delightful concept with cool skill from the moment the narrator realizes that "I was sitting in my own comfortable desk chair with the top of my head blown off" onwards. I suggest that the introduction of the adjective 'comfortable' in that sentence can only be described as elegant. And elegance of wit is characteristic of the British style.

Guy Cullingford's narrator goes on to make another discovery after his ghost has listened to two somewhat inept detectives discussing him over his corpse who have then walked through his invisible self on their way out. "I suppose I should have guessed that if detectives could pass through me without causing any great inconvenience to any of us, I could myself pass through solid objects with equal ease." The casually conversational tone is again typical of British understatement, the quality from which the wit of the sentence derives.

We get, too, of course, in the book that reliance on the longer word we have noted as a factor in traditional British humour, though it is used with more discretion in the service of a sharper humour. An example: "because I had not been emulating the behaviour of an American private investigator and light-heartedly smashing teeth back into their owner's jaws, that was not to say that I had not applied myself to the problem." The juxtaposition here of 'light-heartedly' and 'smashing' is a finely crafted piece of wit.

It remains only to point out that this lightly darting wit can be applied not only to the making of elegant phrases or indeed to dagger-thrust repartee ("And you have no young brothers at home?" a slovenly maidservant in *Post Mortem* is asked. "My parents never had but the one." "I'm glad to hear it.") but can also encompass something approaching the Wildean epigram ("Is one to be saddled everlastingly with the wife of one's bosom like the snail within its shell?"). It can further be used in the portrayal of character, at least for minor figures. Here is Guy Cullingford's description of an acquiescent old lawyer. "If he detected any sign of unease in Sylvia's bearing, he was too well trained an old seal to show it. He extended a ready flipper, barked at the appropriate moments..."

I take my next examples of wit in the British crime novel from an espionage story of recent date. The wit here is sharper. Yet, I venture to state, it is not the sort of sharp wit that one associates with American crime writing as in the novels of Dashiell Hammett, Raymond Chandler and their numerous successors, not forgetting their British imitators like Gavin Lyall (not in the private-eye tradition, but a professed admirer of its great names) already mentioned. The new British sharpness must spring, I think, from the nature of the sophisticated spy novel itself, that genre which British writers, pace Charles McCarry, seem to have made their own.

The work I have chosen, almost at random, is Len Deighton's *Berlin Game* (1983). Here, chosen almost as much at random, are my examples: "My photo stared back at me from its silver frame. Bernard Samson, a serious young man with a baby face, wavy hair and horn-rimmed glasses, looked nothing like the wrinkled old fool I shaved every morning." Or, with the narrator-hero, Bernie, talking about a desk-officer he despises, "How the hell can you explain to a man like Cruyer what it's like to be afraid day and night, year after year? What had Cruyer ever had to fear, beyond a close scrutiny of his expense accounts?"

Do such barbs differ from the barbs of, say, Raymond Chandler? Not very greatly. But then it is worth remembering that Chandler was by upbringing a Briton, educated in England at the same character-stamping school, Dulwich College, as P.G. Wodehouse. Yet I think I can point to a subtle difference in the two random Deighton passages I have quoted from pure Chandlerian wit. I do not see Chandler's Marlowe referring to himself, for all his acknowledgement of his lack of financial success, as a "wrinkled old fool", and it should be made clear that Bernie Samson is a man of fifty at most. Again, there is the reference in my second example to expense accounts. This, of course, is pure Deighton. The unnamed hero of all his early books was the spy who came in with unkept-up expense sheets. But the words do give a tang of realism, of everyday sordidness, to the jibe they are part of. It is a realism well removed from the romantic realism of Chandler.

The Donnish

However, there is a very different sort of British wit to consider when we come to examine the humour of the donnish school of British crime. We have already looked, at some length, at Edmund Crispin as providing examples of the traditional in British humour, all the more telling perhaps for being found in the work of a writer who might be thought to be a good deal more sophisticated, more learned, than your usual run of British humorists in the crime field.

But one more quality of Crispin's writing should be mentioned, one that is not so much to be seen in the work of writers not in the curious sub-genre of the donnish detective novel (a sub-genre which in more recent times than Crispin's has not been without its American practitioners). This is urbanity. It is a marked characteristic of the humour of the donnish school to be urbane, to make humorous points so smoothly that the reader almost fails to take them.

As an example let me go back to the opening words of Crispin's *Swan Song*, "There are few creatures more stupid than the average singer." Almost in reading that mellifluous sentence one passes it over. Then the full enormity of the exaggerated assertion strikes one.

Very much the same effect is to be found in a writer of the donnish school much less known than Crispin or Michael Innes, the school's progenitor. He is V.C. Clinton-Baddeley, once editor of the modern history section of the Encyclopedia Britannica, who in his latter years wrote five novels featuring a Cambridge don, Dr. Davie. Here is Davie, waiting to attend a theatrical performance, at which, of course, a principal actor is to be murdered, and glancing at an evening paper (something which, in fact, does not advance the action in any way, thus emphasizing once again the amateur quality of much British comedy crime): "And then there were the sports pages. Someone had kicked a penalty goal. Better, someone had kicked the referee. This was news for which the people of Britain were avidly waiting." The joke is slipped gracefully in. The urbane is at work.

But, of course, the master of the urbane style is Michael Innes himself. One might almost type out by way of example the whole of his considerable oeuvre. Or at least the whole of *The New Sonia Wayward*, that delightful book, which I have chosen as illustrative of his approach. But I had better confine myself just to its opening words. "Colonel Petticate stared at his wife in stupefaction. He could scarcely believe the evidence of his eyes—or of the fingers which he had just lifted from her pulse. But it was true. The poor old girl was dead."

Compare and contrast this with, for instance, the description of almost every corpse in the works of Ed McBain, the splattered blood and brains, the effect of the relaxation of the anal sphincter described to the last drop of excrement. And the effect of Innes's urbanity is, of course, to produce in the reader a warm spread of amusement, an effect soon reinforced in *The New Sonia Wayward* by the following: "On the ingenious little stove were the sauté potatoes Sonia had already prepared, and beside them were four chops waiting to be grilled. He supposed that he could eat four chops, once his stomach had got over its bad turn."

Innes's style has been characterized, a little acidly, by Julian Symons in his *Bloody Murder* (revised 1985) as giving the books "a very thick coating of urbane literary conversation, rather in the manner of Peacock strained through or distorted by Aldous Huxley." And Symons also claims that the donnish detective story which Innes is generally credited with creating with *Seven Suspects* in 1935 had been anticipated by J.C. Masterman with *An Oxford Tragedy* two years earlier. But Masterman's book lacks the sheer literariness of the true donnish novel and much of its high spirits, too, a quality that has been well characterized by Michele Slung writing in *Twentieth Century Crime and Mystery Writers* (edited John M. Reilly, 1980) as "the piquant spirit of enlightened pedantry." Masterman was, in fact, merely using Oxford college life as a background in much the manner that Dorothy Sayers used the life of an advertising agency in *Murder Must Advertise* also in 1933. His book lacks, too, "the flippant gaiety" (I quote Symons again) that is a strong characteristic, if not the essence, of the donnish detective story.

Often this flippancy and this gaiety are expressed, both in Innes and in his disciple Crispin, as fantasy. Indeed Innes, in a short story under his own name of J.I.M. Stewart called 'The Man Who Wrote Detective stories', says of its hero "He loved absurd and extravagant contexts. There was a strong vein of fantasy in him." That vein could well be labelled the bizarre, and the bizarre beginning of *The New Sonia Wayward* just quoted for its urbanity of style could also be cited as an example, though by Innes's standards it is a mild one.

This element of the humorously bizarre was seized on, and even improved upon, by Edmund Crispin. His handful of books includes such a concept as a whole shop which disappears overnight, in a manner that is eventually explained with certainly enough plausibility to satisfy the reader of detective stories (*The Moving Toyshop*, 1946). Allied to this liking for the bizarre is Crispin's occasional, endearing way of referring to himself during the progress of his story, as when Professor Fen during one of the not infrequent pauses in the action begins "making up titles for Crispin." This is taking the bizarre to the point of the rococo, as in those artists who put a detail of their work out on to the frame supposed to be merely its surround.

The Farcical

That trickiest of all combinations in crime writing, the mixing of farce and murder, is, of course, something that has been attempted, and sometimes brought off, in American writing as well as in British and also in European. Is there a particularly British slant to the attempts by English writers?

I think that there is, at least to the extent that the British attempts tend to have in them a dimension of provinciality. But, having said that, I must at once draw attention to one considerable exception to my dictum, the stories of G.K. Chesterton. Many of these, looked at from a purely formal point of view, can be seen as farce if farce of a rarefied, even spiritual sort, as opposed to the down-to-earthness we generally associate with the mode. Consider the plot of *The Man Who Was Thursday* (1908), in which the poet Gabriel Syme in his role as detective, or Philosophical Policeman, joins a gang of anarchists each named after a day of the week only to discover in the end that they, too, are all detectives. A number of the Father Brown stories have the same cavalier disregard for the probabilities. Yet Chesterton, most English of writers though he was, is in no sense provincial. Indeed the Father Brown stories range nonchalantly over the whole globe. But the particularly English quality I see in Chesterton is the element of fantasy, of whimsicality, we have earlier looked at.

The element of fantasy can be seen, too, in the work of Peter Dickinson, referred to earlier, in so far as that can be categorized as farce. From its settings—an architecturally upsidedown palace in Arabia where an ape is being taught grammar is another—this may surely be considered as farce crime, if, like Chesterton, Dickinson almost always has a deeper purpose in his work than the mere evoking of laughter. Again, the element to isolate is that of fantasy, even a sort of boisterous fantasy very different, for instance, from the arch and airy fantasy of French writers such as, in the theatre, Giraudoux and Anouilh.

Certainly when we come to look at two English writers of recent years who have attempted pure farce in crime writing, Colin Watson and Joyce Porter, we find that boisterousness well to the fore.

Joyce Porter has written farce-crime with two main central characters. First she produced Chief Inspector Dover, a Scotland Yard detective who is wholly unlikely but bursting with so much life that this difficulty recedes into the background. Dover is fat, greedy, inordinately lazy, grossly rude to suspects and inferiors and uninhibited about his bodily functions (Another instance of chamber-pot humour). His cases are generally reasonable as detection puzzles, though the solving of them is often left to his subordinate the put-upon Sergeant MacGregor. But his main function is, once more, to deflate pretensions, something he does in the classically farcical manner. The crimes Dover has to deal with almost always occur, it is worth noting, in provincial settings and they are, too, essentially small affairs. Both these qualities seem to me typically English, modest and unambitious.

Joyce Porter's subsequent hero is the Hon Con, the Honourable Constance Morrison-Burke, large-beamed spinster living in a desperately suburban bungalow with a put-upon companion and amusing herself as an amateur investigator, put off by no considerations of tact whatsoever. The humour is largely on class lines, a subject never far away in British fiction of any sort. It is worth noting, too, that in all the Porter books action frequently takes place in rainy or other unpleasant weather conditions. Mud is much in evidence. The effect is to contribute to the lowering of temperature, the scaling-down which is such a prominent feature of British humour.

Colin Watson's books are, equally, all set in the imaginary provincial town of Flaxborough, a place described by one of his characters as "a high-spirited town...like Gomorrah." Once more we have deflationary humour, though here perhaps the acidic bite is not altogether typical of British humour. But chamber-pot jokes are well to the fore, though they embody a good deal more of the sexual than was to be found in the books of the writers of pre-World War II vintage.

The Flaxborough Crab (1969, *Just What the Doctor Ordered* in America), for instance, has a plot centering on a new drug being dubiously tested on behalf of a pharmaceutical giant by a local doctor which has the unwanted side effect of turning elderly men into raving sexual maniacs. In *Coffin, Scarcely Used* (1958), a title which in itself embodies the deflationary and modest aspects of British humour and which may have been responsible for the book not being published in America till 1967, there is a doctor's surgery which doubles as a brothel. But pure chamber-pot humour is never far away either, as in the small instance of a practical joke which takes the form of wiring electrically a dummy fly and fastening it to the side of a toilet-bowl as a target which, Watson alleges, no man could resist.

Social Comment

In the novels of Colin Watson we get, as well as the strong element of farce, a clear strain of social comment, a factor that has run like a black thread in and out of the fabric of British comic crime writing almost from its very earliest days. Chesterton, of course, wrote his frequently almost farcical stories of Father Brown with the single object of criticizing contemporary attitudes to religion. Bentley's *Trent Last Case* is an urbanely savage attack on the capitalist as embodied in the villainous super-millionaire Sigsbee Manderson. Even in the supposedly anodyne days of the Golden Age it was not Dorothy Sayers alone, in her treatment of advertising ethics, who had social comment to make. Even a writer as steeped in the conventions of Golden Age detective stories as John Rhode, firmly characterized by Julian Symons in *Bloody*

Murder as a supreme example of what he calls the Humdrums and author between 1924 and 1961 of no fewer than 78 detective novels under this pseudonym as well as 63 under the pseudonym of Miles Burton, could on occasion place on the lips of his hero, Dr. Priestley, acidulously urbane criticism of the current state of society.

But it is with the post-World War II novelists that the strain comes fully to the foreground. It is there in much of the fiction of Julian Symons who has said "If you want to show the violence that lurks behind the bland faces most of us present to the world, what better vehicle can you have than the crime novel?" And Symons does more than that: he excoriates, with a cold rather than a warm urbanity, the beliefs and prejudices of bourgeois Britain.

Nor is he alone, though perhaps his is the sharpest voice in this new chorus in British crime humour. But social criticism, often expressed in terms of pointed humour, is patently to be found in the work of Peter Dickinson, in the South Africa-set novels of James McClure, in the class-ridiculing work of Len Deighton (a prickly enough voice here, perhaps symptomatic of the non-middle class writers who have made such an impact in other fields of British literature in the past twenty or thirty years) and in the arts-world novels of Simon Brett with his actor-sleuth Charles Paris.

Conclusion

In the work of the writers mentioned above there may be distinguished a new note in the humour of the British crime novel. But it still has much in it that I have characterized as being aspects of traditional British humour as it manifests itself in the pages of crime fiction.

There is the essential gentleness, still not by any means entirely routed by the new note of late twentieth-century sharpness, still often expressed in terms of smooth urbanity. There is still, frequently, the note of innocent simplicity (I detect this, in my analytical moments, in those of my own Inspector Ghote novels where humour plays the largest part). Perhaps the traditional chamber-pot humour has ceded in these Permissive Society days to sexual humour, but such comedy is still often of a notably mild tone.

Long words are still, half a century after E.C. Bentley pointed out how easily they amuse the average Briton, a staple of humour in the crime novel, as, alas, are funny foreigners, Americans prominent among them, together with funny (in hope at least) personal names and place names. Persiflage and banter have not disappeared from the pages, though few writers today handle this with the light adroitness of E.C. Bentley or Ronald Knox.

The deflationary mode is still perhaps the chief tool of any crime writer needing to lard the pages with a little humour. The fanciful and whimsical are there in full force, too, signs of that essentially amateur quality (not to be despised) which permeates much of British crime writing. Will it ever disappear? I believe not.

Laughing With the Corpses:
Hard-Boiled Humor

Frederick Isaac

I first heard Personville called Poisonville by a red-haired mucker named Hickey Dewey in the Big Ship in Butte. He also called his shirt a shoit. I didn't think anything of what he had done to the city's name. Later I heard men who could manage their r's give it the same pronunciation. I still didn't see anything in it but the meaningless sort of humor that used to make richardsnary the thieves' word for dictionary. A few years later I went to Personville and learned better.[1]

It would be interesting to eavesdrop on a reader opening Dashiell Hammett's first novel on its release in 1929. What is this first paragraph supposed to say, anyway? Is it a simple linguistic joke, played by a sly author trying to unsettle an sophisticated reader? Or is it a swipe taken by the narrator toward his opponents, as yet unseen? It is, of course, hard to tell at this point, before the speaker has even introduced himself to his audience. The real point of the story, that the Continental Op is telling nothing but the truth, is the final irony in Hammett's pattern; the funny anecdote is not, in the end, funny at all, but grimly predictive. With this in mind it would not be surprising to have our reader of sixty years ago throw the book across the room in frustration, vowing never to read another crime novel as long as he lived.

Max Eastman begins his *The Enjoyment of Laughter* with the following caveat:

I must warn you, reader, that it is not the purpose of this book to make you laugh. As you know, nothing kills the laugh quicker than to explain a joke. I intend to explain all jokes, and the proper and logical outcome will be, not only that you will not laugh now, but that you will never laugh again. So prepare for the descending gloom.[2]

Luckily, I have no such designs for the readers of this essay. What I propose is that there is an underlying and generally agreed principle for much of the humor in hard-boiled detective fiction; it is something like the misdirection of a good magician. While there are instances of many types of humor and the comic in the hard boiled, they rely to a large extent on the use of exaggeration and comparisons of incompatible objects for laughs.

I have taken some of my understanding of humor from John Morreall and his book *Taking Laughter Seriously*. Morreall posits that much of what we consider humorous "results from a pleasant psychological shift."[3] Morreall subsumes within this definition three major theoretical constructs: that there is a psychological change within the person, for one of a number of reasons (superiority, release of tension, or perceptual); that the change is abrupt; and that it is pleasant. Morreall utilizes his theory to analyze the work of such comics as Woody Allen, whose best work deals with the logic behind apparently incompatible groupings.[4] While I agree with much of his reasoning and analysis, I believe that Hard-boiled humor deals more frequently in what he terms "the incongruity theory."[5] This sub-division, which Morreall employs as a part of his completed pattern, may best be described using examples. In one case, the entire range of cartoons by Rube Goldberg suggests the extent to which incongruous objects may be joined. Goldberg's humor derives from the utilization of outlandish and complex schemes to accomplish simple tasks. This is far from the *New Yorker* cartoons of Peter Arno, with his sophisticated and witty social comments. But as Max Eastman shows, they both present the world from alternate points of view, each of which is congruent from a particular perspective. It is in fact the discovery of these unapparent likenesses that creates humor in Hard-boiled fiction.

From its beginnings in the 1920s, the private eye story has always had a sense of humor, though the fact is frequently missed by its detractors. The common view of the form by its enemies is somewhat akin to letting a mad dog (the detective) loose in a rat- (villain-) infested alley (Raymond Chandler's "mean streets" are often cited as the best description). The expectation of the reader is that the hero will crush his enemies, thus allowing society to go about its business. The story is viewed as singularly unfunny, little more than murder followed by mayhem, a series of bloody episodes punctuated by gunfire and brawling. Wherein the hero interrupts his massacre of the bad guys only to take a drink or six, and to bed one or another of the beautiful dames he has met along the way. The solution of the original plot is immaterial, so long as there is lots of action.

In fact, there is plenty of fun to be found in the hard-boiled novel. From my perspective, the special joy of the hard-boiled is in its inversion of logic, making things that ought not to work together seem plausible. My reading in the form has uncovered many examples of intended humor, particularly in the work of Dashiell Hammett and Raymond Chandler but also in the writings of all of its best practitioners. There are also elements of the hard-boiled in some books not easily classifiable.

1. Humor In Description

Much of the humor in hard-boiled fiction is descriptive. One of the best examples is at the top of this essay. It is easy to see the humor precisely in the way Hammett talks about the town. When the Continental Op arrives, he is struck at once by the grit that not only fills the air but has also seemingly invaded the people. The portrait is not merely sad, and not quite vicious. Somehow the reader is persuaded to smile at the Continental Op's growing comprehension, even as the complete corruption of Personville is made visually apparent:

> The city wasn't pretty. Most of its builders had gone in for gaudiness. Maybe they had been successful at first. Since then the smelters whose brick stacks stuck up tall against a gloomy mountain to the south had yellow-smoked everything into uniform dinginess. The result was an ugly city of forty thousand people, set in an ugly notch between two ugly mountains that had been all dirtied up by mining. Spread over this was a grimy sky that looked as if it had come out of the smelters' stacks.
>
> The first policeman I saw needed a shave. The second had a couple of buttons off his shabby uniform. The third stood in the center of the city's main intersection—Broadway and Union Street—directing traffic, with a cigar in one corner of his mouth. After that I stopped checking them up.[6]

This description takes us into Personville for a first-hand look at the Continental Op's job. It is, in a very real way, extremely funny. The repetition of "ugly" joins with the imagery to create a sharp picture of the town. The inclusion of the police, the guardians (supposedly) of the townspeople, suggests that at best they do not care about their appearance. At worst (and we will of course find out that this is the case) it points to the evil that pervades the entire town.

The Hard-boiled often uses humor as mocking commentary on what the detective sees. In his first appearance, Philip Marlowe describes the weather and his clothes, and only then goes on to talk about the job. "I was neat, clean, shaved and sober, and I didn't care who knew it. I was everything the well-dressed private detective ought to be. I was calling on four million dollars."[7] This use of self-deprecation includes a second, more biting comment in the dehumanization of the Sternwoods, and wealth in general. The replacement of people, unknown to the detective, by a simple certainty, in this case wealth, is a striking case of humor that is used frequently by Hard-boiled writers.

The exaggerated situation and the overstated description have become trademarks of the private eye story. When done well, however, they leave the reader with a very definite impression. Marlowe first describes Chris

Lavery, the man his client says his wife has run away from at the beginning of *The Lady in the Lake* as "Six feet of a standard type of homewrecker. Arms to hold you close and all his brains in his face."[8] It is a quick notation, but every reader will identify Lavery from that point with a man of his or her acquaintance. The smile is one of recognition, and it is the juxtaposition, the incongruity of the patterns that allows us to make the connection so quickly.

2. The Humorous Character

Perhaps even more commonly recognized than humorous description, though not necessarily more important to its development, is the humorous character. Wilmer Cook, the young gunman in Hammett's *The Maltese Falcon*, is an obvious sort of humorous character. Wilmer is funny because of his actions. He isn't supposed to be, and shouldn't be, but in order to convince the gang hunting the black bird that he is serious, Spade forces Wilmer into making bad choices and then humiliates him. In chapter 13, after disarming Wilmer on the way to see the Fat Man, Spade tells an obvious lie which further disgraces the gunsel in front of his employer:

> Gutman opened the door. A glad smile lighted his fat face. He held out a hand and said: Ah, come in, sir! Thank you for coming. Come in."
>
> Spade shook the hand and entered. The boy went in behind him. The fat man shut the door. Spade took the boy's pistols from his pockets and held them out to Gutman. "Here. You shouldn't let him run around with these. He'll get himself hurt."
>
> The fat man laughed merrily and took the pistols. "Well, Well," he said, "What's this?" He looked from Spade to the boy.
>
> Spade said: "A crippled newsie took them away from him, but I made him give them back."
>
> The white-faced boy took the pistols out of Gutman's hands and pocketed them. The boy did not speak.
>
> Gutman laughed again. "By Gad, sir," he told Spade, "You're a chap worth knowing, an amazing character.[9]

It is worth noting that John Huston's classic movie retained the entire scene intact, with Elisha Cook grimly scowling at Bogart. Both the menace and the laughter are clear for the viewer. The result is a feeling of superiority on Spade's part, which will assist him later in the novel. For us, though, Wilmer becomes an impotent character, only good for a laugh. Earlier in the book Spade warns Joel Cairo that "if he gets to be a nuisance I may have to hurt him."[10] This occurs even before we know that both men are working for Gutman.

Cairo himself can be seen as humorous, though in a far more complex and menacing way. His first appearance (which Huston also kept) features the turning of the hunter on the hunted and then back, within a very few pages.[11] When we see Cairo in later scenes we understand that his place is not comic relief, or the need for an extra body (the place filled by Wilmer) but as one of the key players in the game. The balance has been tipped to the other side, and though he retains a bit of the ludicrous for us, we also understand that in the end he did win his encounter with Spade.

There is also Chandler's classic image of Moose Molloy at the beginning of *Farewell, My Lovely,* gazing from Central Avenue at the place where his "little Velma" used to work:

> He was looking up at the dusty windows with a sort of ecstatic fixity of expression, like a hunky immigrant catching his first sight of the Statue of Liberty. He was a big man, but not more than six feet five inches tall and not wider than a beer truck...
>
> He wore a shaggy borsalino hat, a rough grey sports coat with white golf balls on it for buttons, a brown shirt, a yellow tie, pleated grey flannel slacks and alligator shoes with white explosions on the toes. From his outer breast pocket cascaded a show handkerchief of the same brilliant yellow as his tie. There were a couple of colored feathers tucked into the band of his hat, but he didn't really need them. Even on Central Avenue, not the quietest dressed street in the world, he looked about as inconspicuous as a tarantula on a slice of angel food.[12]

From that point on Moose is etched in the reader's mind. He becomes central to the plot of the book, even though he only returns on the final few pages. And our realization of his importance is only enhanced when, midway through the novel, the police *think* they have found Moose, but have only mistaken somebody else for him. How, we may wonder, can anybody, especially the police, not only not find such a distinctive man, but think another guy who is merely big their quarry. The very possibility reinforces our impression of Moose's special-ness, and the humor of the situation.

It is difficult at times to differentiate between the humorous character and the character described in humorous fashion. The Hard-boiled contains more than its share of wisecracks, and many of them are used in the description of its people. In *The High Window* Marlowe describes Lois Magic, Alex Morny's wife, in terms that indicate both her style and the vapidity that it is supposed to hide:

> From thirty feet away she looked like a lot of class. From ten feet away she looked like something made up to be seen from thirty feet away. Her mouth was too wide, her eyes were too blue, her makeup was too vivid, the thin arch of her eyebrows was almost fantastic in its curve and spread, and the mascara was so thick on her eyelashes that they looked like miniature iron railings.[13]

From another angle he describes Mrs. Florian, who used to employ Moose Molloy's girl Velma, to Det. Nulty:

> She's a charming middle-aged lady with a face like a bucket of mud, and if she has washed her hair since Coolidge's second term, I'll eat my spare tire, rim and all.... She is a girl who will take a drink if she has to knock you down to get the bottle.[14]

While neither of these descriptions are meant to flatter the women involved, they are also not meant to move beyond the physical. The result is that the characters are not comical, but their facades have been removed. Exposing the differences between the superficial, public faces which people show, and their underlying realities is a major element of the humor to be found in the best Hard-boiled. What is common to them as well is the juxtaposition of unlike elements in order to create an effect that is both humorous and immediately apprehended by the reader.

In all of these cases, whether the character is intended to be humorous in whole or is merely described in an off-handed manner in order to put the reader at ease, the repeated element is the seemingly unforced use of overstatement or the development of a sensible mental picture from obviously unlike elements. It should be noted that, in the case of Lois Magic, and in many more descriptions throughout the form, the humorous commentary is used to make a negative statement. There is beneath much hard-boiled humor a realization that the world is a difficult place, and that in order to make it more livable the people who rule it must be stripped of their power and beauty. In talking about Mrs. Florian, Marlowe sees her degradation, and comments on it. His reaction to her, though, differs markedly from his impression of Lois. There is a tinge of regret mixed with his anger at the old woman's alcoholism, but no second thoughts involved with the gangster's wife. The difference between the emotion-engaging and the denigrating effects of humor must be identified and recognized in order to understand the detective's feelings and the author's intent in employing laughter.

3. Humor in Action

A third humorous element comes with the humorous situation, a scene or occasionally a series of scenes, that contain comic elements. We have already noted that the scene early in *The Maltese Falcon* between Spade and Joel Cairo can be used to portray Cairo as at least partially a humorous character. The scene itself is a funny one, though, no matter who takes part, because of the shifting points of danger and the clear understanding that the story is only just beginning. When Cairo points his gun at Spade for the second time and says "earnestly" "You will please keep your hands on the top of the desk. I intend to search your offices", Spade laughs. And so should we, if only in amazement.

It is frequently the abruptness of an act that makes us laugh. Even though we think we are ready for whatever may come, especially in a hard-boiled story, we want to be surprised, and can even be disappointed when we are not. Surprise, as Morreall and others have noted, can be the cause of laughter all by itself, even—or perhaps especially when—the event is far from funny.

Take the example of Nick and Nora Charles, one of the first couples to star in a mystery. In Ch. 8 of *The Thin Man* Shep Morelli is holding a gun on the pair in their hotel bedroom. As they talk and Morelli tries to convince Nick that he has nothing to do with the case, somebody "drummed on the corridor door, three times, sharply...":

> The knuckles hit the door again, and a deep voice called:
> "Open up. Police."
> Morelli's lower lip crawled up to lap the upper, and the whites of his eyes began to show under the irises. "You son of a bitch," he said slowly, almost as if he were sorry for me. He moved his feet the least bit, flattening them against the floor.
> A key touched the outer lock.
> I hit Nora with my left hand, knocking her down across the room. The pillow I chucked with my right hand at Morelli's gun seemed to have no weight; it drifted slow as a piece of tissue paper. No noise in the world, before or after, was ever as loud as Morelli's gun going off. Something pushed my left side as I sprawled across the floor. I caught one of his ankles and rolled over with it, bringing him down on me, and he clubbed my back with the gun until I got a hand free and began to hit him as low in the body as I could.
> Men came in and dragged us apart.
> It took us five minutes to bring Nora to.
> She sat up holding her cheek and looked around the room until she saw Morelli, nippers on one wrist, standing between two detectives. Morelli's face was a mess: the coppers had worked him over a little just for the fun of it. Nora glared at me. "You damned fool," she said, "you didn't have to knock me cold. I knew you'd take him, but I wanted to see it."
> One of the coppers laughed. "Jesus," he said admiringly, "there's a woman with hair on her chest."
> She smiled at him and stood up.[15]

What strikes us about this short scene is the rapidity of the incongruous events, which combine to create a comic effect. That the man would slug his wife is not in itself humorous. Her first words on being revived, though, show Nora to be more than a spectator. She wants to see Nick subdue Morelli. She is aggrieved that she has lost the chance. The finale is given by the cop. It is a case of continual surprises, and the reader isn't sure which is the last one. (Like Huston's *Maltese Falcon*, the movie version of *The Thin Man* starring William Powell and Myrna Loy was surprisingly faithful to Hammett's book. This may have helped convince MGM to continue the characters as a series, though none of the sequels matched the original.)

In a different way Jonathan Latimer writes humor into his masterpiece, *The Lady in the Morgue*. The very concept of a body disappearing from the coroner's office may be ridiculous to some people, but Latimer invests the plot with so many twists that the tale becomes more menacing because of its unpredictability. The things Bill Crane must do to solve the crime and unravel the many situations surrounding it lead to some bizarre and exciting scenes. In chapter 3 he cases the dead woman's room, but is interrupted by the police. He climbs out the window and into the next room, where a couple is asleep. He ties the woman up, carries the man (who is drunk) into the bathroom, and then turns the cops and the night clerk away by acting drunk himself. The chapter carries its share of danger, but Crane pulls it off with aplomb.

4. Irony vs. Cynicism. When Being Funny Isn't Fun.

The hard-boiled novel has frequently been accused of brutality, the belief that the style contains a narrow and nasty view of life itself. Life is so cheap, say those who dislike the form, that the detectives themselves have no sense of its goodness. The nearness and the graphic depiction of death signifies a callousness that these people equate with an uncaring spirit on the part of the heroes. Alternatively, the stories can be seen as life viewed through eyes slightly askew, using humor rather than fury. The genre's finest work is filled with twists of vision and understanding, as we have already seen. In such presentations the detectives establish and repeat the need to observe life's problems from a distance.

Probably the most consistent use of the ironic tone in Hard-boiled fiction is related to the police. As the guardians of the public welfare cops must, as a rule, be obeyed. Yet when they are not the heroes, the traditional detective story makes them the enemies of the protagonist. From Holmes' battles with Lestrade through Agatha Christie's simple dismissal to S.S. Van Dine's gratuitous insults and bullying, the police most often are seen as non-entities, without the mental skill to capture the criminals in the stories. Yet few of these writers comment on the fact. They allow their work, with its lack of mention of the law, to make the point.

In the Hard-boiled, though, the cops are treated differently, if on the surface not much better than before. It is very much worth noting that Sam Spade respects—if he doesn't always trust—his friend Tom Polhaus. And while he has no love for Lt. Dundy, Polhaus' partner,

Spade never crosses him. Also significant is the amount of truth Spade gives the cops. He doesn't tell everything he knows, but he only lies when he feels there is no alternative, and only as much as he must. There is no spinning of yarns in order to put the police off. Spade knows the limits. This wariness has continued to characterize the relation between the hard-boiled detective and the police for the past fifty-five years. The detectives are always cautious, noting the subtlety of the interaction, using wit and wry comments to soften the antagonism.

As with many aspects of the style, Raymond Chandler uses both humor and serious commentary in describing the police. In *The Little Sister* he paints this portrait:

> They had the eyes they always have, cloudy and gray like freezing water. The firm set mouth, the hard little wrinkles at the corner of the eyes, the hard hollow meaningless stare, not quite cruel and a thousand miles from kind. The dull ready-made clothes, worn without style, with a sort of contempt; the look of men who are poor and yet proud of their power, watching always for ways to make it felt, to shove it into you and twist it and grin and watch you squirm, ruthless without malice, cruel and not always unkind. What would you expect them to be? Civilization had no meaning for them. All they saw of it was the failures, the dirt, the dregs, the aberrations and the disgust.[16]

Like much of Chandler's best writing, this passage is neither sympathetic nor pleasant, but it makes several vital points. It notes the utter sadness of the men, and the unhappiness of their condition. At the same time it introduces a true distance between Marlowe and the cops. Finally, it has just a touch of irony, suggesting that Marlowe understands his position, and that this knowledge will protect the law from his most damaging sarcasm. That there is no mockery, no anger but a bleak recognition of the reality of the situation, indicates further Marlowe's awareness that the difference between himself and the cops is tenuous.

Other practitioners have included the slightly mocking tone toward the police in their work. John D. Macdonald has at times turned Travis McGee into more of a vigilante than a "salvage consultant" because of the unhelpful attitude the police have put forward. Robert B. Parker's Quirk and Belsen, Bill Pronzini's Eberhardt, and other present-day cops are not as lax as the bums in Personville, but they cannot be counted on when the detective is in a real fix, even though they may wish to do so. The distinction may be subtle, but it is unquestionably implicit in the work of all hard-boiled detective writers. As we shall see, though, this lack of complete confidence is far from a lack of awareness; the smile is not a sneer.

The best practitioner of the ironic view is Ross Macdonald, whose
Lew Archer always found ways to separate himself from his clients and
their troubles, while maintaining a steady pace toward the resolution
of the problems he has been given. This ability to establish a distance
from his surroundings is especially noticeable in Archer's sense of humor.
Unlike the directness which we associate with Hammett and Chandler,
however, Macdonald has a sly, wry way to make his points. In *The
Wycherly Woman*, for instance, Archer silently comments on the doctor
in Sacramento, asking "if the Sacramento River ran alcohol instead of
Water."[17] Later, he stops a woman he has been following:

> She backed away from me with her fist at her chin. "What are *you* doing here?"
> "Waiting for Godot."
> "Is that supposed to be funny?"
> "Tragicomic. Where do you want to go?"[18]

By constantly interjecting such comments, Archer may judge from
a distance the things he sees and is thus better able to comprehend their
meanings and the connections they make.

Archer's use of humor is not just wry, however; frequently it has
edges to it, making clear his wary nature. At such times his narrative
voice contains small sad smiles, sometimes sardonic, and occasionally
weary, as of a man who senses that his own quests are doomed to fail.
At the same time Archer sees and recognizes his weakness, and knows
that others are even less competent to deal with trouble. As a result,
he is willing for them to lean on him until they can find their bearings.

I do not know anyone who laughs aloud at Ross Macdonald's humor.
There are very few large gestures, and both the issues treated and the
tragic resolution, especially of the later books, are frequently too bleak
for even a smile. At the same time I doubt that any serious reader can
deal with Archer's ironic texture without acknowledging it as a major
aspect of the work.

When there is no complexity, though, there can be no humor. Take
Mickey Spillane and the writers who have followed him over the past
forty years. In his work Spillane employs many of the locutions we have
discussed thus far. Yet the tone of the books imparts a different feeling.
When, for example, Chandler describes Moose Molloy, there is an
impression not of danger but of the comic. After Marlowe sees Moose
tear up the club, he is hardly inclined to laugh; but the aura of humor,
rather than horror, remains with the reader. This is true for much of
the side commentary in hard-boiled humor, especially that of Chandler
and Ross Macdonald. The authors wish to keep the reader off-guard.
The world is a rough place, they seem to say, and men can be menacing,

even dangerous. Do not be put off or deceived by appearances, though. Even amid the grimness of reality, there is something to smile or laugh about. Without this we would all sink to the level of the gangsters and the punks. Spillane goes much farther in his warning. His understanding of the world, as passed through the exploits of Mike Hammer, is that we will *always* be caught by the bad guys. We must constantly keep ahead of the game, always know what is going on. This comprehension of the world carries through the violent action in the books and includes Spillane's attempts at humor. He has no room for weakness or subtle meanings, nor does he hide his feelings behind contrived screens of sarcasm. His smile is permanently grim, and the attitude toward the world uniformly aggressive. The result is a singularly bleak and unblinking view of society. Spillane seldom uses humor on Hammer's friends or clients; instead, the "comedy" is directed toward his enemies, as if the hero's hatred alone could destroy them. In some ways Spillane corresponds to H.C. McNiele and Sidney Horler, who directed their own fury toward England's enemies and their own during the 1920s and 1930s.[19]

The primary use of irony for most hard-boiled writers is as a covering for any fear on the part of the detective, or any uncertainty at the possibilities for success. Spillane, however, over-steps the bounds of this convention by imposing humor beyond the bounds of the reasonable. Hammer despises the criminals he seeks (they are routinely called "slime," "vermin," or other disgusting names) and lets few opportunities to demean them pass unused. The result is an almost unhealthy disdain for the subtleties of society. Where Spillane sends Hammer there is no quarter asked or given. Even humor is no longer funny.

5. Relationships: Pairs As Alternative Views Of Reality

One of the easiest ways to get a laugh is to put two unlike things together. The very premise behind crime fiction as a form is the juxtaposition of men who uphold the moral law and others who would do away with it, either in individual cases or more broadly. The idea of putting unlike people together in detection is of course not new. The joining of Holmes and Watson surely is one of Conan Doyle's greatest gifts to the genre. The humor was not uncovered until 1936, when Rex Stout gave his famous speech to the Baker Street Irregulars proving once and for all time that "Watson was a Woman."[20] Stout's own writing also proved him a genius at the integration of different types. The team of Nero Wolfe and Archie Goodwin brought forth in its forty years many instances of humor allied with serious detecting. Wolfe's delicate orchids and the masterful cookery have given rise to much admiring comment from readers. What seems to have escaped our notice, or—more likely—

has been so obvious as not to need attention, is Archie's role as a hard-boiled detective, and its effect on the series as a whole.

Wolfe's life-style, in fact, is unthinkable without Archie. Who will go out to the store on Sunday when they have had to flee the Brownstone and the police in *The Mother Hunt*? Who is constantly lectured to about various aspects of current events or history? And, above all, who goes out to interview the suspects, make deals, and occasionally get his head knocked on Wolfe's behalf? Archie, of course! The incongruity of the pair creates a dynamic that is by its very nature a comic one. Readers who have only read the later novels may sense this, but in the early books Archie is clearly a young cousin of Marlowe. And while he becomes less brash and more sophisticated over the years, he is always in contact and therefore in contrast with Wolfe, the quintessential armchair detective. Archie knows the streets, Wolfe knows the mind; together, but only together, they outwit the police.

In fact, Archie;s role as a hard-boiled detective can best be viewed in his interactions with the various levels of police in the books. He constantly challenges Inspector Cramer, both at Wolfe's behest and on his own. In fact, in two instructive scenes Wolfe reminds Archie of the need for good relations with the law.

> I have sometimes been high-handed in dealing with...the officers of the law....But I have never flouted their rightful authority, nor tried to usurp their rightful powers.[21]
>
> To bedevil Mr. Cramer for a purpose is one thing; to do so merely for pastime is another.[22]

But while Cramer is treated carefully and somewhat respectfully by the pair, his underlings are not. Archie's relationship with Purley Stebbins indicates his origins in the Hard-boiled; the difference appears because Archie has no compunctions about using Wolfe as a cover when necessary. Further down the line, Archie makes it clear to Lt. George Rowcliffe that he is vastly superior to the ordinary policeman, and drives the point home several times. The result of these relationships is to introduce both tension and humor in the books, as relief from the tiring didacticism and absolute superiority which Wolfe represents.

More ordinary as a pair are John D. Macdonald's Travis McGee and his friend and occasional partner Meyer. McGee has come to be viewed by many readers as the sensitive macho detective. His mixture of two-fisted action blends well with his tenderness (often ending in bed) toward the women who seek his help. Meyer, though, has become personally involved in some adventures, and has been vital to Travis in dealing with financial matters on a regular basis. Macdonald makes the two men's interaction more powerful through humor. Most striking is McGee's own feelings of inadequacy when speaking of Meyer's success at attracting the pretty young girls on the Fort Lauderdale beaches. (A particularly revealing and completely unexpected explanation is contained in the opening pages of *Deadly Shade of Gold*). While McGee is usually prone to think of such situations as cute, rather than threatening to his own sexual prowess, the idea that Meyer is attractive to these women presents Travis with a problem of merging the serious side of his friend with the playful one. When the pair goes out together on an "operation," Meyer and McGee again make a study in contrasts that has its comic elements. In one respect, they are directly opposed to the inter-action between Archie and Wolfe. Here Meyer is the front for McGee's experienced investigative sense, while McGee resolves the problems by allowing people to believe that he is less important than Meyer. This aspect of their cases has few examples of surface humor; once they begin, McGee becomes focussed on his quarry. Even so, the inclusion of Meyer, with his educated air and clear grasp of financial information, is by itself a use of embedded humor in the series. Without him, the books lose a measure of their humanity.

Many people consider Robert B. Parker's Spenser novels the best series developed in recent years. His use of Boston and the seriousness of his plots make him a major force in the genre today. While Spenser may not be able to cook like Nero Wolfe, or become as well-off as Travis McGee, Parker has given him a certain amount of the same humorous content as the other heroes have. Spenser is the central element in a trio whose interaction simultaneously heightens and dispels tension.

Spenser's first encounter in print with Hawk occurs early in *Promised Land*. Later in the book, Hawk meets Susan Silverman in an encounter that establishes the three of them as among the best humorous relationships in all of detective fiction. After the opening encounters have established the two men as nearly equals, they continue their banter as Hawk drives along Cape Cod:

> "I have explained to the people that employ me about how you are. I don't expect to frighten you away, and I don't expect to bribe you, but my employer would like to compensate you for any loss if you were to withdraw from this case."
>
> "Hawk," I said. "All this time I never could figure out why sometimes you talk like an account exec from Merrill Lynch and sometimes you talk like Br'er Bear."
>
> "Ah is the product of a ghetto education." He pronounced both t's in ghetto. "Sometimes my heritage keep popping up."
>
> "Lawdy me, yes," I said. "What part of the ghetto you living in now?"
>
> Hawk grinned at Susan. "Beacon Hill," he said.[23]

From this time on the two men (both with Susan and in her absence) continue the skirmishing through the series, sometimes goading each other, occasionally just to relieve the tension of the ordinary world.

As much as Hawk and Spenser enjoy each other's company and the male bonding, the books would not be the same without Susan Silverman. She and Spenser meet in an early novel, and she becomes his conscience and his partner in thought. Along with the serious work, however, there is a lightness of touch to this couple that many readers have come to take for granted. Their love affair contains a good deal of sexual innuendo that is clearly intended as fun. This sense of joy and excitement travels into the other aspects of their lives together, and we know their commitment to each other because of Spenser's desolation after she decides to leave him in *Valediction*. Both that book and its successor, *A Catskill Eagle*, contain a level of seriousness that is foreign to Spenser's earlier adventures, and Susan's departure is the direct cause of Spenser's change. These two novels, with only small exceptions, are as dark and void of lightness as much of Spillane's work.

Hawk's interactions with Susan are humorous precisely to the extent that they combine the man's brutality with a precise awareness of the formulae of correct behavior. Hawk is always solicitous toward Susan, courteous to a fault; even so, his evil side is evident to anyone who knows his other attributes. This proper relationship, hinted at in the quotation, acts as a contrast to his "massa an' slavey" relationship with Spenser. For her part, Susan defers to Hawk, both out of respect for his own care in her regard and for his physical presence and prowess. The author's ability to move between the three of them and maintain the integrity of each is a mark of his own deftness.

6. Inner-Directed Humor:
or, even the best detective can have a rotten day

The bumper sticker said: JOGGING IS FOR JERKS. I stood there in my brand-new blue jogging suit, panting and dripping sweat on the sidewalk, and I thought: Amen, brother.[24]

Much of the humor in detective stories and novels appears to be directed outward from the protagonist. With a few well-known exceptions, such as Joyce Porter's Dover and Donald Westlake's Dortmunder, the hero is almost always painted as a paragon rather than a chump. Because for the most part we see ourselves performing the deeds we read about, it would not do for the author to create a character through whom we cannot win all of our battles. From the days when Hammett's Continental Op cleaned up Poisonville, the identification factor in the genre has been significant, and almost complete. The detective is a superior man, and I become the detective by virtue of the use of the first person narrative: Therefore, ipso facto, Zowie-zap, I am the same superior man I read about. In fact, I am even better than my alter ego because I can see where he goes wrong. I can therefore escape into the easy and successful world of crime, where everything is tied up neatly at the end. Bill Pronzini's Nameless detective is directly accused by a woman of being in the business precisely because he wants to be like the private eyes in his extensive collection of old pulp magazines.[25]

Here, most readers would agree, is at least one level of association we make with the mysteries we read. In this idealized existence the detective may make jokes about other men and women, but it is at best unusual for them to reciprocate. Carmen Sternwood's verbal posturing toward Marlowe is used by Chandler to develop her character. When we finally find out her secret, we are less surprised than we might be precisely because of her unpredictable behavior. Susan Silverman attacks Spenser throughout their relationship, but we understand that her position is that of a lover. And when Nero Wolfe chides Archie for some dubious word or other malefaction, we put that under the category of employee relations.

Less frequent still is the self-deprecation we think we see hidden within much of the hard-boiled personality. Occasionally there is a self-doubt, but it is almost inevitably swept away. In *The Lady in the Lake* Marlowe comments on his propensity for discovering bodies:

> Nobody yelled or ran out of the door. Nobody blew a police whistle. Everything was quiet and sunny and calm. No cause for excitement whatever. It's only Marlowe, finding another body. He does it rather well by now. Murder-a-day Marlowe, they call him. They have the meat wagon following him around to follow up on the business he finds.
>
> A nice enough fellow, in an ingenious sort of way.[26]

Or take Travis McGee's comments about his friend Meyer, and McGee's complaints about his own efficacy as a lover. They may appear serious at the time, but in fact the situation is a set-up by the author. The story will probably conclude with McGee lounging on the Busted Flush somewhere in the Caribbean making love to the woman he has recently rescued and has taken as his latest "salvage reclamation project." As much as we want to believe him, old Trav always comes out all right in the end.

So what are we to make of Bill Pronzini's detective? He is over fifty, only moderately successful (what he wouldn't give for some of McGee's "early retirement" between jobs), and as we can see, more than a bit overweight. In fact, his life really can be considered quite sad. He has had one serious scare because of a lesion on one lung, and when he went to the mountains to escape he found that an old friend had become very distant. His best friend is a cop who will have to quit the force. And his love life is something short of a complete success.

What Pronzini does in *Scattershot* is to suggest that the old adage "cheer up, things could be worse" is true. Things do get worse throughout this book, and all we can do is smile. *Scattershot* is an expansion of three short stories. Together they tell us that even when things go well for the detective, they really can be getting worse. He goes to a wedding and one of the presents is stolen from a locked room that he is guarding. Even though he has no key, he is accused and almost arrested. Another case finds him trying to deliver a summons to a woman; he discovers her dead. In the third, a woman wants him to destroy her husband; in searching for evidence, however, he finds himself siding with his quarry, instead of his client. At the end of the book he has solved all of the crimes but has been suspended. Now not only can he point to his unbroken success in these jobs; he knows that the police feel the same way. Rotten.

It is not for us to say in this context that Pronzini's detective messes up the cases, as the author himself has claimed.[27] The point to be made here is that the character becomes aware of his lacks and sees them unblinkingly. This entire book recounts the trials of a man who understands his limitations, but who may be unable to change his life. When he sees himself as the hero of one of the pulp magazines he collects, the detective finds not satisfaction, but problems.

Marcia Muller and other women writing currently in the hard-boiled style have taken additional steps to assure their heroines that they are not superior. In *Edwin of the Iron Shoes* Sharon McCone is constantly made aware of her inferiority by police detective Greg Marcus. And in *Ask the Cards a Question* she is interrupted after returning from tailing a suspect:

> "I was in my office, sewing up the rip in the seat of my pants, when Hank barged in. He scratched furiously at his head and muttered, "Oh, you're not dressed."
>
> "No, I'm not." I draped the pants over my bare legs. "Why don't you come back in about five minutes."
>
> "Uh, sure." He backed out the door, his eyes bemused as he tried to act as if finding me half-naked in my office were an everyday event.[28]

Here and elsewhere in the hard-boiled world, the focus is not on the possibility of sexism or of lacks in the make-up of the detective. Rather, it should suggest that these writers know their characters' quirks, the things that make the fictitious people uneasy, and use them to good advantage. One could hardly say the same of Mike Hammer. What would he do if a client found him with a needle and thread in his hand? Operate on sealing the intruder's lips—for good?

7. The Outlandish and the Oddball

We have seen in the above discussions many of the uses to which humor is put in hard-boiled fiction by its best practitioners. We have also noted that there are cross-over elements which allow the detectives to comment on their environments and for them to see themselves in ways that make us smile. For the most part this occurs through misdirection by the writer, the use of incongruous parts to create a humorous effect.

What remains is to examine quickly other writers whose work makes us smile. Some of these write unashamedly comic mysteries; others are far more ambiguous. The result, though, is always the same. As we read their books, we smile. Sometimes this is because of the writing style, as in the case of Robert L. Bellem and his short stories. Bill Pronzini points to Bellem in his book *Gun in Cheek* as "an awesome figure," and continues:

> Those of us in the contemporary world who have read Bellem's work might also be inclined to run screaming into the streets but with laughter, not anguish. Anyone whose sense of humor leans toward the ribald, the outrageous, the utterly absurd is liable to find himself convulsed by the antics and colloquialisms of Dan Turner, Bellem's immortal "private skulk."[29]

It is in fact impossible to read a Bellem story with a straight face. His attraction to—at best unlikely—twists of speech ought to gain him serious consideration for the Humorists' hall of fame.

> I grinned at Mitzi Madison. "Nix, hon. I've been a private gumshoe here in Hollywood too many years to go for a corny gag like that. It wears whiskers."
>
> Mitzi was a gorgeous little taffy-haired morsel, dainty as a Dresden doll in a combed wool ensemble. It was about ten-thirty at night when she ankled into my apartment, making with the moans regarding an alleged fortune in sparklers which she said had been glommed from her dressing bungalow on the Supertone lot.[30]

The piling of unlikely bits of Hollywood jargon of the 1940s into what ought to be complete nonsense is funny in itself. The realization that the hero is serious, and that the speech is totally comprehensible stuns us for a moment. Finally, when we realize that the character is a rough private shamus just like Marlowe, we cannot help but giggle a bit.

In the 1970s Ross Spencer brought his twisted sense of humor into the form, in the shape of the Chance Purdue novels. From their wonderfully improbable titles—*The Abu Wahab Caper* is my personal favorite—to the idiosyncratic style, these books have a bizarre sort of charm. And while Pronzini is correct in condemning them for their utter simplicity (simple-mindedness may be a more appropriate term), they add a new and unexpected twist to the concept of the one-liner.

Two novelists whose work in the Hard-boiled field suggests that its humorous capacity may not have been reached are Richard Brautigan and Thomas Berger. Both wrote single books featuring private eyes, and each uses the form in ways that explore the meaning—and at times meaninglessness—of the conventions readers take for granted. Brautigan's *Dreaming of Babylon* stars a downtrodden schmoo named C. Chance, who has been clobbered on the noggin several times too often. If he doesn't tend strictly to business, his mind wanders off to an ongoing movie he creates in his head that takes place in Babylon (yes, the ancient land, that's the one) and features Card himself. In the single day encompassed by the short novel just about everything happens, nothing is resolved, and Card floats through it oblivious. It is, in a way, as curious a work as anything Bellem ever created.

In much the same way he questions suburban life in *Neighbors* and medieval legends in *Arthur Rex*, Thomas Berger makes mincemeat of the hard-boiled detective in *Who is Teddy Villanova*. From the first page the book follows Russel Wren through a Hammett-and-Chandler-esque adventure as seen through a funhouse mirror. Nothing is as it seems, and nothing is as it doesn't seem. Every way you try to turn, Berger has magically altered your position. The result is a comic work that owes everything to the masters of private eye fiction, but is totally unlike anything they could have come up with.

Frederic Brown is characterized as "paradoxical" by Newton Baird[31] and that can be taken as a summation of his work. Yet it is hard to stop at that single word when such curiosities as *Night of the Jabberwock* are available. Jabberwock is not a hard-boiled story; it is more of a dream sequence, a nightmarish charade perpetrated on Doc Stoeger, editor of the Carmel City *Clarion* one night. The cast includes a mysterious stranger who quotes *Alice in Wonderland* at will, a group of inept but determined bank robbers, and a quiet town that will never really understand what went on. As in the best literary dreams, none of our questions as readers are answered; we merely catch hold of the onrushing narrative and ride it to the end of the line.

I have left the most serious of the contemporary humorists for last. Stuart Kaminsky and his stories about 1940's Hollywood detective Toby Peters, can be seen as simple throwbacks. In the same way Andrew Bergman puts his Jack LeVine into wartime Los Angeles and New York, Kaminsky has Toby acting in a special time and place. What separates this series from most other historical detection is the depth of the author's research. This extends beyond knowing the basic events of the time, as any good writer should. It includes knowing the details of life as ordinary people lived it. Toby's breakfast cereal box has been noted, as have some of the songs on the radio. The verisimilitude of such details allows readers to enter the character's life.

There are of course unique people in Toby's world; Gunther Werthmann, a midget who was accused of murder while working as one of the munchkins in *The Wizard of Oz*; Shelly Minck, the world's least professional dentist; and Jeremy Butler, professional wrestler turned sensitive poet. They could turn the books into a complete parody of the genre; in fact, they are deftly used to complement and assist Toby in solving the peculiar cases he acquires.

In addition to the fictional characters who people Kaminsky's work, there are the real "names." We see Bela Lugosi, trapped in his role as Dracula (*Never Trust a Vampire*), and Emmett Kelly working the tent circus (*Catch a Falling Clown*). Kaminsky has his people in their accustomed places, doing not only what we think of them as doing, but doing what they really were doing at the time. In *You Bet Your Life* Toby's clients are the Marx brothers: Groucho is loud and obnoxious; Chico is gambling and then running out on the debts, and Harpo is quiet and watchful. For anybody who knows about the trio, the vision is as true as anything in their biographies and much easier to follow than any of the movies. *Murder on the Yellow Brick Road* contains several scenes with Toby and Raymond Chandler, who is doing the research that will help him create Marlowe as he should be. As in other instances, the specificity of detail turns absurdity into comedy, ridicule into humor.

There are ludicrous aspects to Toby and his continuing saga. He has been slugged so often on the head one wonders whether he really can think any more. His relationship with his brother Phil, the typical stupid cop with brains in his fists, leaves much to be desired. Last, the queer logic that puts the biggest names in Hollywood in touch with an unknown like him is compelling at the same time that it borders on farce. Through it all, Toby perseveres, and with his motley crew of cohorts, has given us some of the best laughs in all of the hard-boiled.

8. Conclusion

As we have seen, there are several ways in which the hard-boiled detective story can make us smile, chuckle, or laugh aloud. The very thought of Moose Molloy can bring a grin (but if Moose himself saw it he might well break both of our arms). Joel Cairo's persistence with Spade is a moment of high comedy that John Huston transferred whole to the screen. And more recently some of the scenes featuring Susan

Silverman and Hawk should leave a lasting impression on lovers of fictional counterpoint.

Whatever one thinks of mystery fiction, its very premise is so grim that humor is a necessary element. While some writers have used assistants, such as the ordinary Dr. Watson, to set off the heroes, the Hard-boiled has not. The writers and novels we have been examining have created marvelous comic effects by allowing the incongruity of reality to emerge. While the other definitions of what makes us laugh (discomfort, superiority, and the rest) have their place in Hammett, the Macdonalds and the others, what we find funny here is the focus on simple details. At first they may seem displaced, but on consideration they all have two purposes. On one hand they make us look twice at what they show. Pronzini's hero can't really have a week like this one, for instance. But he does! At the same moment they heighten our awareness and force us to analyze what they are telling us; the world really is like this.

The realization of the doubling, and the simultaneous knowledge that it has forced us to think twice about everything we see, creates precisely the pleasant psychological shift that Morreall has identified. But it is the juxtaposition, and results through repetition within the stories, which allows the shift to take place, relaxing us in anticipation of the author's next twist. At the end the very grimness of the stories is incongruous with the humorous images through which it is presented. And therein lies the greatest fun of all.

Notes

[1]Dashiell Hammett, *Red Harvest*, in *The Novels of Dashiell Hammett* (New York: Knopf, 1965), p. 1. This volume contains all four of Dashiell Hammett's novels: *Red Harvest*, *The Maltese Falcon*, *The Glass Key*, and *The Thin Man*. All references to Hammett come from this volume.

[2]Max Eastman, *The Enjoyment of Laughter* (New York: Simon & Schuster, 1937), p. xv.

[3]John Morreall, *Taking Laughter Seriously* (Albany, N.Y.: State University of New York Press, 1983), p. 39.

[4]Allen's movies "Play it Again, Sam" and to an even greater extent "The Purple Rose of Cairo" are based on the entirely plausible effects of ludicrous events.

[5]Morreall, ch. 3. pp. 15-19.

[6]Hammett, *Red Harvest*, p. 1.

[7]Raymond Chandler, *The Big Sleep*, in *The Omnibus Raymond Chandler*, New York: Knopf, 1964. p. 1. This volume contains four novels: *The Big Sleep*, *Farewell, My Lovely*, *The High Window*, and *The Lady in the Lake*. Unless otherwise noted, all references to these novels are from this volume.

[8]Raymond Chandler, *The Lady in the Lake*, p. 527.

[9]Dashiell Hammett, *The Maltese Falcon*, p. 375.

[10]Hammett, *The Maltese Falcon*, p. 329.

[11]Hammett, *The Maltese Falcon*, pp. 323-27.

[12]Raymond Chandler, *Farewell, My Lovely*, pp. 159-160. 15.

[13]Chandler, *The High Window*, p. 380.

[14]Chandler, *Farewell, My Lovely*, p. 182.

[15]Hammett, *The Thin Man*, p. 609.

[16]Raymond Chandler, *The Little Sister* (New York: Pocket Books, 1951), p. 140.

[17]Ross Macdonald, *The Wycherly Woman* (New York: Bantam, 1963), p. 108.

[18]Ross Macdonald, *The Wycherly Woman*, p. 175.

[19]LeRoy L. Panek, *The Special Branch: The British spy novel, 1890-1980* (Bowling Green, Ohio: Popular Press, 1981). Panek discusses both McNeile (as "Sapper," his original pseudonym) and Horler in separate chapters. See also Bill Pronzini, *Gun in Cheek* (New York: Coward, McCann & Geoghegan, 1982) for an extended analysis of Horler's viciousness (pp. 120-130). Pronzini says that "he was sui generis" (p. 122.)

[20]Howard Haycraft, ed. *The Art of the Mystery Story* (New York: Grosset & Dunlap, 1946), pp. 311-318.

[21]Rex Stout, *The Black Mountain* (New York: Viking, 1954), p. 153.

[22]Rex Stout, *Champagne for One*, (New York: Viking, 1958), p. 50.

[23]Robert B. Parker, *Promised Land*, (New York: Dell, 1983), pp. 85-86.

[24]Bill Pronzini, *Scattershot* (New York: St. Martin's, 1982), p. 1.

[25]Bill Pronzini, *The Snatch* (London: Sphere Books, 1975), p. 81-82.

[26]Raymond Chandler, *The Lady in the Lake*, p. 596.

[27]Frederick Isaac, "Nameless and Friend: an afternoon with Bill Pronzini, *Clues*, vol. 4, #1, p. 42.

[28]Marcia Muller, *Ask the Cards a Question* (New York: St. Martin's Press, 1982), p. 103.

[29]Pronzini, *Gun in cheek*, p. 229.

[30]Robert Leslie Bellem, "Diamonds of Death" in *The Arbor House Treasury of Detective and Mystery Stories from the Great Pulps*. Compiled by Bill Pronzini (New York: Arbor House, 1983), p. 290.

[31]*Twentieth Century Crime and Mystery Writers*, Second Edition, ed. John M. Reilly (New York: St. Martin's Press, 1985) p. 113.

"What Fun!":
Detection as Diversion

Elaine Bander

Detective fiction is always fun for readers. Why else do readers so cheerfully feed their addiction? And most detectives in literature, from Dupin and Holmes to Archer and Wolfe, whether amateur or professional, enjoy their vocation. Only in "What Fun!" detective fiction, however, do the *other* characters—official mourners, witnesses, suspects—respond to murder in their midst with gusto and delight. Whereas in traditional detective fiction most characters greet the discovery of a violent crime with expressions of horror and fear, either out of genuine conviction, respect for social conventions, or (in the case of the criminal) as protective colouring, the characters in a "What Fun!" novel rub their hands in gleeful anticipation of a puzzle.

These characters view crime and detection as a diversion at least on a par with tennis, cocktails, and fast cars. Their attitude, as well as their ironic, reflexive commentary on the detection process, increases our own delight in detection, so that readers, detectives, and suspects can all join together to exclaim, "What fun!"

Although elements of whatfunity can be found in many detective novels, the "What Fun!" school of detective fiction really belongs to a particular time and place: England between the wars. H. Douglas Thomson, the man who invented the label in his pioneering study of detective fiction, *Masters of Mystery* (1931), describes the rise of "What Fun!" detective fiction after the Great War:

The 'holiday spirit' permeated the underworld and the annals of crime. By this I mean not only that the detective story was written in a lighter vein as an August companion, but also that the characters of the detective story began to treat the murder just as light-heartedly as the reader, and their desire to solve the mystery did not arise from righteous indignation so much as from the crossword complex.[1]

44

"Detective-fever," of course, was first diagnosed by old Gabriel Betteridge in Wilkie Collins's *The Moonstone*, and the contagion has been around in one form or another ever since. Holmes and Watson were no strangers to the affliction, nor were their scores of imitators. Then just before the First World War, E.C. Bentley wrote *Trent's Last Case*, which came close to being a "What Fun!" novel. The hero, Philip Trent, could qualify as a "What Fun!" detective, for he's an irreverent amateur (a serious painter and occasional journalist). When his publisher asks him "to do some work" by investigating the death of Sigsbee Manderson, Trent replies, "Some play, you mean."[2] He takes the job for a lark, then loses his detachment when he falls in love with the lovely widow. But while Trent is jolly and unconventional, at least until he becomes emotionally involved in the case, the other characters take the business-at-hand in dead earnest. Certainly no one but Trent looks upon the murder investigation as "play."

The distinctive qualities of "What Fun!" detective fiction do not emerge until the post-war publication of A.A. Milne's *The Red House Mystery* (1922). Indeed, this novel gave the sub-genre its name when Thomson wrote:

The Red House Mystery is a fine example of the "Lord, what fun!" type of detective story where detection is the amateur's recipe against rainy day ennui, and the murder is acclaimed as a happy stroke of Providence.[3]

In *The Red House Mystery* the murder of Mark Ablett is solved not by a policeman or professional detective, but by Antony Gillingham, a clean-cut, eccentric young gentleman who has chosen to work variously as a *valet de chambre*, a newspaper reporter, a waiter, and a shop-assistant. He becomes a detective through pure chance. One summer day he leaves a train at Woodham "because he liked the look of the station." Discovering that he is near The Red House, Stanton, where his young friend Bill Beverley is staying, he decides to walk over and call, thus arriving just in time to help discover a murder. Since he is between jobs, Antony takes up the new profession of "private sleuthhound." (No one, it should be mentioned, has offered to pay him a fee.) As an outsider, he can "consider the matter with an unbiased mind." To begin his investigation, Antony questions Bill closely about the household.

Bill looked at him eagerly.
"I say, are you being the complete detective?"
"Well, I wanted a new profession," smiled the other.
"What fun! I mean," he corrected himself apologetically, "one oughtn't to say that...."[4]

Of course one oughtn't—but one does, over and over in "What Fun!" novels of the Golden Age.

The detective novels of Georgette Heyer are typically "What Fun!," beginning with her second, *Death in the Stocks* in 1935, and continuing beyond the interwar period with her final detective novel, *Detection Unlimited* (1953).[5] Many of her characters express the "What Fun!" sentiment outright. In *A Blunt Instrument,* for instance, languid Neville Fletcher remarks, "Aren't we having fun," as he trails a policeman around the grounds of his murdered uncle's house (15). In the same novel, when detective-novelist Sally Drew suggests blowing up the dead man's safe, Neville exclaims, "What lovely fun!" (30). In *They Found Him Dead* young Timothy Harte speculates on the possibility of a murder happening in his grand-uncle's house. " 'Of course, I know there won't be one really, but all the same, it 'ud be jolly good fun if there was,' said Mr. Harte wistfully" (18). Timothy is wrong; two murders ensue, and Timothy, "his blue eyes sparkling with pleasurable anticipation," asks, "I say, do you think there's a Hidden Killer in the house!" (165).

In *Envious Casca* even characters who feel conventional distress at the violent death in their family are touched by detective-fever. Paula Herriard says to sardonic Mathilda Clare, "Do you wonder which of us did it?" Mathilda admits that she does, and Paula adds:

> "I know! Ah, but it *is* interesting, isn't it? Confess!"
> "No, it's vile."
> "Oh—vile!...If you like! But psychologically speaking, isn't there a fascination?" (110-111)

Nearly all of the villagers in *Detection Unlimited* share Terrible Timmy's ghoulish interest in murder and detection. Thus Mrs. Haswell and Miss Patterdale "were agreed that although it was disagreeable to persons of their generation to have a murder committed in their midst, it was very nice for the children to have something to occupy them..." (89). When proper Major Midgeholme remarks, very properly, "Sad business, this," cynical Gavin Plenmeller corrects him: " 'What a mendacious thing to say!' remarked Gavin. 'When we are all perfectly delighted!' " (82).

Agatha Christie also practiced Golden Age whatfunity, less in her Hercule Poirot books than in those novels detailing the adventures of high-spirited, high-born young ladies like Lady Eileen (Bundle) Brent in *The Secret of Chimneys* (1925) and *The Seven Dials Mystery* (1929), or Lady Frances (Frankie) Derwent in *Why Didn't They Ask Evans?* (1934), as well as in the chronicles of Tommy and Tuppence Beresford.[6] In *Chimneys*, when soldier-of-fortune Antony Cade is asked to remove an awkward corpse from Violet Revel's study, he responds enthusiastically: "I've always wanted to do a bit of amateur detective work" (63). Enjoying the Ruritanian intrigue into which he is plunged, he announces himself at Chimneys, after the murder of a Balkan prince, by saying, "Enter suspicious stranger from the village inn" (85). Bundle shares his detective-fever: "We've never had a murder in the house before. Exciting, isn't it?" (111).

Frankie in *Why Didn't They Ask Evans* is just as cool and resourceful about murder. When questioning her childhood friend Bobby about the dying man he found below a cliff, she asks:

> "I suppose nobody pushed him over, did they?...."
> "Pushed him over? Good lord, no. Why?"
> "Well, it would make it much more exciting, wouldn't it?" said Frankie idly. (20).

When Bobby miraculously escapes what should have been a fatal poisoning, she comments: "It's most exciting to have a romantically poisoned friend" (39).

Tommy and Tuppence Beresford enter into all of their exploits of detection and espionage in the pure spirit of "What Fun!" When they take over Blunt's International Detective Agency in *Partners in Crime* (1929), Tuppence anticipates delights to come: "It will be too marvelous," she declared. "We will hunt down murders, and discover the missing family jewels, and find people who've disappeared and detect embezzlers" (8). They pursue their profession for the fun of it, playing games, imitating the Great Detectives of fiction, and (incidentally) solving a few crimes. Tuppence, happily married but bored at the beginning of the book, has found the perfect diversion in detection; it even beats buying hats.

When the Beresfords comically burlesque various styles of fictional detectives, moreover, they exhibit another characteristic typical of "What Fun!" amateur detectives: reflexive comic commentary on detective conventions. Thus Tommy displays "a somewhat futuristic dressing gown, a turkish slipper, and a violin. 'Obvious, my dear Watson,' " comments Tuppence (20).

Ronald Knox's patience-playing detective, Miles Bredon, takes a similarly lighthearted approach in *The Three Taps* (1927) to his job as investigator for the Indescribable Insurance Company. He works only when his imagination is engaged; then, assisted by his resourceful, tolerant wife Angela, he performs virtuoso feats of detection. Like the Beresfords, moreover, the Bredons comically allude to the Great Detectives of fiction:

"Good! The case progresses. Let me call your attention to this singular absence of sangwich-cutting [sic] on the part of Mrs. Davis. Angela, I'm right on the track of the beastly thing, and you mustn't disturb me."

"Have you really worked it all out?"

"No, not quite all; but I'm in the sort of stage where the great detective says, Good God, what a blind bat I have been!"[7]

Dorothy L. Sayers also uses this comic device, particularly in *Have His Carcase*,[8] when detective Lord Peter Wimsey and detective-novelist Harriet Vane trade witticisms as they investigate a murder:

"You aren't suggesting," said Harriet, "that the weapon isn't really the weapon after all?"

"I should like to," said Wimsey. "The weapon never is the weapon is it?"

"Of course not; and the corpse is never the corpse. The body is, obviously, not that of Peter Alexis—"

"But of the Prime Minister of Ruritania—"

"It did not die of a cut throat—"

"But of an obscure poison, known only to the Bushmen of Central Australia—"

"And the throat was cut after death—"

"By a middle-aged man of short temper and careless habits, with a stiff beard and expensive tastes—"

"Recently returned from China," finished up Harriet, triumphantly.

The sergeant. . .now burst into a hearty guffaw.

"That's very good," he said, indulgently. "Comic, ain't it, the stuff these writer-fellows put into their books?" (49)

The joke's on the sergeant, for Wimsey has pretty accurately described the man he's looking for, in an act of deduction worthy of Sherlock himself.

Sayers was practically a charter member of the "What Fun!" school. Wimsey, who makes his first appearance in *Whose Body?* (1923), is a cross between quotation-spouting Trent and Ass-About-Town Bertie Wooster, at least in the early novels. His man-servant Bunter partakes of Lord Peter's "What Fun!" spirit when he replies to his master's announcement of a new corpse, "Indeed, my lord? That's very gratifying" (9). When Wimsey's friend Inspector Parker visits, Wimsey says, "Parker, I hope you're full of crime—nothing less than arson or murder will do for us tonight.... Perhaps you have a body. Oh do have a body" (20).

This insouciance remains in *Clouds of Witness* even though the murder suspect is none other than Wimsey's brother Gerald, Duke of Denver. Bunter, informing Lord Peter of Denver's arrest, says:

"I fancy the investigation will prove very interesting."

"From a criminological point of view, I daresay it is interesting," replied his lordship, sitting down cheerfully to his *café* au lait, "but it's deuced awkward for my brother...."

"Ah, well!" said Mr. Bunter, "They say, my lord, there's nothing like having a personal interest." (9)

In *The Unpleasantness at the Bellona Club*, Murbles, the family solicitor, asks Wimsey to undertake the investigation of old General Fentiman's death; Lord Peter warns him that the truth might prove awkward, but comments, " *I* shall enjoy it all right" (22).

Only later, beginning with *Strong Poison* (1930), does Wimsey express ambivalence about his role of detective, an ambivalence which haunts him for several more novels while he courts Harriet Vane. In *Strong Poison*, for example, Wimsey again has a "personal interest," as Bunter had called it in *Clouds*, for he has fallen in love with the murder suspect, Harriet Vane, and must save her from the gallows. For the first time in his life, however, he recognizes that what has been "fun" for himself has been a life-or-death matter for others concerned: "I'm beginning to dislike this job of getting people hanged. It's damnable for their friends..." (92).

Sayers deliberately transformed the character of Wimsey from a one-dimensional comic instrument ideally suited for "What Fun!" detection to a complex human being, whose flippant wit in the early novels is retroactively cast as a protective pose, a mask worn to disguise a vulnerable sensibility. In subsequent novels like *Have His Carcase*, *The Nine Tailors*, *Gaudy Night*, and *Busman's Honeymoon*, Peter Wimsey and Harriet Vane continue to discuss the ethics of detection; eventually both Peter and Harriet accept the legitimacy of his job—but by this time his "What Fun!" days are behind him, and Sayers's fiction has lost most if not all of its "What Fun!" characteristics.

Heyer's output, meanwhile, remained faithful to the "What Fun!" spirit; her last detective novel, *Detection Unlimited*, was as full of whatfunity as the early *Death in the Stocks*; her characters exhibited the "What Fun!" attitude that criminal investigation is an amusing pastime and that an ounce of cynical wit is worth a pound of trite moralizing. In short, just as the detective problem in the novels frustrates reader's plot expectations, so too the comedy in the novels works by reversing the conventional pieties readers expect in detective fiction.

Gavin Plenmeller and Neville Fletcher are typical of Heyer's unconventional young men, languid, even epicene, whose witty reversals of conventional attitudes sound as though they had wandered off the set of Oscar Wilde's *The Importance of Being Earnest*. Their lives are a series of poses, and they view murder as high theatre. This decadent aestheticism is generally innocent, meant merely to baffle and disconcert the other players, but it can also conceal guilt. The murderer, of course, is by definition playing a role: each of the other characters may appear guilty from time to time, but he or she alone is guilty, yet he or she must always act the role of the innocent; sometimes that role can mean acting the part of an innocent person who pretends to be guilty for the theatrical value, or the fun of it. Confusing? Of course. Since Golden Age detective fiction depends on bluffing readers, Heyer's readers cannot dismiss the whatfunity of her characters as a mere pose; it might also be a most deadly serious disguise.

In *Death in the Stocks*, for example, Antonia and Kenneth Vereker disdain to pretend grief for their murdered half-brother or to disguise their relief at his death. Indeed, they cheerfully assess the evidence against themselves, bristling with indignation at the suggestion that they might not be capable of murder. Their more conventional cousin Giles recognizes what he calls their "purely intellectual attitude," which baffles the police and annoys Kenneth's resolutely genteel fiancée, Violet— ironically so, since she is in fact the murderess. Thus the one character determined to observe the niceties of social hypocrisy is also the one who has committed murder.

Kenneth, a painter, views the murder aesthetically; "I won't have seedy strangers butting in on a family crime. It lowers the whole tone of the thing, which has, up to now, been highly artistic, and in some ways even precious" (85). His perspective is similar to De Quincey's in *Murder Considered as one of the Fine Arts*:

Everything in this world has two handles. Murder, for instance, may be laid hold of by its moral handle (as it generally is in the pulpit and at the Old Bailey), and *that*, I confess, is its weak side; or it may be treated *aesthetically*, as the Germans call it— that is, in relation to good taste.[9]

This "aesthetic" view is of course the view of detective fiction readers and writers; it is also the view of many characters in "What Fun!" books.

Typical of this aesthetic detachment in Heyer's novels are Neville Fletcher and Sally Drew. When Neville announces his uncle's murder, Sally says to him:

"You'd better tell me all about it. It might be good copy."
"What a lovely thought!" said Neville. "Ernie has not died in vain."
"I've always wanted to be in on a real murder," remarked Sally thoughtfully (Blunt, 21).

When told that Ernie was killed by the eponymous "blunt instrument," Sally nods "with the air of a connoisseur." She tells Neville, "I hope you get pinched for the murder," and he replies, "It would be awfully interesting" (21). The two compare their real selves unfavourably to the resourceful characters in Sally's books. They enjoy the murder in the same spirit as they would enjoy reading—or writing—a work of detective fiction. By the end of the novel, however, Neville has completely lost interest in the investigation. He doesn't even wait to hear the name of the murderer. Newly engaged to Sally, he tells the astounded Inspector Hannasyde, "I can't be bothered with murder cases now. I'm going to be married" (246). Clearly *his* handle on murder is aesthetic, not moral. Even Sergeant Hemingway partly shares this aesthetic view of crime. Hemingway wants an *artistic* case: "I don't like the setup. Ordinary, that's what it is.... Give me something a bit recherché and I'm right on to it" (34).

In *Detection Unlimited* Heyer really lets loose. The entire village of Thornden succumbs to detective-fever after the murder of the unpopular Sampson Warrenby: hence the title. Everyone has a different theory, and amateur detection becomes everyone's favourite pastime, quickly eclipsing tennis:

> The murder of Sampson Warrenby naturally formed the sole topic for conversation.... Abby said simply that she had never hoped to realize an ambition to be, as she phrased it, mixed up in a murder-case. Miss Patterdale...very handsomely said that she was glad it had happened while she was there to enjoy it. (46)

Here the narrator shares the "What Fun!" outlook of her characters, adding that the murder "naturally" was on everyone's lips and that Miss Patterdale's comment was a handsome one. This satiric inversion of conventional values (one would expect a well-bred maiden aunt to apologize if violent crime marred her niece's visit) is typical of "What Fun!" literature in general, and Heyer's books in particular.

In Heyer's novels, however, the "What Fun!" attitude is not always a genuine expression of cynicism, aestheticism, or satire. It can mask more serious emotions, even blood guilt. In *Detection Unlimited*, for example, Gavin Plenmeller appears to be yet one more of Heyer's clever, cynical, languid young men who scorn social and moral hypocrisy, whereas in fact he is a murderer who tries to divert genuine suspicion from himself by deliberately calling attention to the evidence against himself, such as his lack of an alibi. During one of the general discussions of the case which occupy the villagers throughout the novel, Plenmeller says: "*Surely* the police cannot overlook my claims to the post of chief suspect? I write detective novels, I have a lame leg, and I drove my half-brother to suicide. What more do the police want?" (49). As he anticipates, the others put his remarks down to plain bad taste. The idea that he could be telling the truth is never seriously entertained. He is just one of the villagers making his peculiar brand of fun out of the fortuitous murder, or so they think. So he wants them to think.

It is rare, however, to discover a murderer lurking beneath a "What Fun!" facade. More commonly, a character whose flippancy and cynicism is (at least in part) a pose is disguising more benign emotions, such as fear lest the police wrongly suspect himself, or concern for another character, or even atavistic horror of death. When Neville Fletcher first learns of his uncle's death, for example, he remarks casually to Sergeant Glass, "I don't like murders. So inartistic, don't you think?," thus adopting the aesthetic pose, but "it was plain that under his flippancy he was shaken" (Blunt, 5). Later he tells Sergeant Hemingway, "You mighten't think it, but I'm frightened of you. Don't be misled by my carefree manner: it's a mask assumed to hide my inward perturbation" (114). Kenneth Vereker, too, plays a game with police in *Death in the Stocks*. Like Plenmeller, he calls attention to the case against himself. His sister Antonia recognizes the method to Kenneth's madness: the police don't know how to take him and hesitate to arrest him partly because of his unsettling attitude.

Guy Matthews, weak and dependent, tries a "What Fun!" pose in *Behold, Here's Poison*, but he has trouble carrying it off. After his initial questioning by Detective-Superintendent Hannasyde, Guy remarks to the household, "Aunt was scared..., but personally I found it rather amusing" (47). His next remarks, however, belie his detachment. His cousin Randall's flippancy is more effective, because rooted in a more genuine cynicism. After startling Hemingway and Hannasyde by admitting that he, as heir, had a strong motive for wishing his uncle dead, Randall adds, "Now do let us understand each other! There's not the least need for you to ask me careful questions. I shall be delighted to answer anything you choose to ask me. In fact, I'm burning to assist you to track down the murderer" (63). Ultimately, it is Randall who successfully does the tracking, not in a spirit of "What Fun!" but in order to suppress the fact that his uncle had been a blackmailer. Randall's pose, moreover, unlike Guy's, remains consistent. When asked if he will attend the inquest, he yawns, "If nothing more amusing offers, I might" (90). Clearly, though, he is aware of the stakes. When congratulated upon inheriting his uncle's fortune, he replies "in a bored voice" that "It puts strange ideas into the heads of policemen,...and that, though amusing up to a point, is apt to become a nuisance" (120).

Stephen Herriard in *Envious Casca* also adopts a casual "What Fun!" pose, conscious of the effect he creates. When asked, "Who did it?", he replies, " 'I've no idea!'... He took a cigarette from the box on the table and lit it. 'Interesting problem, isn't it?' he drawled." Stephen then looks around "in malicious amusement at the various countenances turned towards him" (57). His sister Paula's histrionics are instinctive, for she's an actress. Her brother, on the other hand, is conscious that, as his dead uncle's heir and the one to discover the body, he is the most likely suspect. His casual attitude masks anxiety lest police suspicion fall upon himself.

Indeed, with so many characters playing roles, consciously or unconsciously, it's not surprising that murder and detection are often viewed as mere backdrops for theatre. Sergeant Carsethorn, commenting to Chief-Inspector Hemingway on Gavin Plenmeller's perverse behaviour, says it perfectly: "Anyone would have thought the whole thing was a play, and we was having drinks between the acts, and talking it over" (Detection, 59).

In *No Wind of Blame* Vickie Fanshawe is continually role-playing and isn't above casting the police into subordinate roles in her little dramas. After goading Inspector Hemingway to declare her an official suspect, she casts herself "upon the maternal bosom" and plays out a scene for her mother's benefit, accusing her mother's suitor of implicating her. She has a good time acting, and incidentally prevents her mother from marrying a fortune-hunter. For Vickie, her stepfather's murder is a stroke of good fortune, ridding her mother of an unsatisfactory husband and providing herself with scope for her talents.

Perhaps the best explanation for the "What Fun!" pose is provided by Dame Agatha in *Why Didn't They Ask Evans?*. Bobby's conservative clergyman father says of the dying stranger whom Bobby discovers, "What a tragedy!" and he deplores Bobby's own flippant tone. Bobby cannot explain what he really feels, but thinks, "If his father couldn't see that, of course, you joked about a thing because you had felt badly about it—well, he couldn't see it!" (14).

As many commentators have pointed out, Golden Age detective fiction flourished partly because the trauma of the Great War left ordinary, educated readers hungry for a literature drained of profound emotions, a literature which would assuage doubts and reinforce social prejudices, at a time when modernism was stripping "straight" literature of all its familiar landmarks. Detective fiction filled this need. At the same time, the post-War generation could not think and feel as their fathers had done. "What Fun!" detective fiction allowed such readers the best of both worlds: the surface iconoclasm of its characters and the reassurance of a world in which all problems have rational solutions and all evil-doers eventually pay for their crimes. By allowing the reader's own "What Fun!" attitude into the detective story, "What Fun!" authors made explicit the comic world-view implicit in all detective fiction.

Notes

[1]*Masters of Mystery: A Study of The Detective Story* (London: Collins, 1931), p. 72.

[2]*Trent's Last Case*, in *Three Famous Murder Novels* (New York: Modern Library, 1941), p. 247.

[3]*Masters*, p. 164. Earl F. Bargainnier generously attributed the term to me in his article, "The Dozen Mysteries of Georgette Heyer," *Clues: A Journal of Detection*, 3:2 (Fall/Winter 1982), 30. In fact, I took it from Howard Haycraft, *Murder for Pleasure* (New York: Appleton-Century, 1941), p. 151, who was in turn citing Thomson's study.

[4]*The Red House Mystery* (New York: Dutton, 1922), p. 58.

[5]The editions of Heyer's novels cited in this essay are listed below, preceded by the original date of publication. All quotations will be cited in the text using, where necessary, the abbreviation given after the entry:

1935 *Death in the Stocks* (Granada, 1963)

1936 *Behold, Here's Poison* (Granada, 1963)

1938 *A Blunt Instrument* (Bantam, 1973) (Blunt)

1938 *They Found Him Dead* (Bantam, 1970)

1939 *No Wind of Blame* (Granada, 1963)

1941 *Envious Casca* (Panther, 1961)

1953 *Detection Unlimited* (Granada, 1961) (Detection)

[6]The editions of Christie's novels cited in this essay are listed below, preceded by the original date of publication. All quotations will be cited in the text using, where necessary, the abbreviation given after the entry:

1925 *The Secret of Chimneys* (Dell, 1975)

1929 *The Seven Dials Mystery* (Bantam, 1964)

1929 *Partners in Crime* (Berkeley, 1984) (Partners)

1934 *Why Didn't They Ask Evans?* (Fontana, 1956)

[7]*The Three Taps: A Detective Story Without a Moral* (Penguin, 1960), p. 155.

[8]The editions of Sayers's novels cited in this essay are listed below, preceded by the original date of publication. All quotations will be cited in the text.

1923 *Whose Body?* (NEL, 1973)

1926 *Clouds of Witness* (NEL, 1972)

1928 *The Unpleasantness at The Bellona Club* (Avon, 1963)

1930 *Strong Poison* (Signet, 1967)

1932 *Have His Carcase* (Penguin, 1962)

1934 *The Nine Tailors* (NEL, 1968)

1936 *Gaudy Night* (Avon, 1968)

1937 *Busman's Honeymoon* (Avon, 1968)

[9]Thomas De Quincey, *On Murder Considered as One of the Fine Arts*, Vol. XIII, *The Collected Works of Thomas De Quincey*, Ed. David Masson, 14 vols (Edinburgh: Adam and Charles Black, 1890), p. 13.

Farcical Worlds of Crime

Earl F. Bargainnier

And then it all dissolves into farce.

Edmund Crispin, *The Glimpses of the Moon*

The spectrum of comedy is broad and ill-defined. Such terms as *high comedy* and *low comedy* do not say very much about a work. Wit and slapstick may be used as extremes, but both are often found within the same work.

The one constant is the creation of a comic world, however elevated or however gross. In the best sense, the comic writer creates an anything-can-happen world. That world can take many forms, but it always allows for the incongruous, the improbable, the exaggerated, and the hilarious, while retaining enough resemblance to the actual world to be at least possible and to emphasize the comic deviation from that actuality. When crime enters such a comic world, the anything-can-happen possibilities are doubled. (Comic relief in an essentially non-comic work is another matter; though it appears in even such dour works as William McIlvanney's *Laidlaw* and *The Papers of Tony Veitch*, it is never central to either action or tone.) Crimes may be bizarre, characters ludicrous, motives and actions improbable, or detection more luck than logic so long as the author can make readers realize and accept that anything can happen in his comic world of crime.

The specific form that world takes to be considered here, and that in which the anything-can-happen motif has the widest scope, is the farcical. Because farce is so often physical—hence the synonym *slapstick*— its effectiveness for comic crime is obvious. Plot is the dominant element in detective fiction, and plot is action. To make that action farcical is to create a world in which zany happenings so enliven and complicate investigations of crime that both characters and readers must be prepared for *anything*, no matter how absurd. The number of such happenings may range from interspersed episodes in a basically non-farcical work, such as the car chase scene and Nigel Strangeways' initiation into a secret club of prep school boys in Nicholas Blake's *A Question of Proof* to the entire plot of a novel. Richard Hull's *The Murder of My Aunt* is a prime example of the latter: the funniest inverted work in the genre, with one bungled attempt after another to kill an unwanted aunt, capped by an atypical but still farcical conclusion. Though usually described as the "lowest" form of comedy, farce may be combined with other forms, as in the mentioned Blake novel, including its often designated opposite, the comedy of manners. Farce is particularly adaptable for parody and burlesque, as shown in the novels of Leo Bruce and Ross H. Spencer, for there is no easier way to mock the conventions of a form than to treat them in a farcical manner. Farce is also used for satirical purposes, and Simon Brett and Tom Sharpe have successfully done so in quite different ways. Bruce, Spencer, Brett, and Sharpe are four of the ten writers to be examined in this essay. The order follows that slippery scale, already noted, from high to low comedy, and judgment as to a particular writer's placement may differ; nevertheless, it certainly seems in order to begin with Michael Innes and Edmund Crispin.[1]

Julian Symons has written that Michael Innes is "the finest of the Farceurs, a writer who turns the detective story into an overcivilized joke, by a frivolity which makes it a literary conversation piece with some detection taking place on the side."[2] Though I assume intended as a compliment, this statement indicates less than wholehearted approval of comic crime. Yet implicit in the statement is that Innes' work can be considered only as comic detective fiction. That work generally includes a great deal of comedy of manners, but always more than enough farce to justify calling him a farceur. Four novels, chosen at random from the forty-year period 1942-1982, illustrate some of his methods of combining farce and crime: *The Daffodil Affair, Appleby's End, One-Man Show*, and *Sheiks and Adders*. Innes sets the tone for the zany action by the names he gives places and people. One can expect the fantastic to occur in such places as Sneak, Snarl, Yatter, Boxer's Bottom, or the Forest of Drool. Similarly, the inhabitants' names sound like a cross between P.G. Wodehouse and the Marx brothers: Hildebrant Braunkopf Brown, Mervyn Twist, Tibby Fancroft, Mr. Beaglehole, Brettingham Scurl, Sir Mulberry Farmer, Inspector Mutlow, a butler named Rainbird, and Gregory Grope—the last an engineer who schedules his train to please his mother.

Such eccentricity runs rife. The Raven family of *Appleby's End*, which furnishes John Appleby, Innes' series detective, with his wife Judith, includes a mild-mannered man who always looks ferocious, another totally preoccupied with his own death, and a third who singlehandedly is writing the *New Millenium Encyclopaedia* and planning *The Revised and Enlarged Resurrection Dictionary*. Appleby's introduction to his future bride is a daffy beginning to romance. After a bumpy ride in a vegetable-laden stagecoach, they are swept down a river—calmly chatting atop the coach—and then spend a hour warming up inside a haystack, before discovering a dead man's head peering at them from a snow bank. After such an opening to the novel, it is not surprising to find lifesize waxworks of Mongolian warriors in the Ravens' front hall or to learn that farm animals have been stolen and replaced by corresponding marble statues, which action causes an elderly cowmaid to become demented when she tries to milk the statue of a cow, her dementia taking the form of believing she is a cow herself. The other novels provide similar examples. In *One-Man Show* a duchess serves as waitress in her castle tea-shop, and another noblewoman crusades against vice in spy novels by providing homes for elderly spinsters since her theory is that only such women write about "the activities of seductive women in the pay of foreign powers" (110). Eccentricity as producer of farce is a favorite technique of Innes, and one that has been employed again and again by his successors in farcical crime.

His works also contain farcical incident based upon some initial absurd premise. *Sheiks and Adders* presumes that a millionaire would combine an outdoor public masquerade with a crucial business conference. The results include Appleby and the Chief Constable, both dressed as Robin Hood, trying to prevent the assassination of a sheik amid people disguised as Teddy bears, deep-sea divers, clowns, golliwogs, and witches. The host's son shows up, "a spectacle of the most horrendous and revolting sort," as one of the Seven Deadly Sins—only he has not decided which (41). There are also seven phoney sheiks wandering around. If this were not enough to create chaos, the situation becomes even more out of kilter with the arrival of the Basingstoke Druids to perform their "Perlustration" of the manor house, which translates into their attempting to make off with every valuable they can. How does Appleby prevent murder and robbery? He has the boy scouts present to perform in a pageant charge the crowd with bayonets from one side and an Oxford herpetologist release the snakes he has gathered in the Forest of Drool from the other, while he and the sheik commandeer a hot-air balloon from its drunken owner and sail away to his wife's rose garden. From the original premise, the farcical complications mount until that truly appropriate ending. *Sheiks and Adders* is the *reductio ad absurdum* of mystery action.

A third principal farcical method of Innes is literary allusion or parody. The Thomas Carlyle nightclub in *One-Man Show* offers an instance of the former. Its tables are covered with cartoons of Victorians so that one sets "down one's glass on Tennyson's nose or tap[s] one's cigarette-ash into Browning's ear" (103). The club's band is dressed "as Eminent Victorians. Florence Nightingale was at the piano, Cardinal

Manning discoursed upon a saxophone, Dr. Arnold fiddled, and General Gordon operated a battery of drums" (107). The image is too ludicrous to have any relation to life or literature, past or present; it is not even mockery, but farce for the sake of farce. However, genial mockery, that is parody, of crime fiction appears in the same novel. Appleby's fight in a dark antique-junk shop becomes less a life-and-death struggle than a knockabout parody of such a struggle, with flying objects and unknown obstacles, while the final three-way gun battle between two sets of crooks and the police is so exaggerated that it too becomes parodic. In *The Daffodil Affair* Innes offers an extended farcical parody of the mad scientist plot, only here making that stereotype a mad metaphysician: a man who wishes to control the world through possession of all paranormal phenomenon from his Happy Isles retreat two thousand miles up the Amazon. To accomplish his plan, he persuades, coerces, or kidnaps mediums, witches, schizophrenics, speakers in tongues, etc. He also steals a horse that counts and even a haunted house. All of these are transported to the Happy Isles. The reaction of a mother whose daughter is persuaded to go is combined with the comments of neighbors and the frustration of a police inspector to form not a scene of grief, but of grotesque farce. Likewise, the death and consumption by cannibals of one of a pair of psychics and the resulting mental breakdown of her partner is treated as merely morbidly ludicrous. Appleby's thoughts are "The mortal remains of Miss Molsher departing to stew-pots at various points of the compass and the resulting bafflement of Mrs. Gladigen's psychic perceptions: the notion was rather more absurd than horrible" (184). This fantastic thriller parody shows Innes at his most extreme in creating wildly comic novels of crime and farcical action, but it is only one of more than forty that do so.

His success as farceur of crime is unquestioned, and the techniques he has used in his long career have been influential. For instance, the following exchange occurs in *The Daffodil Affair*:

"We're in a sort of hodgepodge of fantasy and harum-scarum adventure that isn't a proper detective story at all. We might be by Michael Innes."

"Innes? I've never heard of him." Appleby spoke with decided exasperation. (234)

Such disparaging references by a character about his creator has become one of the most noted devices of the next major farceur to appear: Edmund Crispin.

Gervase Fen, Crispin's detective, realizes he is fictional and does not hesitate to comment on his creator's presentation of him and his cases. He speaks of Crispin writing up the cases "in his own grotesque way," and when he is tied up in a cupboard in *The Moving Toyshop*, he spends time making up such suitable titles for Crispin as "The Blood on the Mortarboard," "Fen Strikes Back," and "A Don Dares Death (A Gervase Fen Story)" (81). After a long period of no detective novels, Crispin wrote his last, *The Glimpses of the Moon*; that hiatus is noted by Fen in the following manner:

In the fifteen years since his last appearance, he seemed to have changed very little.... At this rate, he felt, he might even live to see the day when novelists described their characters by some other device than that of maneuvering them into examining themselves in mirrors. (43)

In the same novel, another character shows his awareness of its fictional nature; when Fen says that he does not know the identity of the murderer, that character replies, "But you must know by now, my dear fellow.... We're practically at the end of the book" (211). These comments even include the political views of a book's publisher; when Fen and a friend are undecided as to which road to take in *The Moving Toyshop*, the friend says "Let's go left.... After all, Gollancz is publishing this book" (87). Such deliberate joking with narrative reality helps to set the tone of the novels, and that tone is farcical.

Like Innes, Crispin employs comic or absurd names, another contribution to the farcical tone. He particularly enjoys giving characters, and animals, inappropriate—and often allusive—names: a cowman is named Enoch Powell, a nobleman Henry Fielding, an office boy John Wilberforce Mornington, and a private enquiry agent Bartholomew Snerd. Two children are christened Anna May and John Will Bust. Others include Jane Persimmons, Ortrud Youings, Father Hattrick, Titania and Tatiana Bales—known as Titty and Tatty, a revolutionary butler Syd Primrose, a male mystery novelist who writes as Annette de la Tour, and Lavender, a cat which sees Martians in unexpected places. Lavender's peculiarity is matched by an inn's nude parrot, which when prompted by two lines of Mallarmé recites Heine's *Die Lorelei*, or a "non-doer" (non-growing) pig, which always makes its way back no matter how many times its dissatisfied owner sells it. Such names and odd animals add to the fun, as does Fen's fondness for puns. In *Buried for Pleasure* the following outrageous exchange occurs:

"For a time I worked in Boots—the book department. But it didn't suit me, for some reason. I used to get dizzy spells."
     "Inevitable, I should think, if you work in a circulating library." (12)

Though a farcical tone is produced by such devices, it is the novels' action that makes Crispin the superb farceur he is. His novels move with the same plot precision as the great farces of Feydeau or Labiche.

For instance, the chase scenes in *The Moving Toyshop, Buried for Pleasure*, and, especially, *The Glimpses of the Moon* are almost choreographic. The chase at Parson's Pleasure, the Oxford "nude beach," and then another through the streets of Oxford ending on a merry-go-around provide a hilarious conclusion to *The Moving Toyshop*. (Ten years after *The Moving Toyshop*, Robert Robinson's *Landscape with Dead Dons* took the Oxford street chase one stage further by having interrupted naked bathers from the same Parson's Pleasure chase a killer through the main streets of the town.) The chase in *Buried for Pleasure* includes that "non-doer" pig, a poltergeist, and an escaped lunatic who thinks he is Woodrow Wilson, and it ends atop a vicarage. The longest—more than forty pages—and most complex is in *The Glimpses of the Moon* and involves foxhunters, hunt-saboteurs, a herd of cows, motorcycle racers, an exploding power pylon, a booby-trapped strong-box, and policemen, with Fen and a companion viewing the action from an overhanging tree limb. The characters vary from the barely normal to such grotesques as a hunter "with waist-length hair, who was wearing a hoicked-up caftan and prayer beads above his shining riding boots" (209). Shorter but similar is the confusion arising from Fen's disruption of a chorus rehearsal in the Sheldonian Theatre while chasing a girl in *The Moving Toyshop*. These scenes are comic romps, but every movement is as carefully planned as those of a classical ballet—no matter how chaotic at first glance they may seem.

Though the chases are perhaps the most obvious elements of farce, Crispin's works offer numerous other examples. The parliamentary election in *Buried for Pleasure*, which Fen wins by one vote over two other candidates by giving an insulting speech to assure his loss, certainly qualifies, as does his encounter with Dr. Boysenberry, the director of an asylum who should be one of the patients and would have been a perfect role for Groucho Marx. Often described as his masterpiece, *The Glimpses of the Moon* is the most consistently farcical of Crispin's novels. It opens with a sort of Three Stooges act, including Fen, in a pub, and from then to that final, long chase, it is truly an anything-can-happen novel. One meets a tortoise named Ellis whose favorite food is premasticated pansy petals, a pathologist named Honeybourne whose ranch house is at the bottom of a limestone quarry, a composer who would rather set *A Child's Garden of Verses* but writes scores for such horror films as *The Mincer People* and *Bone Orchard*, and the most likeable rector in detective fiction, who tells fortunes in drag and says that since he bought "a forty-two bra, C cups" the bosom has been no problem. He is corrected when he addresses a policeman as inspector with the reply "Superintendent, sir. I smoke a pipe" (147). Pigs again have a part to play. Fen muses on the fact that "west-country sows often [bear]

the same sort of names as the higher-born women in Thomas Hardy,"
as Wilfreda, Eusalie, and Bathsheba (37). A pig's head is given to Fen
in honor of his having an M.A., and it and a victim's head wander
variously around the countryside, being exchanged several times—the
victim's head last being seen floating down a river on a raft, while his
body has had arms and legs reversed. Finally, a female killer's attempt
to escape in a Volkswagen, a Gas Board hole in a street, other drivers,
and bystanders create another choreographed scene of utter wackiness.
Crispin takes "high" farce as high as it can go.[3]

Writers contemporaneous with and coming after Innes and Crispin
have used the same farcical devices and techniques, but with the exception
of Colin Watson, have combined farce with other forms of the comic
or have employed it for some purpose other than farce for farce's sake.
Therefore, most do not require as much comment, but before Watson—
and Ross H. Spencer and Tom Sharpe—brief consideration of Peter
Dickinson, Simon Brett, Leo Bruce, Charlotte MacLeod, and Jonathan
Gash seems appropriate.[4]

If all of Crispin's novels can be described as farcical versions of
Golden Age detective fiction, the same cannot be said of Peter Dickinson's.
From his first work, he has been experimenting with ways of expanding
the range of both the detective novel and the thriller. Whether in the
five cases of Inspector Jimmy Pibble or the others among the first ten,
he plays with the conventions he is using, stretching and twisting them,
though never allowing them to break (his last four are outside the comic
mode). In such novels as *The Glass-Sided Ants' Nest*, *The Old English
Peep Show*, *The Lizard in the Cup*, *The Green Gene*, and *The Lively
Dead*, Dickinson exhibits a playfulness in staying within the formulas
of detective and thriller fiction, while incorporating into those formulas
a mass of diverse, incongruous, and often farcical elements even though
he cannot be called a farceur as such.

Jimmy Pibble is not a character of farce himself, but he must deal
with cases, which he calls "kinky," that are filled with other characters
and situations which are. *The Glass-Sided Ants' Nest* takes place in the
London house to which an anthropologist has transported a New Guinea
tribe known as the Kus. Their cultural differences with this environment
offer all sorts of possibilities for zaniness. One instance is the acceptance
of the position of tribal witchdoctor by Robin Ku, a teenager, on the
condition that he will be allowed to play drums like Ringo Starr. *The
Lizard in the Cup* takes place on a Greek Island where someone is
attempting to steal the entire mosaic wall of a chapel piece by piece.
Its characters include a beautiful terrorist, who is both the girlfriend
of a millionaire and the bomber of the Folger Shakespeare Library, a
homosexual secret agent, a legless physical culturist named Buck

Budweiser, alcoholic monks, and decadent expatriates. Multiple plots keep the action spinning, while the assorted characters create havoc with logic and problems for Pibble. *The Old English Peep Show* has more farcical elements than any other Pibble case: a stately home as amusement park, a tiger-pit decorated with a huge eighteenth-century pornographic frieze, a man-eating lion named Bonzo, the macabre deaths of two British heroes—of one of which Pibble thinks, "There could be a grand state funeral of the unconsumed portions" (166)—and Pibble's being saved by a Texas Minuteman tourist, who has him pose for photos on the scaffold from which a few minutes earlier he was to be hanged by a murderer. Indeed, Pibble's cases are kinky; they combine comedy of manners, satire, wit, and farce to form a unique anything-can-happen world.

The same is true of the early non-Pibble novels, only they contain even more farce. *The Green Gene* is a mordant fantasy-satire of racism in which all Celts are green. Its unlikely hero is Pravandragasharatipili P. Humayan, an Indian mathematical genius, who is also a devout believer in horoscopes, almost perpetually in a state of sexual excitement, and avidly desirous of publicity. Among his adventures is his apparent control by a teenage witch who has made him impotent, except in the shower, leading little Pravi to visit a large prostitute for what becomes a hilarious sex-in-the-shower scene. The alternate England that Dickinson creates in this novel is both funny and horrifying, and it is the farce which prevents it from being as depressing as Orwell's *1984*. Much lighter in tone is *The Lively Dead*. The death of Mrs. Newbery, housekeeper of the Livonian government in exile and mother of Procne Newbery, one of London's more famous call girls, is its starting point. The Livonians have their embassy on the top floor of Lady Lydia Timms's townhouse, where they keep the body of their national hero pickled in "Varosh," that country's vodka. Lady Lydia is a cheerful, fiercely independent young woman, whose philosophy is to accept people as they are. This attitude is severely tested by those with whom she comes in contact, particularly when Mrs. Newbery's body turns up in her rosebed. A gangster, a foreign agent, and an arrogant policeman, plus her assorted tenants, make her life less than serene. She describes it as "an absurd situation. It is like a sort of French farce for moral philosophers" (182). The same could be said of such other Dickinson novels as *The Poison Oracle* and *King & Joker*. Farce is only one element of many employed by Dickinson to produce his bizarrely comic worlds of crime—but is far from the least important.

If Dickinson uses farce for moral philosophy, Simon Brett uses it for social satire. His series of novels featuring actor-detective Charles Paris present the world of show business as a microcosm of contemporary

British society, and farce is one of his means of presenting that society. Paris' bumbling detection, his excessive drinking and its effects, and his relationship with his ultra-conventional daughter and son-in-law create continual farcical situations. Also farcical are the puns, stale jokes, mock reviews of Paris' performances, capsule summaries of inane sitcoms, and the boyish enthusiasm for detection of Paris' stuffy friend Gerald Venables. The overdone Dickensian motif of the Great Expectations restaurant in *A Comedian Dies* is nearly as absurd as Innes' Thomas Carlyle nightclub. Scenes of farcical action abound. Paris' confrontation with two union men and a food-fight between a television crew and slum dwellers in *Situation Tragedy* are pure farce, as are BBC committee meetings in *The Dead Side of the Mike* and the deserved on-air comeuppance of an arrogant talkshow host by an elderly comedian in *A Comedian Dies*. In every case, the farcical event reinforces some satiric point. Brett can also effectively join such events to crime. The food-fight scene, with its flying glazed chicken wings and coleslaw matted hair, is abruptly ended by a scream and the discovery of a corpse. In *Cast, In Order of Disappearance* the rehearsal and filming of Paris' big scene as Tick the deformed coachman in a horror film *The Zombie Walks* is another piece of pure farce, but it ends with Paris' being shot. But whether the farcical incidents are joined to crime or remain just set-pieces—Paris as babysitter, his suffering from the "dreaded Distiller's Droop," or his grandson urinating on that pompous son-in-law—they always produce laughter.

The eight Sergeant Beef novels of Leo Bruce employ farce as a part of the author's double trick of writing classical British whodunits while parodying the very conventions of the type by turning them topsyturvy. His creation of works which comment upon themselves through the arguments of Beef and Lionel Johnson Townsend, his Watson, as to how the cases should be presented as novels, bears some resemblance to the Fen-Crispin byplay, but Bruce uses the device as his major structural principle, and used it first. Since there is little action in the Beef novels, it is through the characters and their dialogue that farce enters. The plebeian Beef, with his "look of beefy benevolence," and the snobbish Townsend perform like Laurel and Hardy or Abbott and Costello. Townsend is a burlesque of every stupid, pompous Watson since the original, while Beef is the shrewd Cockney who uses his "loaf" and is uncaring about the proprieties of dress, manners, or food. Adding to the farcical element are the Dickensian names of their supporting cast: Mrs. Scuttle, Miss Pinhole, Wellington Chickle, Hilton Gupp, Constable Watts-Dunton, and a number of others. *Case for Three Detectives*, the first Beef novel, permits him quickly to solve a murder that has defeated the skills of Lord Simon Plimsoll, Monsieur Amer

Picon, and Monsignor Smith. These accurate and hilarious parodies of Wimsey, Poirot, and Father Brown, with their convoluted theories, in contrast with the humble, commonsensical Beef are the basis of this novel's farce. In such other novels as *Case Without a Corpse, Case with Ropes and Rings*, and *Cold Blood*, Beef's chief opponent, aside from the murderers, is Townsend, and even though Beef always triumphs— even in *Case With No Conclusion*—Townsend continues to worry about the Sergeant's appearance, drinking, astuteness or lack thereof, and, most of all, the sales that "novelization" of the present case will bring when written. All of the Beef novels are examples of the conjoining of farce, parody, and crime to form clever examples of classical detective fiction and, at the same time, good-natured mockeries of it.

Leaving England for New England, we find Charlotte MacLeod's zany world in *Rest You Merry, The Luck Runs Out*, and *Something the Cat Dragged In* at Balaclava Agricultural College. The College's power, and source of extra money, is produced by the Cookie Works, which is run on the manure of the College's animals. The College is famous for the Balaclava Buster, a rutabaga developed by Professor Peter Shandy, the series' amateur detective; its Grand Illumination at Christmas, another paying project; its prize sow Belinda; and the Balaclava Blacks, champion horses all named after Norse gods. Its president is Thorkjeld Svenson, whose sighs blow unabridged dictionaries across his office and who fights the villain in *Something the Cat Dragged In* with antlers and tusks torn from the wall. As a gigantic, intelligent "Hagar the Horrible," Svenson's only master is his beautiful wife Sieglinde, the mother of their seven daughters. When he is not tearing doors off their hinges, he relaxes by singing "I'm an Old Cowhand" in Swedish. Caricature though he may be, his famous decree that "Agri isn't a business, it's a culture," delivered with rostrum-shattering force, has made BAC an academic success, which is no farce in these times.

Whenever the deaths of staff, faculty, or their wives prove to be murder, Svenson demands in less than gentle terms that Shandy clean up the mess without scandal. Among those with whom Shandy must deal are Heidi Heyhoe, a coed siren; Idura Bjorklund, an Amazonian buggy whip heiress from South Dakota; Hjalmar Olaffsen, the clumsy campus heartthrob; the Viggies, the militant campus vegetarians; Fred Ottermole, the local police chief who watches reruns of *Barney Miller* "for professional instruction;" the porcine Professor Stott of animal husbandry; and Cronkite Swope of the *Balaclava County Weekly Fane and Pennon, a magna cum laude* graduate of the Great Journalists' Correspondence School. Needless to say, death among such people is more the cause of zaniness than grief. *Something the Cat Dragged In* opens with Mrs. Lomax's cat bringing her the hairpiece of her murdered lodger, a retired BAC professor; from that absurd beginning to the novel's solution, farce is rampant, as in the following account of how a house fire started: "A helicopter from the air base flew over the house and dropped a bolt or something right down our kitchen skylight. I was frying doughnuts. Whatever it was hit the kettle of fat and sent it all over the hot stove" (69). In *The Luck Runs Out* there is as much concern for the pignapping of Belinda of Balaclava as for the murder of Miss Fackerley, BAC's female farrier. All in all, murder seems to provide entertaining disruption of academic routine at BAC for faculty and students—if not for Svenson and Shandy. It is easy to understand why one of the chemistry professors finds the excitement exhilirating; after all, he realizes, he would never have a chance to be made a deputy sheriff at CCNY.[5]

The comic thrillers of Jonathan Gash are unlike any of the novels considered thus far. The adventures of Lovejoy—antique dealer, unkempt lout, womanizer, and risk-taking coward—include detection of murderers, but they are more of the caper or scam type. The humor is most directly the result of Lovejoy's being the narrator. His combination of brashness and continual apology ("It wasn't my fault! Honest!") compel the reader to laugh at, rather than criticize, his often less than honorable actions. His wheeling and dealing, his unfair fights, his chauvinistic treatment of women, his lies, and his cowardice are all grist for Gash's farcical mill. Even his terror when in some life-threatening situation becomes farcical because of his wildly frantic efforts to escape—*and* the fact that they are told in retrospect. His slovenly appearance; his rattletrap automobile, which is an object of derision to his acquaintances; and his rarely clean cottage, entrances and exits to which match those of a nineteenth-century French sex farce, also contribute to his image as the ne'er-do-well of traditional farce, who somehow always manages to survive, whether a quadruple doublecross, as in *The Sleepers of Erin*, or being embarrassingly trapped by several of his former bedmates at once, as at the ends of *The Vatican Rip* and *The Gondola Scam*. There are also farcical set-pieces, not absolutely necessary. One of the best occurs in *Gold by Gemini* when Lovejoy is earning a little money by babysitting the infant Henry and is interrupted by one of his women friends—a scene which surpasses Charles Paris' similar experience. From more than four pages, a few excerpts give some idea of how farcical Gash can be and the effect of Lovejoy as narrator:

"This is all your fault," I hissed at Henry. He was rolling in the aisles again, thinking it another game. "Look." I pushed my fist threateningly at his face. "One sound out of you, that's all. Just one sound." It didn't do much good. He was convulsed, cackling and kicking. I told him bitterly he was no help but anything I say only sends him off into belly laughs. He never believes I'm serious.

* * *

"You're not giving him *that!*"
"What's wrong with it?" It looked all right to me. I poured the sardine oil on the egg to save waste.
... I shook sauce on. Henry was all on the go.
"Dear God!" she exclaimed faintly. "Does his mother know?"

* * *

Janie watched in horror as I fed him. All this mystique about feeding babies is rubbish. It's not difficult. You prop them up in some convenient spot and push bits toward their mouth. It opens. Slide it in lengthwise but remember to snatch your fingers back for further use. The inside looks soft and gummy but it works like a car cruncher...it's not the sort of thing you can do while reading.
"His face gets some too," I told her.
"So I noticed." She looked stunned.
"It's all right. There's no waste. I scrape it off and put it in afterwards. It's his big finish."
"My God. I feel ill." (35, 36, 37)

Colin Watson comes closer to writing "pure" farce than any of the other writers, excepting Crispin. Where he differs from Crispin, and Innes, is in the bawdy, "bloody-minded"—a favorite Watson term—nature of his characters and their actions. The twelve novels composing his Flaxborough Chronicles are filled with people whose concept of life (they would never use such a posh expression) is simply to have as much fun as possible, whatever the expense to others. That desired fun if not strictly illegal is almost always immoral. Flaxborough is "a town of earthly misdemeanors," a place of "endemic sexual impetuosity." Whether among such lower-class tribes as the Trings and O'Shaunessys or the upper-class families of Jubilee Park Crescent, shenanigans of all sorts abound: a probation officer sells obscene postcards to his clients, a brothel hires efficiency experts, a Baptist lay preacher is drummed out of the church for "his liberal interpretation of the word 'lay,' " and an alderman drugs the Amateur Operatic Society's cast of *Rose Marie* on opening night. The list could go on and on.

Inspector Walter Purbright has the responsibility of solving murders amidst the farcical goings-on of his fellow townspeople. As with Dickinson's Inspector Pibble, Purbright is in no sense a farcical character himself. He is the single point of stability around which revolves the lunacy of others. Purbright must clean up the messes the Flaxborovians deposit at his police station; he is as much public sanitation officer and general nursemaid to his town as policeman. At the same time, he must deal with colleagues who are much like a British version of the Keystone Cops. His sergeant, Sydney Love, is a middle-aged and comically inept boy; the coroner is crankily senile; the forensics man, whose name is Warlock, is so facetiously breezy that he makes Purbright feel like a straight man in a comic routine; and in *Hopjoy Was Here* "the man named Ross," a parody of James Bond, is so obtusely sure of himself as to be ludicrous. Purbright's principal problem, however, is his superior, Chief Constable Chubb, who is either lazy or stupid—it is never clear which. Chubb upbraids Purbright for poking his nose into other people's business, and since he raises terriers, he believes that the world should be "a great dog show with policemen having nothing to do but guard the trophies and hold leads" (*Coffin Scarcely Used*, 17). Though Purbright does solve his cases, he must do so surrounded by this zany pack of townspeople and other policemen who rightly make him feel, as he says in *Blue Murder*, "like the visitor to a closed ward in a psychiatric hospital who notices...none of the doors has a handle on the inside" (75).

It is impossible here to examine all the plot bases and specific situations of Watson's novels that are farcical, for that would require covering all of the action, but a few may be noted as illustrations. *Lonelyhearts 4122* concerns two swindlers each posing as a love-lorn person desirous of marriage and each trying to out-con the other. One of them is Miss Lucilla Edith Cavell Teatime, Watson's feminine version of the gentleman-crook who aids the police when such aid does not interfere with personal schemes. She appears in eight of the novels and dominates three: *Lonelyhearts 4122*, *Just What the Doctor Ordered*, and *It Shouldn't Happen to a Dog*. A superb comic figure, Lucy Teatime's peccadilloes contribute much to the fun of the novels. In *Just What the Doctor Ordered*, she is running Moldham Meres Laboratories, which makes Samson's Salad, a preparation for the impotent, and thus becomes involved in a series of attempted rapes by elderly men. The action from beginning to end—including the attempted rapes and several deaths— consists of one farcical incident after another. An exceptionally funny one is an excursion-picnic forced upon a group of reluctant, cantankerous elderly people; it is a hilarious warning to overly zealous do-gooders. The most farcical, and probably the single most laugh-producing, incident in any of the novels occurs in *Six Nuns and a Shotgun*. The Floradora Club, a bordello posing as a restaurant-nightclub, provides mock medieval dinners, complete with costumes for guests. The description of such a dinner, with the diners becoming drunker and more lascivious by the minute is uproarious, but the comedy is doubled when a group of thugs, dressed as Vikings and hired by an enemy of the owner, raid the place. For over twenty pages, the insanity of the situation produces continuous laughter. Many other examples could be given, but it is hoped that enough have been mentioned to indicate that though Watson's death in 1983 ended the Flaxborough Chronicles, they remain the most outstanding series of farcical mysteries since those of Crispin.

Though the farce in Ross H. Spencer's "Caper" novels is as bawdy as that in Watson's, its purpose is to support Spencer's burlesque of American hard-boiled detective fiction. Through the misadventures of inept Chance Purdue in his fight against the dreaded DADA's attempt to conquer America for communism, Spencer's five novels mock both the image of the private eye and the spy-thriller plot. Purdue's sexual exploits, drinking, fighting, strong silent manner, continual shrugs, and crumpled cigarettes are so exaggerated and so repetitious that he becomes that familiar character of farce, the self-assured bumbler who cannot solve anything but plows ahead anyway, getting himself into one hilariously messy situation after another. Much of the action is purposely nonsensical and is presented by Purdue himself in a parody of the laconic, clipped style associated with the hard-boiled detective, but reduced to the level of the Dick-and-Jane reading texts of elementary school. It is this style—no internal punctuation, each sentence a separate paragraph, etc.—which gives each novel some semblance of "unity," for they are actually "loose" comic novels, with supposed crime as scaffolding: loose in the sense that Spencer throws in whatever he wishes whenever he wishes.

Spencer employs nearly every device and technique of comedy and humor in the novels, including, from among dozens, such staples of farce as puns, bathos, hyperbole, comic names and similes, the comic pause and added comment, invective, ethnic humor, comic misunderstanding, understatement, vaudeville routines, comic reversal and repetition, malapropisms, and comic definition and description. Some of these are devices of language and for their effect have to be seen in context, but others, such as names and the personalities that go with them, can be easily abstracted. The world of Spencer's novels is one in which is found the 000th Field Artillery, Old Wachensachs Beer and Comrade Terrorist Vodka, a mare named Ecstatic Climax, a football-playing gorilla named Zanzibar McStrangle, the Wisconsin Beanie (as opposed to the Kentucky Derby), and Schweinschwanz's Super Discount Drugs. Into this world Spencer places characters just as suggestive and bizarre. There is Myrtle Culpepper, a great-grandmother rapist who leaves her victims money commensurate with her pleasure and has songs written about her exploits. A quite different female is Brandy Alexander, a beautiful, sexy young woman who describes herself as "the head bitch" of the CIA hounds, and it is she who solves most of the cases. Orientals include Admiral Yogo Takashita, who writes poetry for the *Kamikaze Veterans' Digest*. In *The Radish River Caper* Spencer, with a facetious bow to Sax Rohmer, transforms Sir Lenox Nilgood Fiddleduck of Scotland Yard into the ageless Chinese Doctor Ho Ho Ho, "the most savage and merciless creature in all of history," the man who tricked an enemy into "visiting a WCTU meeting shortly after the Superkola had been spiked with Spanish fly" (59 & 54). Spencer follows Damon Runyon when naming his gamblers: Bet-a-Bunch Dugan, Oratory Rory McGrory (who poses as Detective Sergeant Holmes with his partners Ellery and Queen), Opportunity O'Flynn, and so on. He is at his most inventive with athletes. The football players of Radish River include Slippery Sleighballs, Barracuda Barinelli, and Half-Yard Bunderfoot, and their coach is Suicide Lewisite. The coach of The Stranger City Strangers, in the Caper of that name, is Rube Mountainstill, and his all left-handed team consists of, among others, Gaylord Messerschmitt (a catcher with a wooden leg), Barnaby Klutz, Opus Ganderneck, and Attila Honeywell, who fights a battle against 96,000,000 black ants who have a commune under his first base position—and loses.

The activities and experiences of such characters is what might be expected—or perhaps not. What is one to make of a six-piece combo with three bass fiddles, an "angry" rabbit chasing two "terrified" Great Danes down the street, a football score of 359-0, a lawn mower that peels oranges and skins alligators, or discussion of ABC's televising the Battle of Armegeddon and of the possible point spread? What is Suicide Lewisite's ancestry since the only member of his family not to commit suicide was his grandfather who was hit by a truck when he was five? Such anomalies abound. The chase sequences involve Roman chariots, animals, and even a ferris wheel and are always farcical, as are the athletic encounters. The practice session of the Stranger City Strangers and their baseball game with the Creepy Hollow Vampires and the football game between the Radish River Possumcats and the Sycamore Center Ridgelings, as well as the surprising halftime ceremonies at that game, are grotesquely comic travesties of their sports. Probably the funniest, and certainly the most biting, episode in any of the novels occurs in *The Stranger City Caper* when Purdue visits a revival meeting, the Bobby Crackers' Blitzkreig for Christ; the commercialism, self-righteousness, and sheer tackiness of an evangelistic "crusade" is satirically skewered through farcical presentation. Since most of the characters are less than brilliant, their conversations are as zany as their actions. Two instances of lack of communication leading to hilarity are:

He said there's a pitcher down there what is wilder than a tiger with a knot in its tail.

Moose said who would tie a knot in a tiger's tail?
Rube said at the moment his name eludes me.
Moose said well if he keeps it up he gonna get reported to the SPCA.

(*The Stranger City Caper*, 71)

She said if we're successful the Desert Sands might junk their *cause celebre* and stop
trying to start their *coup d'etat*.
I said yeah well those foreign cars have always been a big pain in the ass.

(*The Abu Wahab Caper*, 32)

Spencer's Caper novels provide another instance of an alternate, anything-can-happen world: in his case, a world of slapstick action, of ridiculous characters, of outrageous distortions of language—a world of farcical belly laughs.

Watson and Spencer are bawdy, though differently so. Tom Sharpe is gross and obscene—and very funny—but not without reason. *Riotous Assembly* and *Indecent Exposure*, his two novels of the South African police and apartheid, present a world of paranoia, stupidity, cruelty, violence, and cupidity, which always defends itself as preserving "Western Civilization." However, rather than preach, Sharpe ridicules with laughter; his purpose is satire and his method farce—farce in its most extreme, its "lowest," form. Much of the farce results from the theme of lunacy running through the novels. To Sharpe, South Africa is a lunatic state, where irrational conduct is the norm. References to insanity are continual, and separation of the sane from the insane is impossible. Lunacy reigns supreme, controlling every aspect of life. In *Riotous Assembly*, a prison chapel is decorated with stained glass windows by an "insane" genius, depicting various forms of execution, including one by electric chair: "the figure in the chair was portrayed encased in an aura of electric-blue sparks" (168). Such is art, such is the comfort of religion in Sharpe's South Africa. In the same novel, Miss Hazelstone, a leader of South African society, is put into an insane asylum by police order; her comment after a few days is that "there didn't seem to be any significant difference between life in the mental hospital and life in South Africa as a whole. Black madmen did all the work, while white lunatics lounged about imagining they were God" (149). Miss Hazelstone makes another analogy which is almost surreal in characterizing the lunacy of South African life:

That is life, a black man pretending to be a white woman, dancing steps of a ballet
he has never seen, dressed in clothes made of a material totally unsuited to a hot climate
on a lawn which was imported from England, and kissing the stone face of a man who
destroyed his nation, filmed by a woman who is widely regarded as the arbiter of good
taste. Nothing could better express the quality of life in South Africa. (143)

It is hardly surprising that the novel's climax is a pageant on the history of South Africa presented by the inmates of an asylum which ends in a chaotic, bloody, and fiendishly comic free-for-all.

The lunatic activity in both novels revolves around and includes three policemen: Kommandant van Heerden, Lieutenant Verkramp, and Konstable Els. Van Heerden is the stupid bully of farce. As commander of the police in Piemburg, a city of seventy thousand, he is overlord of six hundred policemen, yet within him is a "kernel of servility" which is his "innermost self and which no amount of his own authority could ever erase" (*Indecent Exposure*, 37). But this servility exists only toward the British: his sentimentality toward them and their snobbishness, which he thinks of as breeding, is a sign of his stupidity and leads him to accept phonies as aristocrats and even to attempt to have an unnecessary heart transplant, the new heart being a desired British one. On the other hand, any mention of color, particularly black, however innocuous, sends him into a frenzy. In fact, to everyone except admired Englishmen, his attitude is "It's dog eat dog and I'm the bigger dog" (*Indecent*, 106). His blustering and bullying leads him into situations from thinking a health farm is a hotel and being put into a room labelled "Colonic Irrigation No. 6" to his total puzzlement but acceptance at being tied to a bed in a rubber suit by an elderly fetishist (and eventually hanging in it from a second-story window still attached to the bed), or participating in his first foxhunt on an uncontrollable horse, the hunt ending with him and his host's wife having sex surrounded by the pack of slobbering foxhounds.

Van Heerden's immediate subordinate Verkramp is also stupid, but he is even more vicious and devious—and he hates the British. His masochistic puritanism and his paranoia about communist spies and miscegenation create most of the farcical action of *Indecent Exposure*. His view is that his "professional task was to root out enemies of the state and it followed that enemies of the state were there to be rooted out" (34), and so in van Heerden's absence, he puts into effect Operation Red Rout and Operation White Wash. The first intends to expose the communists in Piemburg; its results are the destruction of much of the city by his secret agents, who mistake each other for communists, and "hordes of self-detonating ostriches," which have been fed gelegnite-filled condoms by those agents. At the same time, Verkramp, aided by the Amazonian Dr. von Blimenstein puts into effect Operation White Wash, whose purpose is, by the use of aversion therapy, to insure that no member of the police will engage in miscegenation with black women. The therapy is so drastic and so successful that half the men become gay, no longer wanting any woman whatever her color. A bare summary of Verkramp's two pet projects gives no conception of the chaotically farcical events which comprise their action. As black as the humor is (the pun is unavoidable), it is literally riotously funny.

Though he appears in both novels, Konstable Els is more prominent in *Riotous Assembly*. He is a sub-human sadist, who happily kills twenty-one fellow policemen in one afternoon with "a magazine-loaded multi-barrelled elephant gun" (21). Whenever in a fight with man or beast, he likes to bite; when he thinks he has rabies, a doctor says, "You'll live to bite another day" (85). He wins a battle with a doberman by the unfairest, almost unspeakable, means, and then has the creature stuffed as a souvenir. At the end of the novel it appears that he has died in the collapse of a scaffold, on which he was to be acting hangman, but he returns in *Indecent Exposure* having enjoyed himself for awhile as a black convict and is as randy and mindlessly cruel as ever. If farce must be described as "low" comedy, one can hardly find a lower farcical character than Els.

Van Heerden, Verkramp, and Els are the central characters, but they are surrounded by many others whose personalities and actions contribute to the lunatic farce. Scenes such as that of a woman who has "Blackcock Fever" being interviewed by Dr. von Blumenstein in *Indecent Exposure* is as obscenely wacky as anyone can—or cannot—imagine. Similar ones include a lisping lawyer and deaf judge, the misfortunes of a vulture, a machinegun battle in a stately mansion owned by a family whose crest is a wild boar "rampant" with the motto "Baisez-moi," penises being kept erect with novocaine, the Bishop of Barotseland confessing to lesbianism, and an affair between a transvestite native and that elderly rubber fetishist in *Riotous Assembly* ("I might almost say that our love affair was cemented over a Michelin X" [90]). There are dozens of others, but let Els have the last word as he consults the Bishop in *Riotous Assembly* on stuffing Toby the doberman:

> "I believe it had a pedigree,"...
> "What's a pedigree?" Els asked.
> "A family tree," said the Bishop...
> "Fussy sort of dog, having a family tree," Els said to the warder. "You'd think it would pee against lamp-posts like any other dogs." (136)

It is necessary to repeat an earlier statement: the farce, and the obscenity, serve a purpose other than just laughter—though that is present in massive amounts. Farce is often considered the most mindless form of comedy, yet a writer such as Sharpe can use it in its lowest form to make a statement on a basic political and social issue: that is not a negligible task for either farce or crime fiction.

This brief survey of ten writers has not attempted to prove a thesis as such; rather, its purpose has been to demonstrate that farce has a place in a significant amount of fiction about crime. Much more space has been given to the farce than to the crime, which seems justifiable, for crime in the mystery and thriller is a given. The laughs and how they are produced have been the focus of what has been said. The forms that farce takes vary with the individual authors, and the fact that nearly all combine farce with other types of the comic also creates a variety of forms. But whether farce is incorporated into comedy of manners, is an element of satiric purpose, or is present for its own sake, each author has to create that anything-can-happen world to make such high jinks acceptable when in combination with what would normally be a grim situation. With the exceptions of Crispin and Watson, the authors considered are still writing, and so readers who enjoy laughter amidst murder and its investigation may confidently anticipate more examples from them, as well as from others not considered, such as Robert Barnard, Ron Goulart, Frank Parrish, Lawrence Block, and Donald Westlake. In fact, if the past is any indication, as long as there is fictional crime, there will also be farcical crime.

Notes

[1]The novels considered in this essay are listed below by author, preceded by the original date of publication. All references will be cited in the text.

Richard Hull:

　1934 *The Murder of My Aunt* (New York: International Polygonics, 1979).

Michael Innes:

　1942 *The Daffodil Affair* (New York: Garland, 1976).

　1945 *Appleby's End* (New York: Harper & Row, 1983).

　1952 *One-Man Show* (New York: Garland, 1983).

　1982 *Sheiks and Adders* (New York: Penguin, 1983).

Edmund Crispin:

　1944 *The Case of the Gilded Fly* (New York: Avon, 1980).

　1946 *The Moving Toyshop* (New York: Penguin, 1958).

　1949 *Buried for Pleasure* (New York: Harper & Row, 1980).

　1977 *The Glimpses of the Moon* (New York: Avon, 1979).

Robert Robinson:

　1956 *Landscape with Dead Dons* (New York: Penguin, 1984).

Peter Dickinson:

　1968 *The Glass-Sided Ants' Nest* (New York: Harper & Row, 1968).

　1969 *The Old English Peep Show* (New York: Harper & Row, 1969).

　1972 *The Lizard in the Cup* (New York: Harper & Row, 1972).

　1973 *The Green Gene* (New York: Pantheon, 1973).

　1975 *The Lively Dead* (New York: Avon, 1977).

Simon Brett:

> 1975 *Cast, In Order of Disappearance* (New York: Berkley, 1979).
>
> 1977 *Star Trap* (New York: Scribner's, 1977).
>
> 1979 *A Comedian Dies* (New York: Scribner's, 1979).
>
> 1980 *The Dead Side of the Mike* (New York: Scribner's, 1980).
>
> 1981 *Situation Tragedy* (New York: Scribner's 1981).

Leo Bruce:

> 1936 *Case for Three Detectives* (Chicago: Academy Chicago, 1980).
>
> 1937 *Case Without a Corpse* (Chicago: Academy Chicago, 1983).
>
> 1940 *Case with Ropes and Rings* (Chicago: Academy Chicago, 1980).
>
> 1952 *Cold Blood* (Chicago: Academy Chicago, 1980).

Charlotte MacLeod:

> 1978 *Rest You Merry* (New York: Avon, 1979).
>
> 1979 *The Luck Runs Out* (New York: Avon, 1981).
>
> 1983 *Something the Cat Dragged In* (Garden City: Doubleday, 1983).

Jonathan Gash:

> 1978 *Gold by Gemini* (New York: Harper & Row, 1978).
>
> 1981 *The Vatican Rip* (New York: Penguin, 1983).
>
> 1983 *The Sleepers of Erin* (New York: Dutton, 1983).
>
> 1984 *The Gondola Scam* (New York: St. Martin's, 1984).

Colin Watson:

> 1958 *Coffin Scarcely Used* (New York: Dell, 1981).
>
> 1963 *Hopjoy Was Here* (New York: Walker, 1963).
>
> 1967 *Lonelyheart 4122* (Chicago: Academy Chicago, 1983).
>
> 1968 *Charity Ends at Home* (New York: Dell, 1983).
>
> 1969 *Just What the Doctor Ordered* (New York: Putnam, 1969).
>
> 1974 *Six Nuns and a Shotgun* (New York: Putnam, 1974).
>
> 1977 *It Shouldn't Happen to a Dog* (New York: Putnam, 1977).

The Comic Village

Mary Jean DeMarr

The generally well accepted differences between typically English and American mysteries are often defined by their settings. Thus the generic locus for an "American hard-boiled" mystery is the "mean streets," while English "cosies" are most frequently, or so it is thought, set in English country houses or in apparently idyllic villages. These assumptions about place are associated with further assumptions about tone. The American novels of the mean streets are expected to be gritty, realistic, harsh in tone, frank if not vulgar in language, and pessimistic, even naturalistic in their view of humanity and society. Quite to the contrary, the English genre is expected to be light, even frivolous in tone, genteel and witty in language, and optimistic about human nature and society, revealing that order can be restored to a basically humane society once the perpetrator of the crime has been detected.

These generalities hold truest for the period prior to the Second World War, when the English type was in what has so often been called its Golden Age and when some of the leading practitioners of the American form were also active (although there had long been Americans working in the more cerebral "English" form). In the more recent period, however, boundaries have tended to blur, and the English treatment of the village has often become sardonic, even bitterly satiric, instead of light and basically favorable as in earlier days. Meanwhile, on the opposite side of the Atlantic, Americans have adapted the form in various ways: such varied writers as Phoebe Atwood Taylor and Charlotte MacLeod have comically used New England small town settings, and more exotic locales, such as Carroll in Crawford County, Texas, in D.R. Meredith's *The Sheriff and the Panhandle Murders* (1984), have made the form seem even more elastic.

The accepted mother of the comic village form, of course, is Agatha Christie in her Miss Marple stories. Christie represents the optimistic view that order can be restored by the revelation of the criminal and his or her removal from that society. Since her mysteries are almost

75

paradigmatic for the contemporary form, other works by other authors can best be studied as they relate to her novels. Another particularly helpful novelist is Edmund Crispin, for his village mysteries contrast particularly with hers in tone. In fact, these two writers may be taken to provide the tonal parameters between which most other comic mystery novelists of village settings have tended to move.

Christie's villages generally seem orderly places; the church and vicarage, the local aristocrat's estate, the doctor's office, the greengrocer's shop, the tearoom, and the local constabulary are all in their appointed places carrying on their appointed functions. The crime generally upsets the proper functioning of one of these, with the result that doubt is cast on many of the apparently blameless and normal citizens of the village. And these citizens are often comic either because they are exaggerated examples of the types they represent or because they meet the sudden disorder of their world by inappropriate responses to it.

Crispin's villages, on the other hand, tend to be collections of eccentric, even degraded people. Many of the same stereotypical characters are present and many of the same institutions occur. But his approach, while more highly and obviously comic, is also much bleaker. His depictions of village life are sharply satirical, jaundiced, even embittered— charged with biting humor.

For Christie, however, in such novels, spaced throughout her career, as *The Murder at the Vicarage* (1930), *The Body in the Library* (1942), and *The Mirror Crack'd* (1962), the village has always been more complex than it seems, and the view of her mysteries as presenting an idyllic rural England of a lost past is oversimplified. Her villages, under their surface veneer of respectability, teem with potential and actual sin. Miss Marple, whose St. Mary Mead remains the quintessential village of the English mystery, repeatedly stresses the passions and jealousies and guilts that are rife in this apparently simple world. And in the discordance between the appearance of light and the actual darkness lies much of the comedy. Miss Marple is herself an excellent example of discordance: appearing weak, fluttery, innocent, and incompetent outside her very limited sphere of house and garden, she actually has a deep (if second-hand) knowledge of an incredible variety of sins, all learned by close observation of her fellow villagers. Appearing the stereotype of the foolish old maid, Miss Marple through her characterization sets the comic tone for these novels.

A novel that well exemplifies Crispin's sardonic view of English village life is *The Long Divorce* (1951). The title refers not to marriage but to murder (the epigraph, from *Henry VIII*, act 2, scene 1, reads "The long divorce of steel"—title page);[1] the murder weapon is a "butcher's steel." This particular village, Cotten Abbas, is the home of a mixed group of people—a schoolmaster, one male and one female doctor, an attractive young girl and her angry and embittered father, and others, of both working- and middle-class, play important roles.

Crispin's village, when first observed, is being torn apart by the presence of a writer of scurrilous anonymous letters which eventually lead to murder. The village itself, "sixty or seventy miles from London," we are told,

> obscurely conveys the impression of having strayed there out of a film set. As with most show-villages, you are apt to feel, when confronted with it, that some impalpable process of embalming or refrigeration is at work, some prophylactic against change and decay which while altogether creditable in itself has yet resulted in a certain degree of stagnation. But for all that, its charm is undeniable. (22)

More recent village mysteries have tended also to deny the village's idyllic appearance; they thus, despite their variety in tone, present the unvarnished village. Robert Barnard's *A Little Local Murder* (1976), whose title hints at its attitude, is particularly astringent in its treatment of village hypocrisy, much more like Crispin than Christie in tone. In this novel, more than in most, the village itself is a central subject, not just the backdrop for the strange actions of some eccentric (or even degenerate) characters. The appropriately named Twytching is awakened from its usual somnolence by the news that a radio documentary, to be broadcast in its namesake, Twytching, Wisconsin, is soon to be made. Immediately, the jockeying for position begins, since most of the village leaders are persuaded of their indispensability to the broadcast and the necessity that they control it if it is to present their village in the proper light. Thus we quickly meet a number of the leading citizens, are inducted into a number of the less savory secrets about their activities and relationships, and are able to observe them with the objectivity of the outsiders who come to Twytching to make the documentary. Even before a rather unpleasant local woman is killed, we have begun to learn of the "deceptions of simple village life" (90).[2]

These truths about village life contrast starkly and comically with the pleasant picture that all assume Twytching, Wisconsin, to have of its namesake and to expect to be presented in the documentary. The producers are quite aware of what they must reveal: it is their "duty (for commercial reasons)" to reveal "a cosy image.... Twytching's American cousins would expect it to be quaint, friendly, and impregnated with history and folk-culture, and that's how it was going to be" (87-88). The truth, of course, is far different, and a police inspector gives us the truth beneath the veneer:

Parrish did not think of Twytchingites as being particularly close to the soil (close to the telly would be nearer the truth), or as anything other than slovenly shoppers who could be deceived by the most patently bogus special offer, the most obviously inflated packaging device. (105)

Another recent novel with a tone more similar to Crispin's is Martha Grimes' *The Man with a Load of Mischief* (1981). Although written by an American, it is consciously in the tradition of the British mystery, and not only so in its English village setting. It even includes a map of the village ([8-9])[3] which is not unlike that supplied by Christie in *The Murder at the Vicarage* (60). Some of Grimes' descriptions of Long Piddleton stress by implication its similarity to St. Mary Mead, its encompassing the usual stereotypical figures:

As the Dorking Dean Road became Long Piddleton's High Street of rainbow shops and houses, Jury passed the Church of St. Rules and the vicarage on his right, then drove to the square. There was the tea room and bakery, where he supposed Miss Ball was up to her elbows in flour. After he drove over the bridge, Jury saw Marshall Trueblood standing behind his fancy window, and returned a brief salute when Trueblood waved. The Jack and Hammer was closed like a clam, with that air of desolation some pubs have prior to their 11:00 A.M. opening. (85)

It must be acknowledged that the English mystery has tended to be very class conscious. Christie here is typical in seeming to accept in some respects even while denying implicitly the class distinctions so automatically assumed in much of English fiction of her earlier period. Christie's mysteries take place among respectable middle- and upper-class people, but Miss Marple's village parallels generally relate to servants and tradespeople. It is comically surprising for the reader to learn of the parallels between rather stupid servants and perhaps equally obtuse members of the gentry. Miss Marple, herself a highly respectable maiden lady of independent if limited means, moves socially among educated, professional, and wealthy people as well as among other elderly women, both widows and spinsters rather like herself. But she observes the lower world of the serving class, those whom her middle- and upper-class friends tend to take for granted. And in observing she learns. Her special knowledge is only what was available to them all—and yet they must come to her for elucidation of their mysteries, adding another layer of gentle comedy to the novels.

Indeed, the main point about St. Mary Mead is that it is a microcosm. By studying it, Christie—and Miss Marple—can also study the wider world; it is only that the village gives a more limited and therefore manageable focus. Miss Marple moves easily beyond the world of her village; just because St. Mary Mead *is* a microcosm, it has prepared her to meet and even to outwit more sophisticated outsiders untrained in her intimate knowledge of the depths of the human heart. Thus some of her exploits take place elsewhere—but Miss Marple continually refers to parallels in the current case from that village life—and it is these parallels which enable her to solve the mysteries.

Although she finds useful her appearance of comic helplessness and incompetence, for it misleads her adversaries into not taking her seriously, Miss Marple consistently denies the accusation that she is unworldly and naive because of her village background and her apparently constricted opportunities for observing human nature. Her nephew, Raymond West, a sophisticated writer and man of the world, refers scornfully to St. Mary Mead on one occasion as a "stagnant pool." Miss Marple gently replies, "Nothing, I believe[,] is so full of life under the microscope as a drop of water from a stagnant pool" (Vicarage, 149).[4]

In observing her microcosm, Miss Marple often seems to have met a great variety of human behavior; at any rate, she is almost always able quickly to adduce some village parallel to just about any character or action she observes. And these parallels, often cited off-hand, revealing her gossipy, old-maidish qualities as well as her keen powers of observation, are comic because of their very triviality. Others are amused by them, not taking them seriously, and therefore they have yet another reason not to take *her* seriously. Those who do know her, however, do take her seriously and are wont to ask her for her parallels, hoping that in them may lie clues to present difficulties, even if the parallels seem silly. The point is that, however comic they may be, they do shed light on people's behavior. For example, just after the incongruous discovery of a body in the library at Gossington Hall, Mrs. Bantry, the troubled wife of the owner of the hall, sends for Miss Marple.

Mrs. Bantry said hopefully, "Doesn't it remind you of anything?"... "No," said Miss Marple thoughtfully. I can't say that it does—not at the moment. I was reminded a little of Mrs. Chetty's youngest—Edie, you know—but I think that was just because this poor girl bit her nails and her front teeth stuck out a little. Nothing more than that.... Mrs. Bantry felt slightly disappointed. The village parallel didn't seem to be exactly hopeful. (Library, 18-19)

But this is early in the novel, and, as it turns out, those bitten fingernails actually are a significant clue. Miss Marple, in her apparently fuzzy way, has already observed a telling detail and begun to interpret it, although it seems at this point an irrelevancy because neither she nor anyone else understands its meaning. Thus Christie is able to use this parallel, like so many others, in a variety of ways at once: it helps to characterize Miss Marple and to emphasize her contention that the village is a microcosm, it helps to create the gently comic yet loving tone with which

Miss Marple is always treated, and it both reveals and conceals an important clue.

As she is about to reveal her solution to the crime in question, Christie draws together the various strands of village incongruities and wickedness, Miss Marple's deceptively frivolous and even dotty appearance, and her ability to see through surfaces to the truth beneath. In an extended passage Miss Marple defends herself even while behaving at her most fluttery—and the incongruities in her behavior and in the world she observes are both comic and deadly serious.

> "You see," she began..., "living alone as I do, in a rather out of the way part of the world, one has to have a hobby.... [M]y hobby is—and always has been—Human Nature. So varied—and so very fascinating. And, of course, in a small village, with nothing to distract one, one has such ample opportunity for becoming what I might call proficient in one's study. One begins to class people, quite definitely, just as though they were birds or flowers, group so and so, genus this, species that. Sometimes, of course, one makes mistakes, but less and less as time goes on. And then, too, one tests oneself. One takes a little problem—for instance the gill of picked shrimps that amused dear Griselda so much—a quite unimportant mystery, but absolutely incomprehensible unless one solves it right. And then there was that matter of the changed cough drops, and the butcher's wife's umbrella—the last absolutely meaningless, unless on the assumption that the greengrocer was not behaving at all nicely with the chemist's wife—which, of course, turned out to be the case. It is so fascinating, you know, to apply one's judgment and find that one is right." (Vicarage, 194-95)

She maintains that what works in small cases is also valid in large. In her ordered—and therefore comic—universe, rules apply equally well for little peccadilloes and large crimes, equally well in the microcosm and in the macrocosm.

> "After all, a tiny working model of a torpedo is just the same as a real torpedo.... The—what one used to call the factors at school—are the same. There's money, and mutual attraction between people of an—er—opposite sex—and there's queerness, of course—so many people are a little queer, aren't they?—in fact, most people are when you know them well. And normal people do such astonishing things sometimes, and abnormal people are sometimes so very sane and ordinary. In fact, the only way is to compare people with other people you have known or come across. You'd be surprised if you knew how very few distinct types there are in all.... Of course, I wouldn't dream of saying any of this to Colonel Melchett—such an autocratic man, isn't he?—and poor Inspector Slack—well, he's exactly like the young lady in the boot shop who wants to sell you patent leather because she's got it in your size, and doesn't take any notice of the fact that you want brown calf." (Vicarage, 195-6)

Her concluding illustration here returns the reader to the obviously comic—and clearly recognizable—and thus both creates a laughter of recognition and underlines Christie's serious point. With great consistency, it also continues accenting Miss Marple's comic attributes. The village parallels, then, are thus not only central to Miss Marple's method of detection, a method that she defends as more intellectually rigorous and respectable than it might at first appear, but are also structurally valuable as they enable Christie to plant clues unobtrusively and then to unravel the mystery neatly and surprisingly. Additionally, because they are so often based on apparent incongruities and trivialities, they are comic.

Miss Marple's unorthodox methods of detection and her comic appearance and behavior are sufficient to place her squarely within the tradition of the eccentric detective. Crispin's Fen is, if anything, even more odd. Tall and thin, he has brown hair that constantly stands in "spikes," and he is prone to such exclamations as "Oh, my ears and whiskers." Abrupt and often appearing ineffectual, he somehow seems to carry on a career as an Oxford don without much liking what he does. Literary quotations and allusions pepper his conversation, and he generally engages in one long, hilarious chase in each novel. Unlike Miss Marple, an outsider to village life and in appearance at an opposite extreme from her, he is yet like her in using his appearance of incompetence to hide his very real abilities. So for him, as for her, the discordance between comic appearance and real abilities creates humor.

Another more recent eccentric village detective is Anthony Oliver's Mrs. Thomas, who appears in *The Property of a Lady* (1983). She is an indomitable, gossipy, aggressive, and wholly engaging Welshwoman who serves as half of a detecting pair (her colleague is a retired police inspector whom she is hoping to entice into marriage). Much of the novel is seen through her point of view, and much of its humor comes precisely from her blunt honesty and her entirely modern perception of the world. She has made her choice of village quite consciously, it would seem.

Like so many of her countrymen, she knew instinctively that she was wasted in Wales. Cardiff was full of Mrs. Thomases, leaving her talents largely untested and unstretched. Flaxfield, she had recognized, was ripe for a takeover, and like a general surveying the field of battle, she had established her headquarters in a cottage strategically placed in the centre of the village and on ground marginally higher than that of her neighbours. It was more of a hump than a hill, but in the flat East Anglian landscape it gave her a decided advantage. From the bedroom windows and armed with binoculars, she was situated in a position of some importance. (4)[5]

Mrs. Thomas, by her appearance, speech, and behavior often becomes an almost farcical character, always saved from descending into slapstick by her self-confidence and self-knowledge and by the insouciance with which she carries off her most outrageous actions.

The village is usually presented as a closed community; for the mystery form it is thus useful in creating a restriction of suspects similar to that of the even more tightly limited "country house" type. This restriction also relates to the comic presentation of the village as a microcosm, a theme stressed overtly by Christie but largely assumed by other writers. A closed society may be warm, enfolding its inhabitants, as St. Mary Mead, in its better guise, seems to do—or it may be cruel, filled with gossip, malice, and enmities from which there is no escaping, simply because the society is closed.

Barnard's Inspector Parrish, of *A Little Local Murder*, is aware of petty gossip and sees his town as unhealthily turned in on itself, even lacking libido: "A more lethargic and conformist town would be hard to find this side of the iron curtain, and most of the energies which might have gone into sex in fact went into tittle-tattle, back-biting and petty conspiracy" (40). He would find Miss Marple's nephew's image of stagnancy an appropriate one, though he would also agree with Miss Marple's understanding of its full meaning: "These little towns," he says, "can be full of little unpleasantnesses under the surface, and if once they're stirred up, nasty things can happen" (41).

The comedy in Barnard's treatment of village life comes partly from his satiric pictures of petty individuals and partly from the irony of his style. His keen eye for detail picks out many motifs similar to those in Christie, but he treats them without her gentleness and her assurance that once the crime is solved, all can settle back into a generally tidy life, with only minor mysteries disturbing the even tenor of the days. His vision is more akin to Crispin's, stressing the evil undercurrent rather than the restored order. At the end, the villagers smugly reflect on their virtue. " 'There's one mercy,' " says one of them. " 'It's no reflection on the town. Because they weren't locals, were they? He was a nice chap, but he was never one of us. Nor was she' " (Local, 184). Thus they revert to the hypocritical behavior the novel has emphasized. The outsiders, not having served "the fifty-year probation period imposed on newcomers to the village" (108), can be safely blamed for whatever has gone wrong, and the documentary can tell all the expected lies:

[the listeners] sat through an impressionistic rendering of a typical British pub at closing-time; they sat through a typical British fish and chip shop on a Friday night; they sat through swelling oceans of cliché from Hank on the concern of the British for their senior citizens. They sat through... 'An English Country Garden'. (189)

Catherine Aird's village in *Harm's Way* (1984) also satirically reveals the dark underside of this closed society. Like Crispin, Aird sees clearly the stagnation and in-grown malice that can result from villagers knowing each other too long and too well. Detective Inspector C.D. Sloan, Aird's detective, observes, "One thing...was certain about villages and that was that news spread like wildfire" (147),[6] and his associate muses over the related if obverse phenomenon: "Clams...don't have anything on people in villages. Touch 'em and they close up" (148). Christie has the same awareness, but Miss Marple is an insider, and thus to her these characteristics of villagers create useful sources of information she can tap merely by going to some one of the Florences or Claras who had once been in her service. Sloan, on the other hand, must maneuver and manipulate.

A local associate of Sloan's, Police Constable Ted Mason, reveals the contrast between civil servants on the local level and those called in from outside—and in so doing he represents the village mentality. We are told, "His working life had been centered round the skilful referral to higher authority of anything involving any effort. Knotty problems arising in Great Rooden soon found themselves dispatched to the substation at Almstone" (Way, 153). More serious, however, is his misunderstanding of the basis of his profession.

> With some good cause he had long ago decided that civil rights were a purely urban nicety and he had remained untroubled by them. Essentially rural devices like man-traps might be illegal and putting the villain in the stocks no longer a fashionable punishment, but the public pillory still existed in modern guise and Ted Mason had no hesitation in using it as a weapon. A threat to tell the world at large and the village of Great Rooden in particular—and for some the two were indivisible—about a breach of tribal behaviour kept many a petty law-breaker toeing the line.... Only when he couldn't think of a way of making the punishment fit the crime did Ted Mason invoke the due processes of the law.... He was, in short, a believer in the white-glove treatment rather than the kid-glove variety. (Way, 153-54)

Aird, then, like the others, indicates that village life is no idyllic existence. Sloan's awareness of the evil present in the village under its apparently peaceful surface is no less than Miss Marple's—the difference is simply that she learned of evil in the village and carries that awareness with her when she moves outside her native surroundings. She always returns to the village, however, emphasizing her clear sense that life there, despite the wickedness always ready to break out, is smoother in the village than in the city. And, from her point of view, the outside world has nothing better to offer her than what she has in the village. Indeed, her studies of human nature can be most easily carried on there. And one should not overlook the fact that her village parallels are almost always to relatively minor matters. Those murders that do occur in her village are presented as unusual breaks in the usually smooth fabric of village life. Inspector Sloan, on the other hand, is the professional, always involved with crime and bringing his knowledge of it to the village, where he finds the solution if anything especially difficult because of the secrecy and distrust of outsiders that is endemic in the village.

One theme that is notable for its frequency of appearance in the comic novels of British village life is that of change—the intrusion of the contemporary world or the degeneration of a now-lost peaceful existence—but at any rate, an obvious alteration in the fabric of village life affecting both the appearance of the village and the behavior of its inhabitants. For Christie, as suggested by the title and problem of the earliest of the novels we have been using here, *The Murder at the Vicarage*, the church was at the center of village life and the vicar played an important role in the life of the village, carrying a special authority by virtue of his position. In later novels, the central position of the church is taken over, ironically, by the public house.

Crispin's late novel, *The Glimpses of the Moon* (1977), is a case in point, although Crispin balances church and pub, granting each a significant place in village life. The novel opens in a pub, and a long, central scene occurs at a church "Fête" (significantly, however, not within the church—even for Crispin the village church no longer seems significant for any spiritual reasons!). The rector, while as likable as Christie's vicar, is an extremely comic character, regularly described as a "great bandy-legged ape" (66), who happily poses, during the Fête, as a fortune teller wearing an "ankle-length woman's black bombazine dress and carrying a cricket bag" (66).

Although the tone of many of Grimes' descriptions is more like Crispin's because of its wry, almost naturalistic realism, Grimes seems consciously indebted to Christie. One of her characters, Lady Agatha Ardry bears Christie's own first name and, what is more, considers herself a writer of mysteries. However, she is also a comic character—an American who has married into an aristocratic family and become more noble than the nobles (she particularly scorns and marvels at her husband's nephew who has renounced his title). Like Christie, Grimes stresses the changes that have come to the village in recent years, and like her she concentrates also on class differences that both divide and unite the village. However, while Christie seems to show her village society as centering around the church (or really the vicarage) and the great hall, Grimes' villages find their focus in the pubs—it is no accident that all of Grimes' novels are named for pubs which serve as central settings. Like the other recent novelists, Aird describes village life as centering around the pub rather than around the church. Indeed, she presents the church as now simply irrelevant.

The Lamb and Flag was the only public house in Great Rooden and as such was in many respects the centre of village life—the church being open only on Sundays, so to speak. As a place where information was exchanged it came second only to the village general store and post office—but then that was presided over by a woman. (Way, 32)

In Barnard's village, like Grimes', the church no longer plays an important role. The local police inspector, who knows his community well, is of the opinion that "there was very little difference between a clergyman in possession of all his faculties and a clergyman in possession of none of them, since in the context of modern village life both were equally irrelevant and ineffectual. The difference between a good vicar and a poor one could, in his opinion, be measured by the takings at a church bazaar" (Local, 39). The loss of position and authority by the church in contemporary life, even conservative village life, is here comically rendered through the viewpoint of an intelligent non-believer.

This shift from church to pub is a telling comment on the social change of the period since the Second World War, but the pub settings are quite useful to the later authors in creating comic scenes. As gathering places for the villagers where they may reveal their idiosyncrasies, the pubs are surely superior to the church.

A companion image, appearing with rather surprising frequency, is that of the supermarket. Such markets represent modernity and ironically tend to be seen by the villagers not as bringing greater convenience; instead they are rejected simply because they are new. The authors imply that these symbols of modernity are incongruous in their village settings. In *The Mirror Crack'd*, for example, a late Christie novel and one in which change becomes a particularly crucial theme, we are told that change has come even to St. Mary Mead:

when shops changed hands...it was with a view to immediate and intemperate modernization. The fishmonger was unrecognizable with new super windows behind which the refrigerated fish gleamed.... At the end of the street,...where Mr. Toms had once had his basket shop stood a glittering new supermarket—anathema to the elderly ladies of St. Mary Mead. (3)

This repellent supermarket has introduced other changes, changes that alter the very fabric of village life—at least in the view of some of those same elderly women.

"Packets of things one's never even heard of," exclaimed Miss Hartnell. "All these great packets of breakfast cereal instead of cooking a child a proper breakfast of bacon and eggs. And you're expected to take a basket your self and go round looking for things— it takes a quarter of an hour sometimes to find all one wants—and usually made up in inconvenient sizes, too much or too little." (3)

Barnard does not give us much extended physical description of his village, preferring to characterize it and its life instead through the persons who inhabit it. One passage, however, picks up the motif of the intrusion of the supermarket. Like Christie, Barnard combines comic characterization with his thematic point.

Mrs Leaze piloted her massive and ill-co-ordinated frame around the shelves of the Twytching village shop, keeping an eye on her customers in a manner she found much more satisfactory than what she called 'one of them two-way mirror things.' The village shop had recently been slightly redesigned and rechristened the village supermarket, and this reorganization meant that instead of Mrs Leaze getting things for her customers, she now told them where everything was that she felt they might or ought to need. This change suited Mrs Leaze for the retailing of information was her forte, and she had a variety of different tones for the assorted items of information, ranging from a breezy cackle to a choked whisper. It was not for nothing that she was known to the village wits as 'Mrs Sleaze', and there were many who contended that one could judge the staple of village news by the length of petticoat showing under the hem of her dress: on dull days she remembered to hitch it up, but when there was a juicy item to be circulated from customer to customer it was allowed to drift down and down, like the floating pound. (Local, 13)

Additional reference to the flavor of contemporary British life, including its representation here in the village, is given by the information that the refrigerator contains "grubby packets of cheese, and...tasteless Cheddar and tasteless Wensleydale" (64), corruptions of what should be English specialties.

What we tend to see of the village in Miss Marple's stories is the people. True, a map of the village is given to us in *The Murder at the Vicarage*, her first novel, but the village setting consists more of people than of buildings and landscapes. While the people may be both ordinary and, under the surface, seething with passions and possibilities of evil, the life itself there is pleasant and comfortable. Once the mysteries, either major or minor, have been solved, life can go on in a very congenial and secure fashion. Thus, it is, at least in the early novels. By the time of the later stories in Miss Marple's series, change has become an almost obsessive theme—change in village life as in Miss Marple herself.

The Body in the Library (1942) and *The Mirror Crack'd* (1962) serve as companion pieces. Both have crucial settings (either the discovery of the body or the locus of the actual murder) in Gossington Hall, an institution in the life of St. Mary Mead and thus well within Miss Marple's usual sphere of knowledge and activities. But the inhabitants of the Hall differ: in the earlier novel, Colonel and Mrs. Bantry are the owners, a couple who belong to the life of the village and seem to belong there, even though they have only bought, not inherited, it. Colonel and Mrs. Bantry could not be any more quintessentially English, any more at home in the countryside. Indeed in her characterization, Christie is playing about with the familiar stereotype of the gruff but good-hearted British military man. But by the time the later novel takes place, the Hall has been sold to people who are—and always will be—outsiders: filmmakers.

Other changes, also for the worse, parallel the changes in ownership of the Hall. Miss Marple's physical condition, always frail, has declined with the passage of time.

> One had to face the fact: St. Mary Mead was not the place it had been. In a sense, of course, nothing was what it had been. You could blame the war (both the wars), or the younger generation, or women going out to work, or the atom bomb, or just the Government—but what one really meant was the simple fact that one was growing old. Miss Marple, who was a very sensible old lady, knew that quite well. It was just that, in a queer way, she felt it more in St. Mary Mead, because it had been her home for so long. (Mirror, 2-3)

The changes in the appearance of the village echo the changes in modern life. Their cumulative effect is to cheapen and make ugly what had been in appearance an idyllic village (readers know, of course, how deceptive that appearance always was). Though much has changed, something remains—but the tone is gently mocking.

> St. Mary Mead, the old-world core of it, was still there. The Blue Boar [pub] was there, and the church and the vicarage and the little nest of Queen Anne and Georgian houses, of which hers was one. Miss Hartnell's house was still there, and also Miss Hartnell, fighting progress to the last gasp. Miss Wetherby had passed on and her house was now inhabited by the bank manager and his family, having been given a face-lift by the painting of doors and windows a bright royal blue. There were new people in most of the other old houses, but the houses themselves were little changed in appearance. (3)

The most offensive intrusion of modernity is the Development, a large housing complex just outside the village proper, and when Miss Marple escapes her watchful nurse (a hated result of her enfeebled condition), for several hours of freedom, she goes to the Development to explore it as she would a foreign land. What she discovers is "planned, antiseptic, happy messy, and *new*." Searching for parallels, as is her wont, Miss Marple compares Cherry, who lives with her husband in the Development and comes in to clean for her, with the myriad of Florences and Amys and Claras who had worked for her in the past. Where Cherry is cheerful and understanding, they had been obedient and rather stupid. They knew how to wash dishes properly and make beds, tasks which Cherry performs hastily and sloppily, but they had lacked her open-hearted friendliness and concern. "It was odd," she thinks, "that nowadays it should be the educated girls who went in for all the domestic chores. Students from abroad, girls *au pair*, university students in the vacation, young married women like Cherry Baker, who lived in spurious Closes on new building developments" (6). Thus while the changes may often pain her, Miss Marple is obliged to recognize that they are not all for the worse. And when, at the end of the novel, Cherry and her husband ask to come to live with and work for and care for Miss Marple (they have felt stifled in the close quarters of the Development and yearn for a freer and more congenial life that they think they can have in the village proper), a happy merging of some of the best of the old and the new occurs. Thus again we have the comic resolution, the restoring—or creating—of order from discord.

The Development is treated satirically by Christie, as are the filmmakers who now inhabit the Hall. But whether in village or hall or Development, indeed wherever Miss Marple goes, people show the same traits, the same greed and pettiness and lust. And Christie's detached yet affectionate treatment of her villagers and the detective who knows them so well gives us a wry, loving, and comic depiction of the world of the English village.

Crispin's Cotten Abbas, like St. Mary Mead, cannot forestall inevitable changes—although it may be more able to cover them over:

it was essentially a residential village for members of the cultured upper middle class— intelligent company directors, fashionable portrait painters and so forth—who needed to be within reach of London but who could dictate their own time of arriving there; and it was they who had been responsible, at some sacrifice to themselves, for preserving the village's amenities. They had restricted new building, and dictated its style when it proved inevitable; they had sat in judgement on inn-signs; they had pestered the Vicar to remove the Victorian pews from the great church, and had paid for better ones to replace them; they had supervised restoration and rebuilding. . . . they had ordained a minimum bus service from Twelford, and stringent anti-charabanc laws, in their determination to keep trippers at bay. But their best efforts had not succeeded either in preventing the erection of Rolt's saw-mill or in encompassing the destruction of a hideous yellow-brick conventicle, dedicated to the use of an obscure nonconformist faction called The Children of Abraham, which affronted the eyes not twenty yards from the church. Against these two edifices the animus of the intelligent company directors, not less than of the fashionable portrait painters, simmered and bubbled perennially. And their schemes for the discomfiture of the persons most closely associated with the offending structures—Rolt himself on the one hand, and on the other the village butcher, Amos Weaver, who preached heterodoxy in the conventicle on Sunday mornings—imparted to the small community a liveliness which it might otherwise have lacked. (Divorce, 63-64)

Thus a good part of Cotten Abbas' charm has now become spurious, and Crispin repeatedly and wittily stresses that fakery. The pub, for instance, is an inn of low ceilings, uneven floors, and massive chimney stakes, whose frontage of irregular beams and plaster, [is] pierced by diminutive leaded windows.... Entering, you crossed a tiny golosh-littered vestibule and came immediately into the Lounge Bar.... The hunting-prints on its walls, and in general its rather ostentatious rejection of modernity, gave it a vaguely self-conscious look.(23)

Repeatedly, then, Crispin stresses the clashes between the genuinely old and charming and the modern sham which vulgarly apes it and between the genuine villager and the outsider who makes of the village a bedroom community and yet wishes to control its destiny. But the genuine villagers are no disinterested preservers of a lovely way of life; rather they are apt to be ignorant—prejudiced blindly against anything new and, to them, strange. Thus their cruel treatment of the competent woman doctor who hangs out her shingle among them and thus also the enmity between classes which nearly tears the community apart and which makes it a fertile soil for anonymous letters.

And in Crispin's worlds, change is not always for the worse. Having just met a literal idiot, as is his wont Fen meditates on his experience:

Fen reflected that village idiots were something of a rarity these days, whereas in previous times the mating of two members of a particularly stupid family (MUM [*on her death-bed, to her eldest daughter* GWLADYS]: And you, Glad my girl, you just see to it, after I'm gone, that yer Da's kept comfy-like. Know what I mean? GWLADYS [*with enthusiasm*]: Oh yes, Mum! MUM: That's all right, then. These nasty things are best kept in the family, that's what I always say. [*Dies; after a seemly interval for weeping,* GWLADYS *hies her blithely to incestuous sheets.*)]—whereas in previous times the mating of two members of a particularly stupid family could virtually be relied on to engender an ament of one sort or another. Now the breed had largely died out, possibly because in 1908 incest was made illegal. (Moon, 255)

In some respects, Oliver's Flaxfield has managed to preserve its appearance, little changed in externals. Oliver, like the other novelists, tends to draw his settings in broad strokes, depicting the village largely by its inhabitants and by brief indications of the presence of such staples of village life as vicarage and pub. He also, however, makes rather more significant use of geographic locale and details than the others do, seeming almost to delight in the typical village mixture of styles. (He agrees, however, with Christie and Crispin in excepting the contemporary from his approval.) Flaxfield is in Suffolk,

small, quiet, compact and almost completely unspoiled by the ravages of the twentieth century. It lies in the open East Anglian countryside, a happy jumble of styles where the earliest traces of Saxon blend happily with the Tudor and Caroline, and the Georgian porches stand content next to the more solid doorways of their Victorian neighbours. Since about 1850 successive parish councils have resolutely set their by-laws against further development and the village looks now very much as it did then. It has been invaded by Vikings, Normans, Cromwell's Soldiers and Mrs. Thomas. (Property, 3)

One of the intrusions of the world of the 1980s upon Flaxfield is the presence, in a former great hall, of a health spa patronized by women of wealth. This reminder of some of the more grotesque aspects of contemporary life contrasts with the novel's antique theme (central characters are engaged in buying and selling antiques)—for one of the problems presented here is that of distinguishing the true and the fake. Thus the theme of change is implicitly present, though not overtly stressed as by Christie and Crispin.

The fact that this treatment of the comic village in mystery fiction is not itself particularly funny perhaps suggests the seriousness with which the few authors studied here take both their craft and their subject matter. All, even if usually taken lightly as writers of a popular genre or, especially in Crispin's case, as writers of farce, have serious comments to make about the state of the English village and of its inhabitants. The comedy is functional, and the comic effects bring not only amusement but also enlightenment. Among frequent themes are those of class relations and the changes that have occurred in the villages and village life in the recent past. While those changes are most frequently regretted, Christie, Crispin, and such of their inheritors as Aird, Barnard, Grimes, and Oliver are too honest not to balance the good with the bad, and their perceptive, witty observations embellish some of the finest of recent comic mysteries.

Notes

[1]The editions of Crispin's novels cited in this essay are indicated below, preceded by the original dates of publication. All quotations will be cited in the text using, where necessary for clarity, the abbreviation given after the appropriate entry:
1951 *The Long Divorce* (New York: Penguin, 1981). (Divorce)
1977 *The Glimpses of the Moon* (New York: Walker, 1977). (Moon)
[2]All citations of Barnard will refer to the following novel, cited in the text using, where necessary for clarity, the abbreviation given below:
1976 *A Little Local Murder* (New York: Dell, 1984). (Local)
[3]All references to work by Martha Grimes will refer to the following novel:
1981 *The Man with a Load of Mischief* (New York: Dell, 1985).
[4]The editions of Christie's works cited in this essay are listed below, together with the abbreviations used in referring to them:
1930 *The Murder at the Vicarage* (New York: Berkley, 1984). (Vicarage)
1942 *The Body in the Library* (New York: Pocket Books, 1965). (Library)
1962 *The Mirror Crack'd* (New York: Pocket Books, 1985). (Mirror)

[5]All references to Anthony Oliver are to the following novel:
1983 *The Property of a Lady* (New York: Ballantine, 1985). (Property)
[6]All references to Catherine Aird are to the following novel:
1984 *Harm's Way* (New York: Bantam, 1985). (Way)

Crime and Comedy on Campus

Wister Cook

The academic world seems to lend itself to murder. Kramer and Kramer's *College Mystery Novels*,[1] listing nearly a thousand titles from 1882 to 1982, surely confirms the academic novel as one of the most common types in mystery fiction. Famous names appear: Michael Innes, Dorothy Sayers, Amanda Cross, Robert Barnard, Robert Parker. As these names suggest, familiar series detectives have solved academic crimes: John Appleby, Harriet Vane and Peter Wimsey, Kate Fansler, Spenser. And many other writers have put detectives to work on the university scene.

Not all college or university mysteries require academic affiliations. Some murder novels set on college campuses—involving simple sex or greed, for example—could happen anywhere. Other novels entangle professors in murder at a distance from the campus—in hotels, on bus tours, at archaeological sites: in fiction, sabbaticals are statistically high-crime events. Yet some mystery novels could occur nowhere else. In them, the academic ranks supply the personnel for crime: victims, suspects, and perpetrators. Though investigators may come from the outside, academics often extemporize as detectives. Books appear as weapons and clues. Most importantly, the crimes themselves are in the intellectual life of the university.

Not all of these latter novels are comic. But, in addition to fusing the components of academic life and those of detective fiction, a number of them bring to university murder a comic view of the relationship between low crime and the group which (nominally) embodies the highest values of the intellectual life. In these novels the judgment passed on academe is a major theme, and through the elements of the murder mystery—the detectives, the suspects, the crimes, and the resolutions—they offer two different comic portraits of the university. In one, comedy turns toward humor, celebrating the university, as its values—summed up in "the grand old fortifying classical curriculum"—survive murder unscathed. In the other, comedy turns toward satire, making the point that, with or without murder, the university may kill; as the values of the university in fact lead to murder, the vote of diminished or no confidence is summed up in the judgment, "God, what a waste!"

"the grand old fortifying classical curriculum"

In Michael Innes's *The Weight of the Evidence*, Inspector John
Appleby investigates a death by meteorite at the University of Nesfield—
a large meteorite pushed from an upper window onto the head of Professor
Pluckrose as he took the morning sun in the Wool Court. It is soon
clear that Pluckrose should have been murdered: not only had he poured
green paint on a bust of the Vice-Chancellor and stolen from the
Chancellor the very meteorite which struck him; worse, an academic
busybody and poacher, "He got up your stuff on the quiet and then
tried to trap you with it" in a fashion "petty, mannerless, and under-
bred" (102).

Appleby explains academe to the local man Hobhouse: "We're
working among a queer lot. Not like respectable thugs and burglars"
(31). His interviews with the suspects seem to confirm this preview. The
Vice-Chancellor, "a handsome old man with philosophic pretensions
and a mass of white hair" (32), assumes his lecturer's manner so
imposingly that Hobhouse takes out his notebook: "So that iss the first
thing about professors; they worry and have preakdowns" because they
are "ampitious" (35-36). Pluckrose, he believes, suffered from a "Sisyphus
Complex." Hobhouse puts away his notebook. Mr. Lasscock has no
theories, though he admits the death is "Disturbin'," with Pluckrose
"Poppin' off in that ojus, messy way" (79). Indeed, the meteor struck
Pluckrose as he sat in the Wool Court next to Lasscock: "Distressin',
of course. But then it was Pluckrose, you know—which made it not
quite so bad" (209). Appleby meets his old tutor Professor Hissey,
finishing his great work the *Annotatiunculae Criticae*, who beams at
him, asks if he remembers Appleby, and reports on the spread of classical
learning: "And do you ever hear from Harrison?... The natives, he says,
are becoming interested—really interested—in Catullus. I can well believe
it" (47).

Sisyphus and Catullus are two strands in the web of literary and
classical allusions in which Appleby finds himself. The "persistent
mythological associations" puzzle him, as do other reminders of the great
world of learning: Galileo, Milton, Hemingway, Aeschylus, "Circean
magic," modern art, "Classical statuary: hounds and boars, nymphs and
satyrs, Laocoon and Hercules and Niobe all tears" (113), Professor Prisk's
"Cyprian experience," *The Pickwick Papers* and the thirty-nine steps,
Shakespeare, *Zuleika Dobson* and the "Pickwickian core" of the case,
The Pickwick Papers again, and finally "the grand old fortifying classical
curriculum" (250).

Appleby follows academic red herrings which take him off the
campus—the Chancellor's grandson's unfortunate initiation into
"Cyprian experience" under the tutelage of Professor Prisk, and the odd

presence of German girls at a women's finishing school; but he finds the murderer at the University of Nesfield and the motive at the heart of academic life. The selfish, mean-spirited Pluckrose, who "in addition to being a busybody, was a chemist," abused science and abused knowledge, planning "a futile and disgusting experiment" (245-246) which would bring discredit not only on this university but on all scholarship and learning. With the purest detachment and love of truth, the murderer had remonstrated with him; that failing, he "punched him on the jaw" in the university forge-room, whereupon Pluckrose fell under the steam hammer and was irrevocably "pulverised." Recognizing his situation as "awkward," the murderer used Pluckrose's own stolen meteorite to construct an alibi. Only then did the rest of the dead man's plan appear—a plan "of the most extreme ingenuity and malice" (248) for a cruel academic hoax on the murderer himself.

In the ending in the university board room, Professor Hissey, warmly congratulating his old pupil on solving the mystery, credits Appleby's success to "his pursuance as an undergraduate of the grand old fortifying classical curriculum" and, as his former tutor, reminds the gathering of his own modest contribution to Appleby's "straight thinking."

Like *The Weight of the Evidence*, a number of novels about academic murder have less to do with death than with life. Offering more to rejoice about than to mourn, they turn murder into a celebration of the university. In such novels as *Gaudy Night, The Mummy Case, Landscape With Dead Dons, Poetic Justice*, and *The Memorial Hall Murder*, [2] the detectives, whether academics themselves or not, endorse the values of the intellectual life; and the academic suspects embody them. The crimes—as the connection with books and learning suggests—attack those same values; and when a criminal is caught and order restored, the festive endings commemorate their vitality.

Assistant policemen see the university and its inmates as dead to the possibilities of real life—"Not like respectable thugs and burglars," in Appleby's tongue-in-cheek description. As when Hobhouse eloquently closes his notebook on the Vice-Chancellor, they dismiss this world of unpredictable responses, incomprehensible interests, and unaccountable tastes. Inspector Dodd, assisting Appleby in *Seven Suspects*, is momentarily swept off his feet by the university—"It suddenly occurred to Dodd to rejoice that he was not a policeman in Chicago or Sydney"— and he falls to "Praising heaven for his lot" (98). But his attitude is exceptional among assistant policemen, perhaps unique. Sergeant McCarthy asks to be let off from questioning professors, who "wouldn't mind a bit going to gaol" where it's "Quiet and peaceful" (Quadrangle, 95). Contemplating university crime, Inspector Dorcas doesn't "know when I've been mixed up in anything like this before, s'elp me God,

I don't" (Landscape, 54). With his fly-like vision, he sees much to suspect, even in the women's college of the university: " Ever noticed the way they never have outside conveniences in ladies' institutions?" (55-56) Police find academics "not fit to be trusted without the supervision of normal, sane human beings" (Mummy, 184). Writing letters to the *Times* for "their principal recreation—that and doing crossword puzzles," they are seen as "Queer blokes, the whole lot" (Head, 87), a "peculiar lot" (Head, 80), a "very odd lot indeed" (Landscape, 22)—in fact, "all a bit touched" (Quadrangle, 85). In an American idiom, Harvard contains "many fruit cakes" (Memorial, 40).

But these are minority views. Principal detectives, whether amateur academics or professional policemen, conduct a love affair with the university. Far from disdaining it, they respect and embrace it as it embodies the values of the intellectual life. Kate Fansler, who loves few things, admits to "a love for the University...as irrational as it [is] unrewarded" (Justice, 11). Harriet Vane sets out to solve the Gaudy Night mystery for the sake of her college where "integrity of mind [means] more than material gain" (28). Inspector Mild, a Balliol man "dealing with an Oxford murderer" in *When Scholars Fall*, defends the honor of the university in the person of the murderer, "a scholar and a gentleman," and—too optimistically—in his own person; he reminds the undergraduates, "When [an Oxford] graduate is on a case he does not require amateur assistance" (67). Inspector Autumn, measuring himself against Oxford, is appalled at his "lower-middle-class upbringing" (Landscape, 19), his lack of a university education, his career's experience of ordinary crimes, and the consequent damage to his intellectual life: "God, how it narrows a man, a daily round of theft, murder, and rape" (20).

They all attack detective work as an intellectual pursuit. While Dr. Davie enjoys the pose of enfeebled old man ("In a considerable decline, Godfrey," he reports to a former pupil. "You feeling terrible too?"), he admits the excitement of a challenge "for my failing intellect to enjoy" (Dart, 30). Peter Shandy's colleague Timothy Ames launches him as a detective by reminding him of his commitment to truth: "You're a scholar. If one of your plants died, you'd think it was part of your job to find out why. If somebody gets killed in your house, the same principle has to apply" (Rest, 52). Two dons solve *The Mummy Case* out of "Pure intellectual curiosity." Appleby, himself a credit to university education, is "shocked at the quality of pure intellectual pleasure" (Suspects, 124) he gets from the hunt.

Homer Kelly, the manic Harvard guest professor and detective in *The Memorial Hall Murder*, brings a tremendous amount of intellectual as well as physical verve and commitment to the job. Irrepressibly curious, he looks at everything, including the upper reaches of Memorial Hall: "If there's one thing in this life I'm really crazy about, it's crawling around on the tops of vaults"; and he "beamed and shook everybody's hand" (14). He drops in on the remote and peculiar President of Harvard, shakes hands, grins, tilts back in a "fine needlepoint chair," spots the symbol of the Presidency, the "Great Salt": "Good heavens, what's that thing? Some sort of silver spittoon? Haven't you got it upside down?" (97) Lectured by the President on the Great Chain of Being, he takes sides as he walks home: " 'Oink,' said Homer aloud. 'Oink, oink' " (105). In *The Moving Toyshop*, Gervase Fen, pursuing truth with similar gusto, discourses on Shakespeare, disrupts the Handel Society rehearsal, endangers many lives in his car, and captures a murderer on a runaway roundabout while singing "the finale of the Enigma Variations."

Detectives do not always successfully meet the challenge posed by university murder. Inspector Mild, the *ne plus ultra* of university-bred C.I.D. men, gets an Oxford case on the strength of his book—on the lesser seventeenth-century religious poets. "Oxford murders," he explains, "are literary murders. To deal with them you have to have literary policemen.... I wouldn't be much of a detective if I let a murderer beat me to a quotation" (65). Even with these credentials, however, he loses the trail among literary red herrings, and undergraduates and dons beat him to the murderer. The diffident Inspector Fairford, investigating a woman's head found in a biscuit-tin while "the rest of the lady may be somewhere in the college" (Head, 30), supposedly can "stand up to" Oxford; he always draws the wrong conclusions, however, and finally his chief university suspect solves the case while taking a bath. Still, these two failures point up the university's success and, in Inspector Mild's case, the dangers of intellectual pride. And however well or badly they themselves measure up, the detectives never doubt the values of the university: the tradition of learning, the life of the mind, the worth of "intelligence and athletic thinking" (Suspects, 68).

Neither do the murder suspects, the academics themselves. While their behavior may confirm outsiders' worst suspicions about the university, they are loyal to the intellectual life. With few of them killers and by no means dead themselves, in their own individual ways they stand for freedom, growth, and possibilities. As Homer Kelly says of his beloved Harvard, it is "Just a miscellaneous batch of mortal souls scattered all up and down the great chain of being from the bottom to the top" (187); but taken as a class the academics aspire toward the upper end.

It is true that their responses to everyday life range from the merely inattentive to the certifiably mad, and their tenuous grasp of the relevant understandably causes suspicion among the police. Mr. Lasscock, for example, fails to mention the dead Professor Pluckrose and the meteorite when he finds himself late to his lecture. Similarly, Mr. Paltock, having come upon a woman's head in a parcel, leaves it there until after his class. Professor Haveland, who may have murdered President Umpleby, was once found "behaving very oddly among the sarcophagi in the Museum" (Suspects, 61). Professor Delaney, suspected of murdering President Brantley, has been a "border-line case" for a long time, though "that in a professor is scarcely noticeable" (Quadrangle, 143).

Though such responses suggest that—whether murderously or not— "some academic minds move in very small circles" (Don, 165), they also reflect certain priorities. Most academics, like Lasscock and Paltock, take only a marginal interest in crime. However eccentrically they do it, they give their most passionate love and attention to the life of the mind; and pure language, rigorous thought, and exact scholarship command their attention more compellingly than murder. The Master of St. Simon's in a speech to his undergraduates after a murder inadvertently "[utters] several *cliches*, the thought of which [pains] him for days after the event" (Head, 158). Professor Daly, recovering a manuscript briefly misplaced during a murder, "[seizes] it, like a mother recovering a lost child, and almost [covers] it with kisses" (Quadrangle, 80). By contrast, faced with reclaiming his agreeable former wife, he has to conceal a palpable lack of enthusiasm. While Mr. Lasscock may feel a limited interest in the meteorite which mashed his colleague, he has strong views on humbug. He takes leave of the Vice-Chancellor: "You silly old goat.... You fuzzy headed, muddle minded, muddy thoughted leek-eater.... You ode bawlin', chapel crawlin' upstart. Afternoon to you" (Evidence, 212).

Aspirations to the higher life of the mind touch the peripheral characters whom the university gathers to itself. A murder suspect reproaches Gervase Fen for "speaking disrespectfully of the immortal Jane" (Toyshop, 54). A lorry driver who comes to his aid pulls out a copy of *Women in Love* and warns him: "We've lorst touch with Nachur.... We've lorst touch...with the *body*" (87).

The crimes in which the academics figure, innocently or guiltily, are crimes of the intellectual life, as the books and literary references attest. In *Weight of the Evidence* Appleby finds the crucial clue in *The Pickwick Papers*; well-read in detective fiction as well as the standard authors, he notes, in *Seven Suspects*, the significantly literary style of President Umpleby's murder. In *Rest You Merry*, the clue to murder at Balaclava College lies in the Balaclava Buggins Special Collection at the college library. Inspector Autumn pursues a murderer across the book-strewn *Landscape With Dead Dons*, where the basement recesses of the Bodleian are used for storage by an enterprising pornographer, its *Paradise Lost* is mutilated, and books are burned in the Square. A lost work by Chaucer appears, *The Book of the Lion*, "The biggest literary find since..." (19). Dons publish copiously: essays, here and there "a standard work and several editions." When Manchip the Vice-Chancellor appears propped on the chapel roof with "a dessert-knife in his back—one of his own" (31), even his diary becomes material evidence. Mr. Bow-Parley rhapsodizes: "Dahries! One has not read widely in the detective authors, occasionally, on trains, the longer journeys, but one is perfectly well aware of the position, the—ah—key position occupied by dahries" (78). When Inspector Autumn finds his last clue on the diary's last page, he sees that a book is the key to murder. Even the murderer produces a literary masterwork, one into which he pours all his learning: "all my mind," he says, "all my liberality" (191). Finally, in *Poetic Justice* and *The Memorial Hall Murder*, chapter headings from Auden and Handel are reminders of the finest products of the life of the mind.

For the stake in these bookish murders is not merely a book; it is the intellectual life itself—literature, art, the integrity of scholarship. Murder points toward the larger issue, the survival of the values of the university, as someone involved in murder perverts, subverts, mutilates, misapplies, or otherwise abuses learning. Among the murdered, for example, is a poisoned ambitious president who tried to turn his staff into research machines, "reproaching them for lack of devotion to their work,...urging them to wilder and more impossible feats of research... [reducing] everyone to a state of nervous exhaustion" (Quadrangle, 143). A world-famous Egyptologist, suppressing scholarly evidence, is mummified. President Umpleby, like Professor Pluckrose playing games with other men's work, "running an intellectual man's somewhat morbid recreation" (Suspects, 142), is shot. Among the murderers, an obsessed historian who misunderstands both Oxford and history starts a "Tory crusade" at Oxford, two centuries too late. His epitaph explains his problem: he "got it wrong" (Scholars, 224).

In *The Memorial Hall Murder*, when the President of Harvard gives new meaning to the word "contract" by putting one out on the Director of the University Chorus, he suggests the lengths to which a misunderstanding about learning can go, and he spells out the life-or-death conflict of all of these novels—intellectual life or intellectual death. To President James Cheever, Harvard means tradition, the past, and closed doors. Harvard's gate is "something that [contains], guarding and protecting the Yard" (105). The memorial Cheever wants for his presidency—a "jewel" of a museum for the decorative arts, "in the shape of a small triumphal arch" (76)—sums up his need to embalm the university. His mortal enemy, Ham Dow the music director, is leading the barbarian hordes straight into Harvard Yard, for he is obese, has a "rather too catholic" taste in music, and knows very peculiar people, who participate noisily in such events as the Hallelujah Chorus sing-along. A big man in a big body, Dow in fact has "tried to throw open all the gates" (105): "Let everybody in. Admission free for all" (23). As Cheever's symbol is the dead museum, Dow's is the living performance of the *Messiah*. When a contract killer buries him alive in the basement of Memorial Hall, Dow concludes that he can die or "grasp at life by every handle he [can] find" (149). Cheever means to suffocate learning, life, and Ham Dow; Dow, the proponent of learning and life for all, sets out to rise from the dead. Cheever never sees where he "got it wrong"; but his case is closed when, pursued by Homer Kelly, he throws himself from the top of Memorial Hall, and Ham Dow emerges from the bottom. And his fate exemplifies the fate of those characters in all the novels who abuse learning and reject "straight thinking." The abusers are expelled, often feet first; the best of the university values survive; and the life-or-death conflict is resolved in favor of life.

The seasons rejoice, as mysteries are solved in summers when "gardens [yield] themselves languorously behind stone walls" (Landscape, 163) or in the holiday spirit of Thanksgiving and Christmas. Romances occur between young men and generic young women of "reasonable features, equable disposition, and sufficient intelligence" (Evidence, 86) and sometimes between couples who transcend the stereotype—Harriet Vane and Peter Wimsey, for instance, and old Professor Duncan-Smith and "a lady in Slough" (Don, 187). Love and the weather testify to the fertile university life, as it embraces all.

Festivals celebrate, as life's possibilities are fulfilled—sometimes astonishingly—within the university. In the finale of *Landscape With Dead Dons*, Apollo meets Dionysus when a host of naked dons enlarge the imagination of the city of Oxford and help Inspector Autumn capture a killer. *Gaudy Night* ends with music, the promise of marriage, and the unblemished integrity of the academic life. In *The Luck Runs Out* President Thorkjeld Svenson presides over a great solstitial celebration. Ham Dow rises from the dead during a performance of *The Messiah*:

The audience saw Ham first, and a few of them shouted and rose in their seats. The basses and altos were standing on the right side of the stage, and they all began surging forward, blundering between the chairs and music stands of the second violins. Mrs. Esterhazy was screaming. [Vick] dropped her arms and burst into sobs....*The trumpet shall sound*, sang Mr. Proctor, *and the dead shall be rais'd incorruptible.*(243)

As poetic justice is achieved, life expands: a murderer is found, a book is written, a college survives. Professor Castelman and his wife attend the theater, where they see "Dionysian rites.... Nude young women...nude young men.... Oceans of blood" (Justice, 175). Professor

Cartier makes Kate Fansler an offer: "Hope you will sit on my lap one day" (176). Life and art meet in W.H. Auden's speech, and Kate and Reed Amhearst get married.

In a lower key and on a smaller scale, other communal celebrations testify to the vitality of university life. Professor Hissey invokes "the grand old fortifying classical curriculum" at the final gathering in the university board room. *Death of a Don*, on the whole not very comic, has a cheerful Common Room ending where, despite the depredations of dry rot and murder, it is clear that the college will survive. *The Mummy Case* concludes in the Senior Common Room—in the very same room and with exactly the same dons as in the opening chapter. There the ancient Provost, Mr. Lacy, suggests the life-giving properties of the university when he querulously describes the burdens of responsibility he bears: "My dear Benchley, you...cannot imagine the complexity of the problems of thought and conduct that beset the mind of the Head of a House. Believe me, I have often thought of retirement, at any rate when I reach the age of ninety-five" (303). *Seven Suspects* ends with an invitation into the holy of holies of academic life: "The door of the inner common room opened. *'Coffee is served!'* " (268)

"God, what a waste!"

To go from *Landscape With Dead Dons* or *The Memorial Hall Murder* to *The Godwulf Manuscript* or *Close His Eyes* is to enter a smaller, less celebratory, not necessarily pleasant realm of academic murder where humor turns to satire. The university no longer embodies the rich possibilities of the intellectual life. With or without murder, in fact, in such novels as these two, *Deadly Meeting, Tuesday the Rabbi Saw Red*, and others,[3] it seriously diminishes them. In satire which ranges from mild to harsh, the detectives embody the best intellectual values, while the murder suspects—the academics themselves—abuse those values; and murderers, rather than attacking the university, mirror it— by carrying its worst tendencies to their logical conclusions. A murder solved is not necessarily an unqualified victory for life; depending on the harshness of the satire, these novels end in very modest victory, escape, or crushing defeat.

In *Close His Eyes*, when Andrew McNeill the poet is thrown out of the University Tower and the newly-hired bibliographer John Dryden sets out to find the murderer, Dryden discovers the motive in the pervasive misguided ambition of the university. The president fills the university catalog with illustrious Eastern names: with Dryden's own hiring, "He needed someone from [Columbia]. For the catalog.... we didn't have anyone from Columbia. You don't know what a fuss there was when he realized" (35). Members of the English Department serve the life of the mind by "[rushing] around and [writing] critical articles for the quarterlies and [reading] papers at the MLA convention and [knowing] a lot of famous people" (28). In this intellectual context, some motives for murder are self-explanatory. The murderer, at any rate, believes his own logic inarguable: "[McNeill] was going to keep my book from being published.... He was about to write a letter to his publisher, asking them to refuse quotation rights for his books" (162-163).Of all the academic characters, only Dryden and the campus policeman Harvey Kritchner pursue truth for itself rather than for promotion and praise. Kritchner, in fact, rejects the idea of promotion to the downtown police: "The pace is too hectic. It's more interesting here with the towing truck"; like Dryden, he wants to find the murderer "for [his] own satisfaction" (55). Having sorted the McNeill papers and solved the crime, Dryden leaves, but plans to finish his dissertation, marry his girlfriend Gwyneth, and come back to the academic life.

In these mysteries many detectives themselves stand for the intellectual life. Among the academics, Dryden the bibliographer seeks unadorned truth: "Facts are what interests me. I like finding out all I can.... I even like footnotes" (2). David Small, rabbi and part-time professor, is a student and teacher in both his roles, and his method of solving a crime is the intellectual method of the Talmud: "examining every aspect of a problem from every possible point of view" (Rabbi, 261). Among the outsiders, even the most analphabetic-looking policemen and private detectives, as students of literature and language, love learning and respect truth. In Blood Is a Beggar, Chief of Police Cleveland Jones—who enjoys "a bit of literary discussion"—attends a college lecture on poetry, recites "The Lady of Shalott," and, examining forged letters in a campus murder case, admires the writer's epistolary style. Sheriff John Macready reads books from the college library; when invited to sit in a college class, he declaims a passage from The Canterbury Tales and explains, "I always liked Chaucer in spite of his language" (Way, 85). Matt Ruffins, a policeman who likes to look "tougher and stupider" than he is, revels in the pose of boob as he inspects a library—"History of the French Revolution. And here's another with the same name, and my God, there's another!... Do they say the same thing?" (Silent, 48)—but takes extraordinary literary measures when pursuing a killer: "bring me the explanations [of Freud] and then bring me the interpretations of the explanations" (87). Spenser meditates on the language: "It's whom, who is employing whom? Or is it? Maybe it's a predicate nominative..." (Godwulf, 75). Only occasionally, among inside-outside teams, does the outsider intellectually let down the side: Lieutenant Kelly bellows ungrammatically at suspects—"How you happen to go into that there locked press this morning?" (Stain, 32) "Djever see this before?" (Stain,

145)—while librarian Gilda Gorham solves a murder alone; and Inspector Royle speculates dimly about "some kind of sexual prevert" (Goat, 105), while lecturer Bill Bascomb uncovers an academic motive for murder.

But detectives, insiders or outsiders, do not identify the university with the intellectual life, do not identify themselves with the university, and do not solve crimes for the sake of the university. The outsiders seek answers out of their own principles and love of truth: Sheriff Macready tells a group of academic suspects, "I ain't goin' to bite you" and "I'll do my best to treat you right," although "you college folks ain't never voted for me worth a durn" (Way, 21). They set themselves apart from the university by grammar or irreverence or both; and, as with the campus cop Harvey Kritchner, their love of learning, not tied to academic badges, is pure. Among the insiders, John Dryden loves the intellectual pursuit—the "private mystery-story game" (Eyes, 92), not the honor of the university. Henry Dane, who sets aside his paper on Dylan Thomas to hunt a murderer, does so because as a veteran of wartime espionage he has the know-how—not because he loves Collins College, where not only are department heads killed but "leaping, flashing words" of literature expire under the "dehumanizing treatment" of academic life and he feels "imprisoned in hallucination" (Midyears, 31). Bill Bascomb's is an anti-Drummondale University quest: "the thought of finding one of his colleagues out to be a brutal murderer [is] not without its attractions" (Goat, 99).

In fact, detectives who love learning do not love the university, for it up-ends the values they hold dear. The murder suspects—the academics themselves—flatly confirm their worst suspicions about academic human nature. Detectives groping for *le mot juste* label professors "bats, any way you look at it" (Midyears, 91), with "All the neuroses in the canon and a few besides" (134); "neurotic academic types" (Albatross, 32), "flakes" (Godwulf, 69), and "two-bit bookworms with complexes" (Silent, 105), and generally all unflattering judgments are right. Matt Ruffins starts to change his mind—"He'd always thought of teaching and reading for a living as rotten, in fact, queer, work for a man. Yet now he wasn't so sure"—but when he sentimentally concludes that his three suspects are "no pansy," "a straight fellow," and "probably a decent person underneath" (Silent, 83), he is wrong on all counts.

Nor do the academics have redeeming intellectual gifts. Rather than defending the life of the mind, they attack it from within. Intellectually speaking, they themselves constitute the criminal class; and whereas detectives find only a handful of murders, they find many crimes against the intellectual life by academics who value neither the "fortifying classical curriculum" nor "straight thinking." Insteading of learning for the love of it, like Chief Jones or Sheriff Macready, academics who don't "seem able to enjoy reading" (Eyes, 90) publish for jobs, tenure, and rivalry and revenge: Professor Casti, for example, looks forward to settling some scores with his "little article" on phonetics: "There are certain people whose faces will be very red" (Stain, 28). A department head confers the highest accolade on a future member of his department: "did you see his bibliography?" (Meeting, 41) While a few academics make "the natural mistake of assuming that college [is] a place where students come to learn and the faculty teaches" (Rabbi, 127), more common than these mistaken teachers are pedants—the "Academic variety of s.o.b." (Blood, 174)—who transmit the tired old formulas of English Departments: "image patterns...in *Gammer Gurton's Needle*" and "Kittredge's theory of the marriage cycle" (Godwulf, 160, 83). Seminars give them scope for imparting useless information; they approve doctoral dissertations— "original [contributions] to knowledge, on the structure of a grasshopper's tonsils or stuff" (Blood, 155); and at special times such as Ph. D. orals they terrorize graduate students, like "the big Chaucer man" who "made the candidate cry three times" (Stain, 120).

Their non-intellectual activities also show them lost to "straight thinking," and detectives find many problems with perspective among academics—in, for example, a college president who dazzles visitors with his "elocution," while admiring his own reflection in a glass; in another who, during student activism and murder, can be found in his office, "stroking a golf ball across the carpet" (Rabbi, 168); in an instructor mainly concerned with the academic sacrifice attendant upon murder: to commit one, he took an instructor's job "in a holier-than-thou institution of pride and prudery when I could have gone back to Columbia as an assistant professor" (Way, 209). Their convulsive social lives alternate between "stupendous boredom" and "[hangovers] of accusations and recriminations" (Goat, 119, 170). They are over-sexed or under-sexed; though women may have enough strength left over from pedantry and politics (as in *The Widening Stain* and *The Silent Slain*), men may not. When the sleep of reason really brings forth monsters, academics play politics, with departmental in-fighting among professors who "might commit murder just to keep the lower classes out of the Garden Club" (Meeting, 204); "petty squabbles..., petty this, petty that" (Silent, 75). With so much intensity brought to causes of such insignificance, "a flea bite [feels] like the fangs of a rattler" (Blood, 82). Spenser sums up the outsider's contempt for academic quarrels: "You gonna call in some hard cases from the Modern Language Association?" (Godwulf, 150).

But the murders they commit belong to their intellectual lives, not their social lives. Books appear as weapons and clues; and the kinds of books and the relation of characters to them suggest that the basic crime may be against learning itself, with or without murder. An entire library is the heart of one mystery, the home of many readers and few learners. Ignored classical learning furnishes a weapon when a bust of Homer falls on a parasitic professor who expects colleges to "subsidize college professors" (Rabbi, 237). Ignored medieval thought provides a clue to the college mentality as well as murder, when a drug-dealing medievalist steals the "Godwulf Manuscript," a library showpiece, for money, from a college whose main interest in it is money: they don't have a hundred thousand dollars to ransom it. Books and other dubious pieces of academic writing supply motives for murder: plagiarized dissertations (Blood Is a Beggar and The Silent Slain); a critical work which is "nearly half quotations" (Close His Eyes); the *Compendious Bibliography of Prose Fiction in English*, a ten years' monument to "slaving" which not only causes two murders but apparently exhausts "the whole fund of intellectual energy" (Midyears, 94) of its perpetrator; and a grant proposal couched in murderous jargon (Gentle Albatross). Academic efforts which do not directly lead to murder but do severely wound the life of the mind include a much-admired doctoral dissertation which will yield up seven articles on William Michael Rossetti (Deadly Meeting); and the "intellectual highspot of the year" at Drummondale University, Professor Belville-Smith's lecture on Mrs. Gaskell: "He had been delivering that lecture since 1922" (Goat, 12).

These misguided literary efforts are not isolated phenomena. Instead, they point to prevailing values: for the abuse of the intellectual life acted out in murder is not an aberration but the university norm. Murder— which involves misunderstood or perverted learning—reflects the widespread crime of the university. In *The Widening Stain*, for example, murder points to learning misunderstood, when academics mistakenly use it as a refuge from life. Only one professor actually commits murder to protect his chastity, when he kills Mademoiselle Coindreau, "the oomph-girl of the Romance Languages Department" (30), "good-looking, in the smoldering southern incipient-hairy way" (24), in the university library; but sexual fear afflicts them all, and they seek sanctuary from sexual relationships in books. One suspect sums up their choice: deciding between an affair with Mademoiselle Coindreau and a set of the *Encyclopedia Brittanica*, he "thought it all over and decided that [he] would get more lasting satisfaction out of the *Encyclopedia*" (180).

The perversion of learning is not limited to murderers and victims. An untenured assistant professor in *Close His Eyes* kills the subject of his critical biography, the poet Andrew McNeill, when McNeill threatens to stop publication of the book; but at a university where the intellectual life is equated with rushing around and writing articles, he merely carries the perversion of learning to its logical conclusion. As John Dryden the bibliographer-detective suggests, more than one crime is going on: one academic may kill a poet outright, but many more academics bury many more poets under mountains of paper every day; considering the difference in pounds between a poem and "all the critical articles ever written about the poem," he concludes that "There [is] a lack of balance" (15). He himself declines to "add to the side that [is] already overburdened" (67). In *Deadly Meeting*, though the head of the department is murdered for personal reasons, his academic life is a killing offense. An embarrassment to scholarship as well as a "big, over-stuffed son of a bitch" (50), Peter Jackson "may have been murdered by a medievalist. One who had read those articles of his" (127). Or, as he measures the life of the mind by number of publications, he could have been killed for trying to promote a man who "can talk for a whole term about Chaucer without his students ever suspecting that it's poetry" (12), withholding the department's raises to encourage "beefing up" the "amount of publication," or hiring the star job candidate at MLA, a long-winded expert on William Michael Rossetti. But not all academics with paper standards can be murdered, and Jackson shares the standards of the major universities. When someone poisons him, his star candidate is snapped up as an assistant professor by the University of California.

These are specific crimes, and all leave room for hope. In some conflicts between intellectual life and intellectual death, however, the war is over already; with or without murder, the life of the mind is dead. *Blood Is a Beggar* suggests that any academic career is deadly, whether successful or not. Professor Biddler accuses a graduate student of plagiarizing a dissertation, withholds his degree, drives him to suicide, and is murdered in revenge. Emeritus Professor Surtees assures the police, however, that you can't kill a dead man: "There has been no murder except in a very literal sense," for Biddler was "never very much alive." But Biddler represents the values of his department, and it takes an outsider—the superannuated Surtees—to see the intellectual gifts which raised Biddler to professorial eminence: "No real ability to synthesize knowledge, no opinions worth listening to, no spiritual stature, no humor, not even much common sense.... It occurs to no one to shoot him until he is sixty.... God, what a waste!" (181)

Among the murderer and his colleagues, in *The Silent Slain*, the intellectual life is eaten up in venom and spite; in such a viper's nest, murder is redundant. The college president, being blackmailed by the head of the Philosophy Department, in his petty spirit and lack of character sends an assistant professor to make the blackmail payment; as a fair sample of the faculty, the English Department's Wordsworth specialist hates his colleagues and Wordsworth, too; students are academic, intellectual, and sartorial failures, "cheating on examinations, coming up with the wrong answers, abominably clad" (58). This group constitutes the natural home for the plagiarist who murders two people in order to stay with it: a "perverted herd of self-loving rotters" (175).

In the darkest version of the conflict, *Death of an Old Goat*, not only is the intellectual life dead, but so is any distinction between falsehood and truth, except to the murderer. An academic pretender among pretenders, only he has enough sense of reality to kill for it. Murder attends the intellectual high-spot of the English Department's year at the University of Drummondale, when Professor Belville-Smith brings learning from Oxford with his lecture on Mrs. Gaskell—the "same lecture, in the same words" he has been delivering since 1922—to an "unwilling audience," an "uninterested audience," an "over-lectured-to audience" (33), and later has his throat cut at the Drummondale motel. This imposter lectures to other imposters: Wickham, the head of the English Department, an "intellectual booby" while at Oxford, who nevertheless (like the murderer) finds "contact with Oxford pleasurable and flattering" (73); Wickham's wife Lucy, who at Oxford "accommodated a series of dons, . . . all of them, presumably, in a position to further her husband's career" (159); and such colleagues and associates as Dr. Day the Victorian specialist, who does "Research into the poetry of George Eliot. Or the plays of Dickens. . . . I've forgotten which" (122); and Miss Tambly, once a prison warden and now headmistress of the Drummondale Methodist college for ladies—"Those goddam sluts" (44). In this company, a former servant posing as a university man and academic—an Oxford scout disguised as an Oxford graduate—commits murder to hide that former role and hold onto his place in academic life. The context raises the question of who is worse deceived—the Drummondale academics who take a servant for a fellow academic, or the servant who finds a place with them worth killing for.

In the deadly academic realms of these satiric novels, the capture of a murderer does not assure an outcome in favor of life. Given that circumstance, provisional endings match the outcome of the conflicts between life and death. Romance occurs among tired professors who might echo Spenser: "I'm thirty-seven years old and short on rah-rah" (8). Even the weather—fall, winter, and drought—suggests diminished life. In the finales, there is no university-wide rejoicing.

Subdued private gatherings mark the occasions when some positive values survive. At a university where people read but "don't usually do anything," Gilda Gorham, the librarian and detective, finds it is "high time she did something" (Stain, 207); she and three colleagues drink and smoke with impunity in the university library, and she plans to propose marriage. In *Deadly Meeting* with a murderer in jail, a publication-mad department chairman dead, and the Rossetti specialist gone to California, four people celebrate with coffee. John Dryden and his girlfriend dine with a colleague writing "an article on aesthetics...whatever those are" (Eyes, 179). Though the publication mill continues to grind, hope survives in the integrity of such academics as Dryden. With a murderer caught but nothing else changed, others escape the university. Spenser turns his back on university "dope pushing, theft, radical politics, adultery, and murder" (159), not to mention incorrigible vanity and hot air; he has some bourbon and pain pills and calls up a woman with "ripe thighs." Having solved the murder of a disagreeable, lazy professor, Rabbi Small is offered a job as dean by an agreeable, lazy president; but presumably he will decline. Matt Ruffins, ironically acknowledging the education he has received—"what he'd learned here!"—flees Jonas B. Steele College like Lot fleeing Sodom.

At worst, no escape is possible. When Bill Bascomb of Drummondale University looks for Professor Belville-Smith's murderer through "the manifold variety of human folly" (Goat, 157), ironic celebrations mark his uncovering of the truth. In a final gathering, Menzies College of Drummondale University, "in festive mood," hosts a sherry party. At this "Oxonian oasis in the midst of savagery" (171), "barking," "grunting" academics strike blows at the life of the mind with every pretentious and banal, or brutal and savage, word—"Of course, Augustan satire is quite beyond the average student's comprehension" (175); "You bloody toffs from Oxford" (174); "Have you tried the new toffee-flavored laxatives on your girls?" (176)—and confirm themselves as beyond redemption, with or without murder. Another gathering shortly after this one mirrors and comments on it, as Bill Bascomb drinks in a hotel bar with the Neanderthal hired hands from local sheep ranches, "aswill with beer," belching "very loudly every ten minutes or so in the approved fashion" (181). More stupid if possible than the university crowd but appreciably less savage, they fail to grasp the savagery there, seeing nothing more deadly at the university than "Some pretty funny characters," "some real ning-nongs" (182). They also complete the point that, should one wish to escape, there is nothing to escape to: having already portrayed and discredited the university, the gentry, and the law, the novel concludes its panoramic view with these repellent children of nature.

Bill Bascomb, however, never means to escape. The lone believer in truth—besides the murderer—and the lone defender of the intellectual life, at these two gatherings he drunkenly sees the truth and takes it back into the heart of academe, to bring the murderer in. There it betrays him, and in a crushing conclusion he himself becomes the sacrificial goat. When the murderer is caught and sentenced for the murder of

Bill Bascomb, Drummondale University's last ties with truth are severed, and universal darkness can cover all.

In its portrait of the university, *Death of an Old Goat* lies at the outermost extreme of harsh satire. Reviewing the two extremes of this second group of academic mysteries, we note the range of satire which the novels embrace. In the kindly view of the mildest, the major crime of most professors is foolishness; though one of them may commit murder, most uphold a respectable standard of university conduct. Furthermore, though murder undeniably grows out of university attitudes, as an expression of those attitudes it is regarded by many academics as immoderate. In the resolutions, some good survives, as some professors, speaking for the best values, show that they can not only teach but learn. In *Death of an Old Goat*, by contrast, murder is not necessarily the worst of campus crimes. Indeed, judged by the standard of dim viciousness which the academics set, the naive ambitions of a murderer seem almost innocent. The resolution buries the last hope for good—along with the detective—and with the only surviving voice of truth the remote and ironic narrative voice, the novel ends in drought, darkness, and death. The mildest satire, with its amused commentary on university life, is not far from celebratory comedy; while the wicked wit of *Death of an Old Goat* has "little to lose in order not to be comedy at all."[4]

* * * * *

A number of excellent mystery novels combine campus, crime, and comedy. In their treatment of basic elements of mystery fiction—detectives, suspects, crimes, and resolutions—they exhibit the home of the rarefied intellectual life as a natural setting for basic violence, as the university supplies the manpower and furnishes milieu and motives for murder. They encompass a wide range of comedy, from the celebratory, which recognizes the "essential well-being" of the universe and communicates a "happy acceptance"[5] of the way things are, to the satiric, which passes ironic judgment upon the world. Combining a high incidence of unnatural death with a high level of comedy, they celebrate the university and its fortifying values or satirize its waste, which is not confined to murder. Whether they celebrate or satirize, whether academics detect murder or commit it, whether university values survive murder or cause it, whether the university embodies life or leads to death—in their treatment of crime on campus these novels make a rich contribution to novels of academe, to the mystery genre, and to the literature of comedy.

Notes

[1]John E. Kramer, Jr., and John E. Kramer III, *College Mystery Novels: An Annotated Bibliography Including a Guide to Professional Series-Character Sleuths*, New York and London: Garland Publishing Co., Inc., 1983.

[2]All quotations will be cited in the text, using the abbreviation given after each entry. Novels considered under "the grand old fortifying classical curriculum" are

V.C. Clinton-Baddeley, *Death's Bright Dart*, New York: William Morrow and Company, Inc., 1970. (*Dart*)

G.D.H. and Margaret Cole, *Off With Her Head!* New York: The Macmillan Company, 1939. (*Head*)

Edmund Crispin, *The Moving Toyshop*, New York: Penguin Books, 1983; rpt. of Victor Gollancz, 1946. (*Toyshop*)

Amanda Cross, *Poetic Justice*, New York: Alfred A. Knopf, 1970. (*Justice*)

Eilis Dillon, *Death in the Quadrangle*, New York: Walker and Company, 1968; rpt. of Faber and Faber, 1956. (*Quadrangle*)

Michael Innes, *Seven Suspects* (*Death at the President's Lodging*), New York: Penguin Books, 1984, rpt. of Dodd, Mead and Company, 1937. (*Suspects*)

Michael Innes, *The Weight of the Evidence*, New York: Perennial Library, Harper & Row, 1983; rpt. of Dodd, Mead and Company, 1943. (*Evidence*)

Jane Langton, *The Memorial Hall Murder*, New York: Penguin Books, 1981, rpt. of Harper & Row, 1978. (*Memorial*)

Charlotte MacLeod, *The Luck Runs Out*, New York: Avon Publishing, 1981; rpt. of Doubleday & Company, 1979. (*Luck*)

Charlotte MacLeod, *Rest You Merry*, New York: Avon Publishing, 1979; rpt. of Doubleday & Company, 1979. (*Rest*)

Dermot Morrah, *The Mummy Case*, New York and London: Garland Publishing Co., Inc., 1976; rpt. of Harper & Row, 1933. (*Mummy*)

Robert Robinson, *Landscape With Dead Dons*, New York: Penguin Books, 1963, rpt. 1983; rpt, of Rinehart and Company, 1956. (*Landscape*)

Timothy Robinson, *When Scholars Fall*, London: New Authors Limited, 1961. (*Scholars*)

Dorothy Sayers, *Gaudy Night*, New York: Avon Books, 1970; rpt. of Harper & Row, 1936. (*Gaudy*)

Howard Shaw, *Death of a Don*, New York: Charles Scribner's Sons, 1981. (*Don*)

[3]Novels considered under "God, what a waste!" are

Robert Barnard, *Death in a Cold Climate*, New York: Dell Publishing Co., Inc., 1982; rpt. of Charles Scribner's Sons, 1980. (*Climate*)

Robert Barnard, *Death of an Old Goat*, New York, Penguin Books, 1983; rpt. of William Collins & Sons, Ltd., 1977. (*Goat*)

Robert Bernard, *Deadly Meeting*, New York: W.W. Norton and Company, Inc., 1970. (*Meeting*)

Olivia Dwight, *Close His Eyes*, New York: Harper and Brothers, 1961. (*Eyes*)

Elizabeth Foote-Smith, *Gentle Albatross*, New York: G.P. Putnam's Sons, 1976. (*Albatross*)

Hugh Holman, *Up This Crooked Way*, New York: M.S. Mill Co., Inc., 1946. (*Way*)

W. Bolingbroke Johnson, *The Widening Stain*, New York: Alfred A. Knopf, 1942. (*Stain*)

Harry Kemelman, *Tuesday the Rabbi Saw Red*, New York: Arthur Fields Books, Inc., 1973. (*Rabbi*)

Thomas Kyd, *Blood Is a Beggar*, Philadelphia and New York: J.B. Lippincott, 1946. (*Blood*)
Marion Mainwaring, *Murder at Midyears*, New York: The Macmillan Company, 1953. (*Midyears*)
Robert B. Parker, *The Godwulf Manuscript*, New York: Dell Publishing Co., 1983; rpt. of Houghton Mifflin, 1974. (*Godwulf*)
Chad Pilgrim, *The Silent Slain*, London and New York: Abelard-Schuman, 1958. (*Silent*)
    [4]James Feibleman, *In Praise of Comedy: A Study in Its Theory and Practice* (New York: Russell and Russell, 1962; rpt. of 1939), p. 205.
    [5]Ibid., p. 205.

Guises and Disguises of the Eccentric Amateur Detective

Jane S. Bakerman

" 'People don't generally kill for the fun of it.' "[1] This axiom, though taken as elementary by even the dullest Watson, fails to account for such folk as Agatha Christie, who is said to have sealed her betrothal by exclaiming, " '*I adore* corpses and stiffs!' "[2] Why, after all, be satisfied with a conventional embrace (though we hope that Christie and Max Mallowan progressed fairly promptly from conversation to kisses), when one is the Queen of Crime, who regularly "murders" for literary fun and profit? In pursuing her long, successful criminous career, Christie followed a tradition established by Edgar Allan Poe and extended by Sir Arthur Conan Doyle, creators of heroes who solve crimes frequently, who may even support themselves by detective work, but who nevertheless remain amateurs for lack of official status. These authors used eccentric geniuses as their sleuths, thereby dazzling readers not only with the puzzle itself—whodunit?—but also with admiration for the extraordinary skill of their protagonists:

Once you admit the hypothesis that genius and eccentricity stalk hand in hand—and many readers of detective fiction are fortunately credulous enough to believe anything—you are inveigled into concluding that the very mention of the latter presupposes the existence of the former.[3]

Poe summed up C. Auguste Dupin's methodology by coining the term "ratiocination" which has, of course, become part of the crime writer's and crime reader's vocabularies. Ratiocination is dramatized by stressing the detective's extraordinary abilities of observation and deduction coupled with knowledge of psychology and supreme trust in his capability. As he has evolved, the eccentric detective tends to be fully confident in his own concept of justice, and with some frequency, he acts upon his self-determined right to enforce justice when the law is unwilling or unable to do so. All this aggressive brilliance is pretty heady

111

stuff, and Christie exploited it fully in developing Hercule Poirot, the Belgian emigrant to England who figures in so many of her works, and who, like Dupin and Holmes, keeps rather aloof from the society he understands so well.

But the redoubtable Agatha not only followed the lead of such writers as Poe and Conan Doyle, she also did a little leading herself. In the deceptively gentle figure of Jane Marple, the spinster sleuth to whom understanding the villagers of St. Mary Mead is tantamount to understanding any citizen of the world, Christie shifted away from sheer brilliance toward a more homely native shrewdness based upon close study of others' daily routines. As Jane Marple herself once observes, neatly making her point and putting the Vicar in his place all in one stroke,

'Dear Vicar...you are so unworldly. I'm afraid that, observing human nature for as long I have done, one gets not to expect very much from it. I daresay idle tittle-tattle is very wrong and unkind, but it is so often true, isn't it?' (*Vicarage*, 18)

One might say that Agatha and Jane helped domesticate murder.

With Jane Marple and Hercule Poirot, Christie enriched the Golden Age of crime fiction, her specialty being the English cozy murder mystery wherein all hell may (and does) break loose, but tea is forever served; household dogs are always walked, the horses curried, the lawns manicured, the murderer firmly (usually fatally) punished, the plot brought to a full, reassuring closure. In short, Christie's homey little murders fit neatly into the world of Dupin and Holmes, a world which suffers extreme disruption but which nevertheless can be restored and set right.

Because this society seems basically well-ordered, readers love it; it's such a comfort, murders and all! And the traditional amateur detectives—recluse and cosy eccentric alike—cherish and have faith in it. Their respect for the societies they protect and re-order echoes in the words of Charlotte MacLeod's fictional agricultural-college president who proclaims proudly, " 'Agri isn't a business, it's a culture!' " (*Luck*, 75)—and the culture, "constructed out of faith in reason, preference for simplicity, and confidence that leisured upper-class existence...represents civilization,"[4] is precisely what the traditional eccentric is intent upon preserving.

This posh and pedigreed society...offers social forms for the novelist of manners and within those forms, the observable clues to human behavior by which the detective hero can identify the culprit.[5]

But nothing lasts forever, and though Christie's works, like those of Poe and Conan Doyle, are enduringly popular, the world around St. Mary Mead, like the village itself, has changed. New writers' hands grasp pens, rattle typewriters, or click word processor keys, and the brilliant amateur responds to new ideas and attitudes.

Certainly the "aloof sleuths" are still among us, as we shall see, and certainly clever, more domesticated amateurs are still with us, all recognizably related to C. Auguste Dupin, Sherlock Holmes, Hercule Poirot, or Jane Marple. But many of them currently function in a world where rules alter constantly, if, indeed, there be any rules at all. It is as if the carriage ways of country houses are now opening off the mean streets, deepening the shadows, blurring the boundaries of crime fiction subgenres. Literary folk continue to kill for the fun (and the profit) of it, but examining a representative sample of fictional amateur detectives may serve to illuminate some telling changes in the rules of the game both fictional and auctorial.

Generally, the plots of crime novels move swiftly, rushing toward solution of the mystery, honorably supplying clues, true and false, so that if we, the readers, are puzzle-solvers, we can compete with and possibly even beat the detective in a race to identify the villain. This preoccupation with competition, pace, clues, and red herrings is very useful in novels featuring eccentric amateur sleuths for a reason which mystery fans are loath to acknowledge: speedy, compelling action keeps us from thinking too much about the brilliant eccentric. Even though various antagonists denounce the amateur as an interloping pest, the driving force of the action tends to bury those derogations amid galloping gore, lies and logic, terror and tension. But when, in cold blood, as it were, fans and critics do stop to contemplate the personalities and habits of these wildly successful but only marginally adjusted amateurs, they may be stunned to realize that carping, debunking fellow-characters make a valid point. A quick survey of eccentric amateur territory shows that by almost every personal characteristic and by almost every habit and circumstance of life, these eccentric sleuths *are* potentially uncomfortable companions.

Hercule Poirot, Jane Marple, and Peter Shandy are terminally nosy; they can't seem to help it; worse, they don't seem to *want* to change. Like Sherlock Holmes, Nero Wolfe and C.B. Greenfield keep themselves to themselves so intensively that readers are tormented by unanswered questions about their private lives. It is clear, however, that Wolfe is notoriously lazy, that Holmes, a drug abuser, may not always be fit to work, and that Greenfield is obsessively devoted to his personal notion of comfort. Peter Wimsey, Albert Campion, and Melrose Plant, born to the English nobility, reflect some of its less appealing attitudes, and

Plant confuses everyone by renouncing his title; he claims that entering the House of Lords is like walking among a flock of penguins (*Mischief*, 86).

In sharp contrast to these gentlemen, Arthur Crook affirms his lowly origins by an affinity for bombast, appallingly ugly suits, bowler hats, and beer. Going a glass or two beyond Crook, John J. Malone and Charles Paris are more often than not drunk—or should be, given the amount of liquor they consume. Antiques expert Lovejoy and Simon Templar, the Saint, are criminals and boast of it; both, like Paris, are womanizers. Malone and Crook are attorneys who expect everyone to credit their professionalism though they spend precious little time in court and many hours bending the law. And perhaps most alarming of all, Homer Kelly is an academic, a literary critic at that, yet he dares to descend from his ivory tower and tamper with more normal people's lives. In *this* literary neighborhood, the unusual is the commonplace, and these characters can be downright annoying, real pains in the protagonist.

Marked though it may be, oddity is not the only trait shared by these eccentrics. They are all mature or elderly, and most are set in their ways; indeed, it's almost impossible to imagine them as youngsters. In their adult personae, they are like the very rich, perpetually "different from you and me," and therefore, they are distanced from even their most ardent fans.[6] Like Poirot, Wolfe, and Holmes, many of them are arrogant, knowing full well the extent of their powers, and while haughtiness may be justified in a brilliant servant of justice, it is seldom tolerated gladly in daily life. Just as it's fun to watch Peter Shandy ruin his neighborhood's Christmas extravaganza (*Rest*, 1-11), it's funny to observe Jane Marple pry into her neighbors' lives; but it would be infuriating to be the object of Shandy's prank and painful to be subjected to Marple's inquisitiveness. Observing fellow characters bear with Greenfield's carping and Charles Paris' ineffectuality is diverting, but enduring a relationship with either would become exasperating. Imagined eavesdropping upon Wolfe's endless insults or Holmes' detailed explanations is entertaining, but actually listening to such diatribes would be tedious. Reading about the wild auto chases in which Malone and Crook engage is stimulating; riding with them would be terrifying. It's safe to experience Lovejoy's and Templar's shenanigans so long as one knows they are fictional—to be privy to them in real life would be dangerous and unethical.

It is, in fact, very difficult to imagine loving most of these characters, just as it's difficult to imagine being in love with any one of them. Yet love them we do and invite them into our homes and hearts repeatedly, eagerly awaiting the new Peter Shandy, Lovejoy, or Homer Kelly mystery, rereading the Holmes, Marple, Poirot, Wimsey, and Wolfe canons, regretting that new titles are never again to be available. Perhaps the strangest fact about these eccentric, beloved detectives, though, is that we enjoy them for the very characteristics which would make them socially awkward acquaintances, for it is those traits which make us laugh.

Their stories are comic in both the technical and popular senses, and in matters of laugh and death, the humor arises primarily from the character of the hero rather than from the action. They dare to be peculiar—we envy and admire that, and it amuses us in almost exactly the same way the crimes in detective fiction intrigue us. Comfortably sheltered by suspension of disbelief, we can not only afford to observe murder, the only crime in which "society has to take the place of the victim,"[7] but also we can accept, admire, and rely upon heroes whose behaviors we might well reject in real life. By accepting their vagaries as humorous rather than annoying, we distance these traditional eccentrics so that we may well and truly enjoy their adventures.

Moreover, the peculiarities of the traditional mastermind are frequently counterbalanced by the presence of a more ordinary, sometimes rather bumbling, aide-de-camp, commonly dubbed the Watson figure, after Holmes' friend and physician. Author Lucille Kallen reflects many aides' attitudes toward their strange friends when her Watson figure, Maggie Rome, assesses her allegiance to C.B. Greenfield, deciding that their "firmly established relationship" consists "of equal parts of comfortable friendship, grudging respect, . . . simple exasperation, and our mutual unwillingness to disturb a workable status quo" (*Tanglewood*, 18).

These loyal sidekicks offer many benefits. As Dorothy L. Sayers has pointed out, aides are free to praise the detective lavishly without making his ego seem even more inflated than his characterization indicates; readers often feel more clever than the detective's helper, an enjoyable sensation; and discussions between the Watson and his chief allow the author to appear to reveal all clues when actually, he may be less than frank.[8] Watsons also offer readers a further choice. If a fan is too self-effacing, too humble, or even too downright stupid to identify with the brilliant protagonist, the presence of a less clever but very decent secondary figure allows for identification with *him*. If *he* who is frequently involved in criminal investigations cannot crack the case, it's only natural that readers might remain puzzled until the final unraveling. Aides' admiration for the detectives also makes them comforting to those odd souls; their need for detailed explanations makes them convenient for readers and authors.

Similarly, eccentric amateurs often have other friends (or friendly enemies), also continuing characters, who are officers of the law. Their presence, even when it is antagonistic, as in the Wolfe series, lends quasi-official status (or at the least access to the law-enforcement establishment) to the derring-do of the protagonists. They legitimatize as they antagonize or support. Because in even the most orderly of societies, the law is both friend and enemy to the average person, a comfort and a threat, readers align themselves readily with the sleuth in his competition against the police; it's always fun to see the establishment outdone, especially in the cause of truth and justice, the establishment's rightful province.

Just as the presence of ancillary lawmen endorses the detective's propriety of action, so do the friendly aides, police officers or fellow amateurs ratify their likability. If Richard Jury finds Melrose Plant's overwhelming curiosity not only useful but also endearing, if Hastings and Archie Goodwin can remain loyal in the face of their famous friends' enormous egos, so can readers. Friendly aides enlarge readers' perceptions of the protagonists by grounding them in the ordinary world; they are antidotes to both the sleuths' oddity and the criminals' lawlessness. In bonding lies acceptance and *some* degree of normality.

Finally, the patient, almost unfailingly cheerful friends perform another humanizing function in stories of eccentric detectives. They take care of them. Melancholy and withdrawn, Holmes needs Watson for a host of reasons—as a helper, as a listener, as an admirer, as a caretaker. Mary Kelly gently, unobtrusively shepherds awkward Homer through his academic and investigative duties without missing a beat of her own professorial or crime-stopping obligations. Always alert to gossip and innuendo, Miss Marple, aged and fairly infirm toward the end of her career, depends more and more upon her friends for information as she investigates. In many ways, then, the eccentric amateur detective is like an overgrown child, promising but dependent, parented by his best friends who need the detective's stimulating brilliance as much as he needs their salutary ordinariness. It's a strikingly symbiotic relationship and an effective literary device.

Even though their relationships with continuing characters soften their portraits, eccentric detectives remain, of course, extraordinary; yet, their interactions with other subordinate characters (who rarely appear in more than one work) demonstrate ways in which the sleuths' very peculiarities, the distancing factors, serve plot even as they soften the characterizations of the heroes. Because they so are different from other folk, they are, contrary to what one might think, very accessible to other characters.

Though numbers of crime writers stress careful, attentive listening as a necessary skill for their protagonists, critics tend to overlook it when analyzing character development. The eccentricity of the peculiar amateur sleuth sets him far enough outside ordinary relationships that other characters talk to him at length, often about very personal matters, rather in the fashion traveler-strangers talk to one another. Conversation, then, as well as physical evidence often provides necessary clues, facilitating the main plot and generating or illuminating subplots as well.

The most common crime story subplot is a romance (or two or three), and the detective's propensity for bearing patiently with lovers' suffering, doubts, and confessions allows him to learn a great deal about various characters' true personalities. Since most amateur detectives are congenital advice-givers and born-again meddlers, few (apart from Wolfe and Greenfield) hesitate to guide love affairs, either directly or indirectly. Advice, after all, to heartbroken maiden, base seducer, or flawed social order is their stock in trade, and the detectives have earned the right to give it by their patient listening and by their insight into human nature. Though Holmes' brilliant grasp of arcane facts and the minutiae of physical evidence serves him very well, many eccentric detectives also rely heavily on the intuitive leap, imaginatively penetrating the thought processes of the villain and correctly diagnosing the truth about him, his motives, and his crimes. Hours of careful listening and keen-eyed observation of their confidants' behavior prepare them for this exercise from which they learn further lessons of the human heart to pass along to the lovelorn. Hercule Poirot's relationship with Jackie de Bellefort (*Nile*) is an excellent example of intuition and wise counsel. Merely by observing her, Poirot understands Jackie's passionate, uncontrolled nature long before they become acquainted (21-22), and later, he begs her to follow his sage advice (68-74, 101-102). Consequently, tension arises as much from the interplay between these two disparate characters as from the murders which propel the action.

In most instances, eccentricity frees the detective from conducting a viable romance himself. They are not considered eligible, being far too unlike ordinary people, and thus, generally, their sexuality is not a major defining characteristic. Other characters of the same sex, then, find the detectives fairly unthreatening, since they are not competing sexually, and characters of the opposite sex find them companionable rather than alluring; overall, these attitudes prove useful for the crime-buster. Though this device works very well in comic crime stories, it depends upon potentially cruel stereotyping. We are conditioned to believe that as an elderly spinster, Miss Marple is beyond attractiveness and sexuality, and because Wimsey and Shandy are past their first youth, their romances are initially surprising though eventually pleasing. Decidedly mature and a foreigner, Poirot is considered unsuitable for chauvinistic English belles. Perhaps there is some merit, after all, to Holmes' and Wolfe's penchants for isolation over social interaction— the very societies they serve so well perceive the eccentric quite narrowly, often rather cruelly.

Wolfe, of course, is extremely misanthropic, detesting women only somewhat more than he loathes men, and, in the opinion of many of his fans, "To imagine the face of Sherlock Holmes...in close proximity to a woman's is gross degradation" (Thomson, 146), so the absence of any kind of recognizable love life seems to suit them very well. Even when, like Peter Shandy, Homer Kelly, and Lord Peter Wimsey, eccentric detectives conduct courtships, the romance underscores their peculiarities. Only Wimsey would be wise and foolish enough to set his heart upon Harriet Vane, a murder suspect soured on romance. Only Mary Kelly and Helen Shandy would be sensitive enough to understand their homely suitors' true worth.

For many of the same stereotypical reasons, the eccentric sleuth disarms his criminal opponent. No matter how fine the reputation of the detective, the malefactor perceives only the oddities, rarely the brilliance, mistaking uniqueness for ineffectuality. Here again, Hercule Poirot is a prime example. Only the very perceptive soul (like Hastings, like a few others) can recognize the genius hidden within a sausagey body, an egg-shaped head, a flashy appearance; Poirot's dandyish clothing and fussy manner disarm numerous opponents. Further, the initial impression he makes is not much enhanced by Poirot's obtrusive confidence in his "little grey cells." Like the purloined letter, Hercule Poirot's powers are hidden by his obvious display of them. Thus, the traditional eccentric detective is, in a sense, always disguised.

The criminal's habit of underrating the eccentric also helps to make the amateur crime-fighter rather more like readers—who among us isn't unappreciated at least occasionally by the imperceptive?—and so we identify with him in that way. And, because we are "in on the joke," because we anticipate the sure triumph of the sleuth over even the cleverest evildoer, we share his success, an important factor in our enjoyment, a fairly sophisticated deepening of the humor.

Sharing the triumph and feeling superior to the villain are also important in accepting the arrogance displayed by many eccentric detectives, and acceptance is one key to their extended viability as heroes. It feels good to be on the winning side, and embracing the cause of a sure winner guarantees feeling good. It feels especially good, of course, to share in the triumph of justice over evil, and these responses combine to enable us to accept some detectives' behavior which is alarmingly similar to criminality.

If the ultimate act of pride and arrogance is taking a human life, then killing is the ultimate evil, and a detective's behaving as judge, jury, and executioner requires—and usually acquires—some revisionist thinking on the part of readers who must set aside their respect for the law in favor of trust in the detective's judgment and ethic. Fans often commend detectives who "play god" and themselves execute a killer, as in *Curtain* (166-183), to cite the amiable Agatha's most flagrant example. A potent variant of this behavior also occurs with some frequency, and again Christie provides a useful example. In *The Mirror Crack'd*, the killer dies of an overdose most probably administered by another character. Miss Marple understands the situation fully but views the overdose and the survivor's profound grief as acts of retribution sufficient unto themselves. There is no need for the law (198-208).

Justifying such behavior by demonstrating that the amateur sleuth represents absolute justice (Bargainnier, *Gentle*, 42) and that he is with the law if not of it is useful, but strong readerly impulses are also at work here. Because the eccentrics *are* different from the rest of us, because they do stand for justice even more than they stand for the law, and *because we have shared their triumphs*, we accept this irregular behavior, this abuse of their power and powers. Repeatedly, they risk much to protect the basic decencies and the lives of others. In electing to become executioners, they risk all—their prideful reputations and their basic principles—and we admire the big gamble, feel relieved that someone somewhere is willing to wager everything for the good of the social order. Thus, these questionable behaviors strangely enhance rather than limit the traditional protagonist's popularity. And once again, the speed of the action combines with acceptance of the investigators' brilliance to cloud over readers' perceptions which have already been lulled by the humor in the plots.

An obvious service performed by the humor inherent in eccentric characters is, of course, comic relief. Laughter undercuts the horror of the murders (and no matter if some lesser crime occupies subplot or triggers the main plot, murder or the threat of murder is always at the center of the action). Even when the traditional eccentric violates the law by emulating his enemy, the killer, laughter suppresses unease so intense as to make us stop reading. It would be almost impossible to overemphasize this point because fear-but-not-too-much-fear is a major appeal of the formulaic fiction in which eccentric detectives appear.

Commonly dubbed the "country house" mystery, the more traditional of these stories treat a relatively closed circle of suspects, take place in a fairly limited setting, and, as we have noted, posit an essentially orderly society which, though disrupted by crime, can be reordered once the murderer has been identified and removed. Because these settings are limited in both size and social accessibility, they not only circumscribe the investigation (the killer must be one of the inner circle in almost every case) and enable the detective to function, but they also enhance suspension of disbelief. If settings and characters are, in some way, "special," then the dangers of criminal incursion are special also; they are unlikely to affect nonmembers of the circle. The circle members are not, after all, our siblings, parents, friends, or lovers who, we wish fondly to believe, would neither kill nor espouse killers. This reaction permits further reader identification with the detectives whose roles bar them, too, from full membership in the select society though they may qualify for it by birth, social graces, or training.

To solve the mysteries, detectives must alter and diminish the circle by identifying and removing the killer. Because they damage even as they heal, they are kept a bit apart from other circle members and are thus able to look more or less dispassionately at all the suspects. Often, because they *are* separated from the group and because they represent justice, they feel morally superior to the circle members. During their junkets into country houses, readers generally share this sense of redemptive superiority as they share separation from the circle—like the detective, they are in it but not necessarily of it.

Rex Stout exploits the closed circle in a particularly inventive manner. In the Nero Wolfe adventures, Wolfe's obsessively orderly brownstone house with its small, trustworthy, gifted staff represents absolute, ongoing order which contrasts markedly with the mean streets (by definition *always* chaotic and deadly) into which Archie Goodwin makes such successful forays. Goodwin, in effect, brings elements of street life into the house for restoration and redemption so that the Wolfe saga enjoys the best of both major worlds of crime fiction[9]—and Stout thereby establishes a turning point, opening the field for the darker, grimmer visions of writers who follow him.

Lucille Kallen, Jonathan Gash, and Simon Brett do follow Stout's example in exploiting two worlds, the closed circle and the *very* mean streets, but major differences in tone, setting, and some readers' attitudes toward their protagonists—C.B. Greenfield, Lovejoy, and Charles Paris—distinguish these works from those of Christie, Poe, Conan Doyle, MacLeod, and Langton, and set them apart more moderately from Stout's world. As we have seen, order can be restored in the traditional country-house mystery. Stout implicitly acknowledges the inevitable disorder of the mean streets but, as we have also seen, explicitly reaffirms the possibility of order (no matter how wildly idiosyncratic) by making a sort of halfway house of Wolfe's brownstone. Absolutely no such refuge is afforded to Kallen's, Gash's, or Brett's protagonists as their creators take care to point out. Their closed circles whirl terrifyingly up and down ever meaner streets. For example, Maggie Rome, Greenfield's best friend, dearest enemy, and aide-de-camp realizes that the comforting British expression, 'safe as houses,' had become obsolete. Houses were no longer safe. Not even here, forty miles from the urban rot, on a peaceful, upper-middle-class suburban street....a street of well-cared-for lawns and excellent garbage pickup, of dogwood trees and healthy kids on bicycles. There were no longer any safe houses here (*Lady*, 51)

Greenfield's smug, formerly snug, little suburban community is still a closed circle, but he believes that " 'Monstrous behavior is the order of the day' " (*Tanglewood*, 13). Most of his cases to date directly involve acquaintances Greenfield values; once murder is even committed inside his home (*Lady*), and unlike country-house dwellers or Nero Wolfe, C.B. has no sense that he can re-secure his walls. Charles Paris, an actor, almost always works within circles composed of the companies with whom he performs, and even apart from murder, he's conscious of some physical danger in crowded, hectic backstage activities:

Charles instantly remembered stories of flying disasters, of cumbersome pieces plummeting down on actors below, of faulty counterweighting snatching technicians up from the stage to dash them against the chipping machine of the grid in the roof.(*Star*, 68)

Lovejoy operates—in far more ways than one—within the limited, knowledgeable circle of antiques specialists and hobbyists, but he is never really safe, as he bluntly explains:

Antiques is a lovely but murderous game....It's crammed with love, fear, greed, death, hate, and ecstasy. I should know—I'm an antique dealer. And don't chuck this book away in disgust just because I've owned up and told you the truth.
I'm the only person in it you can trust.(*Gold*, 1)

The fact that we accept Lovejoy's proposition that he, a thief and a liar, is the only person we can trust is a telling assessment of the disorderly world wherein some fictional eccentric detectives function; it prepares us for a milieu which "establishes its moral norm within the consciousness of an individual"[10] rather than in a shared concept of decency. "It is not a very fragrant world, but it is the world you live in, and certain writers...can make very interesting and even amusing patterns out of it."[11] Clearly, modern eccentrics like Paris, Lovejoy, and Greenfield, cannot trust society; they certainly aren't proud of it, but it is the only one they have, and so they try, sporadically, to defend it—often in the course of defending themselves. In this way, their attitude differs sharply from that of many other comic amateurs.

Unlike more traditional eccentrics, Paris, Lovejoy, and Greenfield do not truly belong anywhere. Charles Paris' lack of professional distinction bars him from the inner circle of successful theater folk just as Lovejoy's outlawry prohibits him from genuinely supportive relationships among his peers. Indeed, a characteristic of both men's detection is its single-handedness. Though Paris sometimes gains access or information by capitalizing upon old pal Gerald Venables' yen to play cops and robbers and though Lovejoy recruits whatever temporary henchmen (or henchwomen) are at hand, essentially, each man works alone. Greenfield pursues justice by exercising all the cheap "privileges" of male chauvinism, perpetuating one wrong while righting another, so that the Greenfield-Rome relationship is much less comfortable to contemplate than is the Wolfe-Goodwin alliance. Both eccentrics bully; one aide, Goodwin, resists; the other, Rome, tolerates her employer as she might tolerate someone else's spoiled child. Jointly, Rome and Greenfield fight for right, but they do not really stand together; Greenfield won't permit it. This rootlessness has a debilitating effect; it isolates and angers modern eccentrics so that they lose the useful perspective their traditional colleagues use so effectively.

As a consequence of all these factors, modern eccentrics are just as alienated as Sam Spade or any other hard-boiled private eye and therefore differ from even reclusive traditional eccentrics:

given their distrust of organized society and given the absence of social institutions to guide their behavior outside of organized society, the protagonists...have had to create for themselves in little god-like ways their own code of ethics, their own morality![12]

It is noteworthy that Margolies' description of the American hero, especially the tough 'tec, fits Greenfield, Paris, and Lovejoy so neatly. However, even Greenfield, who apparently does see himself as a kind of acerbic knight (*Introducing*, 2), falls well short of the nobility inherent in most hard-boiled private eyes, even though the methodology of the two types also matches exactly: "They think and act in terms of concrete situations and personal involvements, avoiding theory, intellect, and sentiment."[13] The difference lies in the exaggerated characterizations of the modern eccentrics; their portraits are, after all, humorous; those of the traditional private-eye generally are not.

Many other qualities mark Greenfield, Paris, and Lovejoy as proper denizens of the mean streets. For one thing, they lack style. Despite their supreme confidence in their own abilities, Greenfield and Lovejoy cannot carry off arrogance as can Wolfe, Poirot, and Holmes. Greenfield constantly risks his credibility by bemoaning small inconveniences, the unavailability of a favorite cookie, for instance (*Tanglewood*, 100), as vehemently as he opposes injustice; his carping diminishes him. Apart from the fact that Lovejoy regularly compromises his remarkable talent (an innate ability to intuit whether an object is a genuine antique or a phony), he is, to put it simply, a mess. He's tawdry, and why all those female characters fall into his dreary sheets hardly bears consideration. Charles Paris is paralyzed by indecision; he cannot rid himself of an inept agent; he cannot resolve his relationship with his estranged family; he can't even clean up his filthy bed-sitter.[14] Worse, all three men are whiners.

They are petulant and childish, substituting constant fretting or complaint for the awe-inspiring confidence of Poirot, the bellicosity of Wolfe, the detachment of Holmes, or the cheerful forbearance of Shandy. Readers simply have to face it; these guys are not classy, and because they have no panache, they reflect a more fearsome world than do their fellows, a world in which good intentions, even accidental or selfishly motivated good intentions, are vague, unreliable substitutes for order. Consequently, readers perceive that because protagonists such as Lovejoy, Paris, and Greenfield possess no healing powers, they are akin to hard-boiled private eyes nearly as much as they are related to Holmes, Poirot, Wolfe, Marple, Kelly, and Shandy.

Further, each modern eccentric's preoccupation with his own troubles, uncertainties, and self-image precludes full closure of plot: a crime may be solved, but distress and disorder go on and on. Readers are "left with that sense of something profoundly unsolved lying just behind the foreground solution of that particular crime."[15] Our knowledge that Greenfield, Lovejoy, and Paris will *never* be able to distinguish sensibly between minor, self-inflicted disruption and genuine disaster certainly entertains us, but it also engenders the "final dissolution" which Grella identifies as characteristic of the hard-boiled novel ("Mean," 424).

Poirot's first case and an early Paris adventure plainly illustrate varying degrees of closure. In *The Mysterious Affair at Styles*, Poirot not only identifies a murderer but also repairs a marriage ("Who on earth but Poirot would have thought of a trial for murder as a restorer of conjugal happiness!"), unites a pair of lovers, and reassures lovesick Hastings that he, too, will one day make a proper match: " 'Console yourself, my friend. We may hunt together again, who knows? And — then—' " (184-185). Here, Christie neatly ties up all loose ends and confirms society's orderliness with the most traditional of all symbols, marriage, firmly closing this plot while hinting at furture adventures. They are all going to live happily ever after; Hastings can take Poirot's word for it.

In *A Comedian Dies*, by contrast, Charles Paris detects madly but badly, and his word proves questionable. Having arrived at an erroneous solution to the case, he offers succor to the dying killer, only to be belittled. The murderer confesses, not to ease his spirit, not even, really, to set the record straight—but to set Charles Paris straight. Later, Charles *deliberately* misidentifies the murderer as another deceased character (157-160) so that *A Comedian Dies* not only evades full closure but also employs an aberration of the judge-and-jury ploy which Poirot and other traditional eccentrics manage so elegantly in many of their cases. Though there may be merit in protecting the reputation of a dead man with whom Paris sympathizes, it's unlikely that calumny is the best way to go about it. Further, readers cannot be sure exactly why Charles Paris does lie—ragged edges abound; there is no resolution. In both novels, the endings suit the stories perfectly, but only *The Mysterious Affair at Styles* offers readers the reassurance of orderliness.

If Charles Paris and his counterparts are the best there is to offer in the restoration-of-social-order department, society is in sad straights indeed, and that message rings as loudly and clearly through the fun and games of Kallen's, Brett's, and Gash's novels as it does through the gritty works of Hammet, Chandler, Parker, Paretsky, and Valin, creators of hard-boiled, mean-streets fiction. Whether the mean streets dominate eccentric amateur or slogging private detective, they exact the same toll—one cannot expect, much less demand, restoration of order; one must settle for achieving justice, all the while knowing that all settlements are but momentary. Ominous footsteps perpetually sound on the mean streets, and one longs for even a few moments of respite in Nero Wolfe's safe house.

Skewed characterization, the stressful, untidy worlds in which they live, and the absence of true closure of their adventures all affect the humorous tone in novels about modern eccentrics. In the cases (one cannot resist that pun) of such characters as Poirot, Marple, Wimsey, and Shandy, readers almost always laugh *with* the hero. But risky though it be to suggest in the face of possible reprisals from their rabid fans, in the cases of Greenfield, Lovejoy, and Paris, many readers laugh *at* them—or come perilously close to doing so. The prominence of their own troubles suggests an inability (or a refusal) to cope with reality so that we cannot trust and admire them as fully as we do their more traditional colleagues. Even more disturbingly, we cannot suspend disbelief quite enough to be confident that the chaos in which they live does not also affect our lives. As Chandler reminds us, the disordered world is our world, too, as the country house never was, and we further understand that

It is not funny that a man should be killed, but it is sometimes funny that he should be killed for so little, that his death should be the coin of what we call civilization.(398)

In the absence of faith in social order, in the resulting absence of complete trust in or admiration for the modern eccentrics, then, we readers take refuge in laughter which offers little comfort but some relief. We do not share the joke of their sure triumph but rather giggle nervously, perhaps sometimes sympathetically, perhaps sometimes patronizingly, as they flail about, angrily denouncing society while they combat crime. They never heed the wisdom of Pogo—they don't know when "the enemy is us." Traditional eccentrics and traditional hard-boiled sleuths know exactly who the enemy is, and they are able to set aside personal problems in order to confront evil. Characters like Lovejoy, Greenfield, and Paris are very funny; they are wonderful creations, but, with Lovejoy's admonishments ringing in our ears—"My qualities are yours, folks...if...you think I'm lascivious, crude, sexist and selfish, do you know anybody who isn't?" (*Gold*, 9-10)—we cannot be positive that they are truly "different from you and me," and that uncertainty changes the quality of our laughter. If we are all alike, who are the bad guys? Who are the good guys? Who can be healers?

* * * * *

In all his guises, the eccentric amateur detective is, then, an endlessly fascinating character. His behavior comments tellingly upon both ordinary and criminally extraordinary behavior, allowing us to laugh our way safely through one dangerous pursuit after another. Always strangely childlike because of his eccentricities, he is also deeply cynical, for he is aware that everyone, himself included, is capable of killing. He is, perhaps, a distant cousin to the wise clowns of Shakespeare's dramas, enabling us (perhaps emboldening us) to laugh, though he never finds himself at all funny, at the pomposity of nobleman and commoner alike; permitting us, at least while we suspend our disbelief and share his cases, to hope that order can be restored or, more recently, that justice can be temporarily achieved—always assuming that there's an amusing eccentric at hand to work that desirable magic.

Notes

[1]Martha Grimes, *The Man With a Load of Mischief* (Boston: Little, Brown, 1981), p. 86 (*Mischief*). Names of authors and their eccentric detectives mentioned in this chapter are listed below. If quotations or references to specific passages from novels appear in the text, bibliographic information is given, followed by a key word. All further references to these and all but the first references to secondary sources are indicated in the text.

Allingham, Margery—Albert Campion

Brett, Simon—Charles Paris

 A Comedian Dies (London: Futura, 1985) (*Comedian*).

 Star Trap with *An Amateur Corpse* in *Murder—Double-Billing* (NY: Scribner's, 1978) (*Star*).

Charteris, Leslie—Simon Templar/The Saint
Christie, Dame Agatha—Hercule Poirot, Jane Marple
  Curtain (NY: Dodd, Mead Book Club Edition, 1975) (*Curtain*)
  Death on the Nile (NY: Dodd, Mead, The Greenway Edition, 1970) (*Nile*).
  The Mirror Crack'd (NY: Pocket Books, 1964) (*Mirror*).
  The Murder at the Vicarage (NY: Dell, 1976) (*Vicarage*).
  The Mysterious Affair at Styles (NY: Dodd, Mead, Book Club Commemorative
Edition, crt. 1920, 1958) (*Styles*)
Conan Doyle, Sir Arthur—Sherlock Holmes
Gash, Jonathan—Lovejoy
  Gold by Gemini (NY: Harper & Row Book Club Edition, 1978) (*Gold*).
Gilbert, Anthony (Lucy Beatrice Malleson)—Arthur Crook
Grimes, Martha— Melrose Plant. See above.
Kallen, Lucille—C.B. Greenfield
  C.B. Greenfield: No Lady in the House (NY: Wyndham, 1982) (*Lady*).
  C.B. Greenfield: The Tanglewood Murder (NY: Wyndham, Book Club Edition, 1980)
  (*Tanglewood*).
  Introducing C.B. Greenfield (NY: Ballantine, 1981) (*Introducing*).
Langton, Jane—Homer Kelly
MacLeod, Charlotte—Peter Shandy
  The Luck Runs Out (Garden City, NY: Doubleday, 1979) (*Luck*).
  Rest You Merry (Garden City, NY: Doubleday, 1978) (*Rest*).
Poe, Edgar Allan—C. Auguste Dupin
Rice, Craig (Georgiana Ann Randolph)—John J. Malone
Sayers, Dorothy L.—Lord Peter Wimsey
Stout, Rex—Nero Wolfe

[2]Paul Gray, "I *Adore* Corpses and Stiffs," *Time*, May 27, 1985, p. 85.

[3]H. Douglas Thomson, *Masters of Mystery* (NY: Dover, 1978), p. 128.

[4]John M. Reilly, "Classic and Hard-Boiled Detective Fiction," *The Armchair Detective*, 9 (October 1976), 290.

[5]George Grella, "Murder and Manners: The Formal Detective Novel," in *Dimensions of Detective Fiction*, ed. Larry N. Landrum, Pat Browne, Ray Browne (Bowling Green, OH: Popular Press, 1976), p. 47.

[6]See also Earl F. Bargainnier's analysis of eccentricity as a humanizing device in *The Gentle Art of Murder* (Bowling Green, OH: BGSU Popular Press, 1980), p. 44. Bargainnier's book has been a helpful resource throughout preparation of this study.

[7]W.H. Auden, "The Guilty Vicarage," in *Detective Fiction: Crime and Compromise*, ed. Dick Allen and David Chacko (NY: Harcourt Brace Jovanovich, 1974), p. 402.

[8]Dorothy L. Sayers, "The Omnibus of Crime," in *Detective Fiction: Crime and Compromise*, ed. Dick Allen and David Chacko (NY: Harcourt Brace Jovanovich, 1974), pp. 355-6.

[9]For detailed synopses which illustrate this point, see Guy M. Townsend, "The Nero Wolfe Saga," *The Mystery Fancier*, 1 (May 1977) through 4 (May/June 1980). See also Reilly, p. 291. Reilly also suggests "a fundamental similarity," including a "tendency to closure" between Golden Age and Hard-Boiled works.

[10]George Grella, "Murder and the Mean Streets," in *Detective Fiction: Crime and Compromise*, ed. Dick Allen and David Chacko (NY: Harcourt Brace Jovanovich, 1974), p. 412.

[11]Raymond Chandler, "The Simple Art of Murder," in *Detective Fiction: Crime and Compromise*, ed. Dick Allen and David Chacko (NY: Harcourt Brace Jovanovich, 1974), p. 398.

[12]Edward Margolies, "The American Detective Thriller and the Idea of Society," in *Dimensions of Detective Fiction*, ed. Larry N. Landrum, Pat Browne, Ray Browne (Bowling Green, OH: Popular Press, 1976), p. 85.

[13]George N. Dove, "Intruder in the Rose Garden," *The Armchair Detective*, 9 (October 1976), 279. Dove identifies four professional investigators appearing in Golden Age mysteries; some of their unappealing traits are shared by untraditional eccentric amateurs.

[14]See also Earl F. Bargainnier, "Simon Brett," in *Twelve Englishmen of Mystery*, ed. Earl F. Bargainnier (Bowling Green, OH: BGSU Popular Press, 1984), pp. 302-325. Bargainnier analyzes the Paris novels as social satires.

[15]Erik Routley, *The Puritan Pleasures of the Detective Story* (London: Gollancz, 1972), p. 210. Routley argues that detective fiction is comic because it allows for absolution and that closure is therefore usually achieved as it cannot be in tragedy; he recognizes some exceptions to the closure pattern, however, citing Margery Allingham's *The Tiger in the Smoke* as one.

The Little Old Ladies

Neysa Chouteau and Martha Alderson

The writer of mystery fiction who chooses to use a comic little old lady as a main character has a rich field to work. To begin with, the notion of a little old lady being mixed up with crime tickles our sense of incongruity. Erle Stanley Gardner has stated that "The real definition of a character is one who stands out from the common run of mankind."[1] Gardner also said that "the reader loses sympathy with a character who becomes too invincible."[2]

Within the three words "little old lady" we have little as opposed to big, strong, or powerful; old as opposed to young, resilient, or sexy; lady, as opposed to a crook or murderer. In the world of mystery fiction the little old lady fits Gardner's remarks nicely. She stands out from the crowd of tough-guy private eyes, and she certainly is not invincible. Further, older women are so often figures of fun that writers have a wealth of stock characters to build upon in developing their particular little old lady characters. Among the stereotypes are the old battle-axe (often played off against a hen-pecked husband or hostile son-in-law), the social climber, the magnificently illogical club woman, and above all, the eccentric spinster. These women are laughed at for a variety of characteristics, depending upon the particular stereotype. These characteristics may include bad temper; greed for status, money, clothes, food, or jewels; gossiping; lack of logic; wearing silly hats or other funny clothes; being too fat or too thin, too lady-like or not lady-like enough; being against, scared of, unduly interested in, or completely ignorant of sex; or simply being unmarried. In this essay we will discuss some of the series characters who are, metaphorically at least, comic little old ladies and explore the ways in which their creators reinforce or revise the common caricatures of older women to achieve comic effect. The discussion will be limited to women who are major characters in a number of books, whose books are reasonably available to the average fan, and whose authors clearly intended them to be comic.

None of the women discussed in this essay begins life in the state of marriage. Their single state effectively prevents a love interest from weakening the plot or hampering the character's freedom of action. It also promotes comic effect. Perhaps because most of the world is married, the unmarried woman has traditionally been a figure of fun, one to whom the marrieds could feel quite superior—or perhaps being married is no laughing matter. Miss Seeton, Miss Withers, Sister Mary Theresa, and Miss Marple are spinsters, descendants of Anna Katherine Green's Miss Amelia Butterworth, and sisters (or nieces, perhaps) of Patricia Wentworth's Miss Silver. The comic widows, including Bertha Cool, Lucy Ramsdale, and Emily Pollifax, come later to the scene.

Bertha Cool

Bertha Cool was one of the first comic old ladies who wasn't a spinster. Bertha, a widow, was created in 1938 because Erle Stanley Gardner needed more money. Through his publisher William Morrow he was cranking out as many Perry Mason stories as the market would bear. Because he could not go to a different publisher, he made a bet with his editor, Thayer Hobson, that he could write a novel under another name and Hobson would not be able to spot it. Within a month the deed was done. Writing as A.A. Fair, Gardner submitted *The Bigger They Come* to Morrow.[3] In his manuscript Gardner introduced a detective agency run by Bertha Cool and Donald Lam, "as unlikely a pair as a writer ever put together to lure readers."[4] Gardner made them an unlikely pair by inverting most of our expectations about male and female roles. Bertha is the boss and Donald is the employee—later the junior partner. Bertha is big, weighing more than 200 pounds in the first book. Donald is small, a pint-sized 127 pounds. Bertha is "old," in her fifties or sixties. Donald is young, 29 years old when the series begins. Bertha is hot-tempered and profane. (In fact, according to Frank B. Robbins, Bertha was the only character in all of detective fiction who was swearing regularly in the 1930s and 1940s.)[5] Donald is cool and a gentleman. Bertha is a first-rate fighter who enjoys slamming people around when the occasion calls for it. Donald is brave, but loses every fight.

Bertha functions as Donald's Watson. Her role as second banana to fast-thinking, risk-taking Donald could have worked—and with few changes—if the character had been male. However, it wouldn't have worked as well.

Gardner wrote 29 novels starring Donald Lam and Bertha Cool, all under the pseudonym A.A. Fair. The first novel, *The Bigger They Come*, was published in 1939 and the last, *All Grass Isn't Green*, in 1970. Over the years, Bertha stays a stock character, but she does change somewhat. She doesn't wear funny clothes, but she begins as a familiar figure of fun, a fat lady who "wiggled and jiggled around inside her loose apparel like a cylinder of currant jelly on a plate" (Bigger, 17). After a long illness, she loses over 100 pounds and takes up deep sea fishing which apparently makes her quite fit. Donald, the first-person narrator in most books, describes her with such phrases as "tough, hard and rugged as a coil of barbed wire" (*Beware the Curves*, 2) or "built like an old-fashioned freight locomotive" (*Cut Thin to Win*, 11). Her clothes are seldom mentioned, but almost every book refers to the diamonds on her fingers which glitter like her greedy little eyes. Bertha is greedy for good food and for every dollar that she can squeeze out of the clients and out of Donald's expense account.

Bertha is the only older woman discussed in this essay who does not behave like a lady. As she puts it, "I can stand a hell of a lot of vulgarity. I adore profanity and I love violence" (*Some Slips Don't Show*, 138). Oddly enough, at times when she might be expected to say, "Well, I'll be damned," she resorts to slang, using such phrases as "fry me for an oyster," "poach me for an egg," or "pickle me for a beet."

Bertha's comical attitude toward sex is not too lady-like either. In Bertha's view, women are gold diggers and men are suckers for good-looking women. Her own history appears to support her view. According to Bertha, she starved herself and tortured herself with girdles and brassieres for ten years until she got a husband. She kept up the dieting and primping after the marriage until she found out that her husband was having an affair with his secretary. For the rest of the marriage, she ate what she wanted and cheerfully allowed Henry his affairs. As she describes it, "Henry seemed happy; and I ate anything I wanted. It was a wonderful arrangement—until Henry died" (Bigger, 24). The cases that Bertha and Donald deal with reinforce such cynicism because many of them revolve around one spouse's infidelity, attempt to manipulate the other for money, or murder of the other.

Bertha is not without sex appeal nor completely impervious to masculine charm. Sergeant Frank Sellers wants to marry her in *Cats Prowl at Night* because he likes her courage and guts. Although nothing comes of Sellers' admiration for Bertha, his affection is genuine. In *Spill the Jackpot* Bertha is momentarily beguiled by client Arthur Whitewell. As the story begins, Bertha has lost over 100 pounds because of illness. When Arthur Whitewell begins to flatter her, she is interested enough to try to keep on her diet and to drag "a coy smile out of mothballs" (16). His flattery and her response last through most of the book until Whitewell tries to "spread a lot a bull" in order to wheedle Bertha into charging less for the agency's services. Bertha sees "through the old hypocrite right away" (254-255) and proves that she is cured of any romantic notions by downing a gigantic breakfast.

Another problem with sex for Bertha is the fact that being female is a handicap in dealing with clients. A number of the books begin with a prospective client's hesitating to engage the agency because Bertha is a woman. As Bertha says of one client, "he got afraid I'd be too soft and easy because I was a woman...." (*You Can Die Laughing*, 3). At other times, clients sign on only when they are assured that a man will handle their case. If the client has enough money, Bertha accepts the client's intimation that a woman is not as good a detective as a man. If there is not enough money involved to compensate for the insult, out goes the client.

Bertha is a comic character because of her physique, her language, her hot temper, her tight-fistedness, her eye for a buck. It adds to the humor that she is old but that she is by no means little, and she fits no one's idea of a lady. She may be Donald's Watson, but she is also a mean streets version of that stock female character, the old battle-axe.

Lucy Ramsdale

Much of the humor in Bertha Cool's characterization lies in the swap of expected masculine/feminine traits between Bertha and Donald. Much of the humor surrounding Lucy Ramsdale, however, lies in the extent to which Lucy is so very feminine. Lucy Ramsdale is the amateur sleuth heroine of four mysteries written by Hildegarde Dolson between 1971 and 1977.[6] She is a widow who lives in the small Connecticut town of Wingate, fifty miles from New York. She is an illustrator, as her late husband Hal had been. After Hal's death, Lucy rents his studio to Inspector James McDougal, the retired head of homicide of the Connecticut State Police. When murder occurs in Wingate, the local police call on Inspector McDougal for help and are stuck with Lucy in the bargain because nobody can stop Lucy from getting into whatever she chooses to get into. Her knowledge of the local scene, her "healthily curious" instinct, and her involvement with the murderer usually get her into danger from which the inspector rescues her.

She is egotistical, expecting to be the center of attention, the sort of person "who never lingered long in a group in which somebody else had the spotlight" (*A Dying Fall*, 20). She is hot-tempered and sharp-tongued, and while her temper tantrums are "usually as brief as a summer storm," her "thunderbolts hurled at random were enough to drive strong men under the table" (Dying, 13). She is bossy. Young Sergeant Terrezi in particular chafes under Lucy's demands at times, thinking "just because I used to weed her garden, she needn't think she can order me around like a kid" (*To Spite Her Face*, 111).

For all her faults, though, Lucy is a good friend, quick to make amends ("I'm always sorry after I've been horrid" [Spite, 114]), loyal, kind, fun to be around. As one character describes her, "She's one of my favorite people....She bawls me out regularly, she can be ornery as hell, and I like her guts" (Spite, 95).

Much of the humor in the Lucy Ramsdale books springs from Lucy's reactions to age and sex. Lucy's reactions to her age are both funny and poignant. For the most part, she copes. "Just as pregnant women develop a protective lethargy, she had developed a shrugging acceptance of whatever facets of old age were inevitable—or too much trouble, too insanely expensive to change" (Spite, 29). She finds "a certain invigorating aspect to reading obituaries of people you'd known, a healthy animal surge: I'm outlasting the lot of them" (Spite, 83). She also has her bad moments on the question of age. In one amusing sequence, she is forced to eavesdrop on a conversation, and one of the statements she hears about herself infuriates her: "She can be quite the prima donna, you know: the old are so touchy" (Spite, 30). She cannot stand for anyone else to think of her as old unless she is using her "poor old lady" act to get them to do something for her, and she thinks of herself as old only when she is feeling sorry for herself.

In a society which values youth and beauty highly, the loss of both can be troublesome, and Lucy had been beautiful. "Lucy had been used to compliments since she was in her crib. At sixty-nine, white-haired, crepey-throated, fingers slightly gnarled by arthritis, she still had the delicately whittled bone structure, the aura—and sometimes the imperious tempers—of a beautiful woman" (Spite, 15).

One of the reasons that losing beauty can be a problem for a woman is that the world tends to assume that as wrinkles come in, sex drive goes out. Not so. Lucy and many of her fellow volunteers at the thrift shop may have lost the beauty of youth, but they have not lost an eye for sexy men. In *Beauty Sleep*, when another of the older women is discussing such a young man, she states, "I swear my nipples stood up and saluted when he passed us" (5). At another point, Lucy states, "When I meet a real male, he gives off a kind of crackle" (Dying, 99). Of course, the opportunities to cause crackles decrease with age, as Lucy reflects after meeting the local gardner. "Sandini had never pinched her behind, but over the years he had often looked as if he'd like to; the older one got, the more gratifying that was" (Dying, 21). There are crackles between Lucy and Inspector McDougal, but they come to nothing more than mutual admiration and fiery arguments.

Lucy is a lady in several senses of the word. She comes from the upper middle class, she has good taste, she has a strong moral code, she has the good manners of kindness as well as those of finishing school.

She is also small, so she is truly a little old lady. She is vain, emotional, and gossip-loving, but she is also intelligent, industrious, and kind. She is little but mighty enough to make strong men tremble, old but earthy, a lady with a salty tongue and a penchant for trouble. Lucy is not a broadly-drawn caricature. She is comic because she is subject to the everyday ups and downs of the ego and to the weaknesses that we all can recognize in ourselves—or at least in others.

Emily Pollifax

If Lucy Ramsdale is most like a person one might know, Emily Pollifax is most like a person one would *like* to know. She appears in seven suspense novels created by Dorothy Gilman.[7] The first novel, *The Unexpected Mrs. Pollifax*, appeared in 1966, and the most recent one, *Mrs. Pollifax and the Hong Kong Buddha*, in 1985. Emily Pollifax is neither a private detective nor an amateur sleuth. She is a spy who works for the CIA, with her age, suburban middle-class background and naivete serving as the perfect disguise. (If this reminds you of the television series *Scarecrow and Mrs. King*, remember that Mrs. Pollifax was there first.) Since she is a "cheerful cozy little woman with fly-away white hair and a penchant for odd hats and growing geraniums" (*Mrs. Pollifax on the China Station*, 1), she is, as she concludes in the first book, unexpected.

In that first book, Emily Pollifax is a widow with grown children, feeling rather useless, bored, and old. A discussion with her doctor reminds her that she had always wanted to be a spy, a notion that sends the doctor into gales of laughter, but sends her to Washington. She has no idea how to become a spy, and so she just goes down to CIA headquarters and applies for a job. Through a series of flukes, she gets one. Her first adventure takes her to Mexico and Albania, and each subsequent assignment takes her to another exotic location.

The earlier books usually include a young-lovers romantic subplot and in *Mrs. Pollifax on Safari*, Mrs. Pollifax has her own romance, which results in marriage by the next book, *Mrs. Pollifax on the China Station*.

Mrs. Pollifax is a nice person, and she therefore finds the world filled with nice people. Of course, this isn't the way spy stories are supposed to work—everyone in a spy story is supposed to be a potential villain, not a potential hero. In a world of secrets, Mrs. Pollifax is astonishingly open, and, as a result, others are open to her. As a result of her unorthodox approach, imaginative actions, and complete fearlessness, she is stunningly successful.

In keeping with her unorthodox methods, Mrs. Pollifax has "peculiar" ways of thinking, attitudes that caused her first husband to call her a "lovable little goose" (Unexpected, 6). She is more than a bit of a mystic, and this mystic feeling not only adds intensity to her encounters with people but also adds meaning to her adventures; "a sense of life being so stripped to its essence that trivia and inconsequentials fell away" (China, 139). Mrs. Pollifax's ways of thinking do not fit society's view of how one should conduct one's life after a certain age, as expressed at the beginning of one of her adventures. Her first thought is conventional. It seems strange to be going off on a spy mission at her age. She then thinks, "But this was exactly the age...when life ought to be spent, not hoarded" (*The Elusive Mrs. Pollifax*, 34).

The comedy in the Mrs. Pollifax stories rests very much in Mrs. Pollifax herself—she wears funny hats, she has a child-like imagination, and she uses highly unorthodox spy methods. Beyond Mrs. Pollifax's zany personality, however, humor lies in the fact that she is so much more than she seems. Allies and enemies alike are flabbergasted when they discover she is an agent. In the sense that she uses her age and background as an effective disguise, Mrs. Pollifax is much like other little old lady characters discussed here, especially Agatha Christie's Miss Jane Marple.

Sister Mary Theresa Dempsey

A stereotype of women perpetuated by wine commercials as well as by folklore is that of the Roman Catholic nun who is cute but distant and absolutely trustworthy. She always behaves with decorum. Sister Mary Theresa Dempsey, the amateur detective of a series by Monica Quill (pen name for Ralph McInerny), typifies some of these notions of a nun as well as many of the comic little old lady of the classic mystery tradition. But this nun proves she is not one-dimensional, and although she is trustworthy in the strictest sense, she has an attraction to, of all things, murder.

Sister Mary Theresa is an elderly (seventy-plus), spunky (of course), and overweight woman who has been featured in four novels from 1981 (*Not a Blessed Thing*) to 1985 (*Nun of the Above*).[8] The first, *Not a Blessed Thing*, introduces the cast of three nuns, Sisters Mary Theresa, Kimberly, and Joyce, who live in Chicago in an old house designed by Frank Lloyd Wright. The house, the three nuns, and enough money saved to support them are all that is left of the Order of Martha and Mary. Kim and Joyce are much younger and former students of Sister Mary Theresa. The stories are all told from Sister Kimberly's point of view. Kimberly is Sister Mary Theresa's assistant and is in the unenviable position of carrying out many of the older sister's ideas of how to catch a villain.

The relationship of the characters is very much like Rex Stout's Nero Wolfe series with Sister Mary Theresa as the Nero Wolfe figure (pun intended). Sister Kim is, obviously, the Archie Goodwin component. Sister Joyce, the quietest of the trio and the cook, parallels the talented Fritz Brenner of the Wolfe series. None of the three is as worldly as any in the Wolfe household. They fall short in many comparisons with Stout's characters. On the other hand, they are more pleasant than the Wolfe group and their motives are wholly humanitarian.

Sister Mary Theresa is not very mobile because of her age and weight but more particularly of her need to stay at home and work on her life's project, a definitive study of the twelfth century. When she does go out or when she is observed in her study, she is an imposing presence. Dedicated to the old values and the old ways, Sister Mary Theresa still wears the flowing black robes and wobbly head wear of the habit designed by the M&Ms' founder. Clearly, a woman in the 1980s wearing medieval clothing when no longer required to do so is comic, especially when that person is unexpectedly concerned with the contemporary world of crime. In an interesting way Sister Mary Theresa's outlandish garb contributes to a certain invisibility as a sleuth. One might reasonably assume that a fat old nun in a ridiculous habit would spend all of her intellectual powers (such as she might have) on good deeds and prayer without a remaining ounce for worldly matters. But, of course, to Sister Mary Theresa, solving crimes *is* a matter of performing good works. She plans to get to the bottom of the puzzles by whatever means cross her considerably well-endowed mind.

A popular perception of nuns is that they are either tyrants or mice. Sister Mary Theresa is closer to the tyrant mold. She is, in fact, as overbearing as Bertha Cool. She is never profane, however, and she never has to rely upon a partner's superior wisdom as does Bertha. She is as devious as any other detective and has no qualms about sending forth the younger nuns to gather information in unorthodox ways. When Sister Kimberly is persuaded by Sister Mary Theresa to answer an ad for a writer on a magazine in order to stalk a suspect, Kimberly correctly muses that "Emtee Dempsey would have had a complicated argument purporting to prove she had a moral obligation to deceive [the editor]" (Above, 73). When Sister Mary Theresa uses the telephone to do some investigating on her own, she is more likely to call herself "Dr. Dempsey" than "Sister Mary Theresa Dempsey" referring quite correctly though misleadingly to her Ph.D. in history. Neither the more realistic younger nuns nor Kim's brother Richard, a police officer who is frequently on the scene, can deter Sister Mary Theresa from the pursuit of dangerous criminals in the ways she chooses.

Unlike many fictitious sleuths, Emtee Dempsey is never wrong. It could be that her purity of body and soul, or perhaps her woman's intuition, makes her an infallible amateur detective, often right where the professionals are wrong. Like Jane Marple, she is proper to a fault—very feminine in that sense, serving tea—or scotch—and approaching people in the most polite manner. Like Emily Pollifax and Hildegarde Withers, she wears a kind of uniform of unusual design which is helpful to her in many ways. Hers is a nun's habit whereas Mrs. Pollifax's and Miss Withers's are hats.

Sister Mary Theresa Dempsey is not little, is in fact quite large, but has that common female experience of having to prove that she is significant. She is old to our youth-worshiping culture. And she is every inch a lady. It is not amusing to consider that her conservatism may represent Monica Quill's complaint about the loss of tradition with passing time. Yet, Sister Mary Theresa is a little old lady sleuth whose adventures we read with pleasure.

Hildegarde Withers

Another female caricature represented in mystery fiction is the old-maid school teacher. Hildegarde Withers is such a character. She is funny if we pass lightly over the embarrassing references to her maidenhood and enjoy her fine qualities of fearless, determined pursuit of criminals, sly wit, and endless enjoyment of a chase. Stuart Palmer featured Hildegarde Withers in eleven novels and several short stories from 1931 to 1969. The first novel was *The Penguin Pool Murder* in 1931, and the last was *Hildegarde Withers Makes the Scene*, published posthumously in 1969.[9] In the first novel Miss Withers is still teaching in the New York City public school system, but she retires along the way. Also during the course of time covered by the novels, Hildegarde moves to California because of her asthma. In *Four Lost Ladies*, Miss Withers explains to Inspector Oscar Piper, her long-time friend and sometimes opponent, and incidentally "the only man who ever proposed to her" (32), that she is quite without excitement after leaving the classroom—except for occasional substituting—and just must continue with her "assistance" in the detection of crime. She is a "self-appointed gadfly" to the New York police department (and later "retired gadfly to the NYPD" [Scene, 12]). Her unapproved methods usually make trouble for Piper but always vindicate him and herself as well.

In her last escapade, as the—at that time—up-to-date title indicates, *Hildegarde Withers Makes the Scene*. The jacket gives the titillating subtitle, "Hildegarde finds murder among the hippies." The jacket artist has rendered Miss Withers with a tall feathery hat and white ruffled dress collar being presided over by a long pointed chin, beak-like nose, and rather sweet smile. Perfect for the image. We know this is right. She is an "angular old busybody" (Scene, 12), sometimes seeming "like a solid Victorian period piece" (Scene, 60) who has the power that such teachers once had over naughty young boys. Miss Withers carries an umbrella and wears ostentatious hats that call attention to themselves not because they are fashionable, certainly, but because they are odd. One such example "must have been designed by somebody who had heard of hats but never actually seen one" (Ladies, 122). Although Palmer does not dwell on Miss Withers' looks or apparel, readers know her for a type—a maiden lady in funny clothes, who though prim is given to unpredictable behavior. Part of the humor of the Hildegarde Withers stories comes from the unlikely situations into which this proper schoolma'am gets herself. In *Green Ace*, she impersonates the wife of a man imprisoned in Sing Sing to try to gain access to the man to hear his own story. Since the real wife is a great deal younger than Hildegarde, and since the warden had met the real wife a few weeks before, Hildegarde doesn't succeed in her charade. In *Four Lost Ladies*, she tries to impersonate a woman who has recently won a radio contest. She hennas her hair, puts on exaggerated makeup, and dons a rented chinchilla coat to register under the contest winner's name in a hotel where she expects to attract the attention of a murderer. Again, her act isn't entirely convincing, but she does indeed attract the attention of the murderer. In *Hildegarde Withers Makes the Scene*, Hildegarde persuades a handsome UCLA drop-out to attach a sidecar to his motorcycle so that she "in the best tradition of chivalry from Camelot to LaMancha, went forth to rescue a fair damsel in distress, riding sidesaddle, so to speak, on a Hog" (23). Off they go from Santa Monica to a "hippie" gathering place in Laguna Beach. None of these situations is believable, but each is fun.

Hildegarde displays her schoolteacher's broad knowledge of facts frequently. To combat sleeplessness, she "counted herds of sheep, she counted to a thousand by fives, she counted famous historical murderers whose names began with A, she declined *amo, amas, amat...*" (Ace, 214). She quotes Burns, Wordsworth, and Shakespeare. She sometimes resists the urge to explain some of the elementary lessons classroom teachers know so well, such as in *Green Ace* when she decides "this was no time to indoctrinate the man about the principle of the siphon" (10). She handles suspects and friends with the same effective methods of psychology that she must have used to handle generations of students. When Miss Withers appeared in the coffee houses of 1960s Los Angeles, "She was a stern apparition who probably caused more than one runaway disciple to remember uneasily the days of rapped knuckles and home arrest" (Ace, 24). As Mary Jane Jones points out in "The Spinster

Detective," the school teacher is a "mental symbol of order" and "This ability to establish order is perhaps the most dominant trait given to the spinster detective."[10] Hildegarde Withers is a benign old gal who describes herself as "a snoopy old maid who looks rather like a fugitive from a rest home" and explains that this appearance "has the advantage in most cases of being what you might call an effective natural disguise" (Scene, 47). She surprises everyone except Inspector Piper with her self-assured competence in concocting outlandish plots to catch criminals. In many ways she is outdated today but not in her ability to amuse detective fans.

Emily Seeton

Heron Carvic first used Miss Emily Seeton in a short story. Some fifteen years later, "Miss Seeton upped and demanded a book." Carvic decided that if "she wanted to satirize detective novels in general and elderly lady detectives in particular," he would "let her have her head."[11]

The first thing Miss Seeton sends up is the convention of quiet lives in a quiet English village. Miss Seeton locates herself in a supposedly quiet English village, all right: Plummergen is a village of about five hundred souls, with some of the buildings over four hundred years old. Miss Seeton, however, is not to the village born; she comes to Plummergen only after she inherits a cottage called Sweetbriars and a small income from her godmother. Worse, she does not arrive quietly to that quiet street (Plummergen is a one-street village). She arrives from London in a great blaze of publicity because she has poked with her umbrella a man who turned out to be a murderer. The newspapers pick up on her presumably heroic attempt to save the murdered girl's life and dub her "The Battling Brolly." Plummergen's malicious gossips, led by "The Nuts," Miss Nuttel and Nora Blaine, promptly turn Miss Seeton into a suspicious character and the talk of the town.

And so it goes through five books published between 1968 and 1975.[12] Almost every case involves a gang whose members repeatedly try to kill Miss Seeton. They don't succeed because she foils them with her umbrella without ever realizing they intend her harm. When the police try to tell her that she is in danger, she knows that they are wrong because "Miss Seeton is capable of dismissing from her mind any occurrence in her life that does not conform with her conception of the life of a gentlewoman. Gentlewomen do not, in Miss Seeton's estimation, become entangled in outlandish situations; therefore, in Miss Seeton's view, neither does she" (*Witch Miss Seeton*, 29).

In her normal state, Miss Seeton is not a good artist. She is, however, signed on by Scotland Yard as an artist because when she relies on her intuition, she creates remarkable drawings that sometimes foretell coming events, sometimes reveal hidden depths of character. Because she does have an official connection with Scotland Yard, the newspapers insist on calling Miss Seeton a detective, and she hits the headlines every time she waves her umbrella. Her every move—for example, a move such as erroneously taking a plane to Genoa when she should have gone to Geneva (*Miss Seeton Sings*)—is seen as a clever ploy by a mastermind. "Even some members of the police force...insist upon regarding Miss Seeton as a subtle investigator" (*Odds on Miss Seeton*, 45). No one except the officers who work closely with Miss Seeton will accept the fact that she is a perfectly ordinary ex-school teacher except for the fact that "she has this strange faculty, one might say misfortune, for attracting crime and criminals" (Sings, 36). Except for her "strange faculty," there is little that is comic about Miss Seeton herself. She is "a very pleasant, ordinary little body, with nice manners, thoughtful...'"(*Miss Seeton Draws the Line*, 22). The Miss Seeton books, however, can be hilarious, even though they tend to be quite predictable: There is going to be a romantic subplot; The Nuts are going to serve up wild gossip; crooks are going to get done in each time they try to do in Miss Seeton; and there are going to be Keystone Cops chase scenes. The hilarity occurs primarily through wild scenes such as Miss Seeton's leading a coven of would-be witches safely through fire while some other citizens of Plummergen sit in a cave awaiting the end of the world, or Miss Seeton's becoming the hit of a girlie show. An added pleasure of the Seeton stories lies in the inside joke available to knowledgeable mystery fans. Unlike Miss Marple or Miss Silver, Miss Seeton is no detective. Not only does she not observe clues, she persists in not seeing the most blatant evidence if she doesn't want to see it. Her only flashes of intuition, her drawings, embarrass her. Furthermore, she doesn't blend into the background but constantly attracts extraordinary attention, not only from the antic villagers but also from the national, and at times international, press. Miss Marple and Miss Silver were never like this.

Jane Marple

Although Miss Silver is amusing to her surrogate nephew, Inspector Frank Abbott, the series is not written with comic intent, and the books make slow reading today. The Miss Marple books are still very much good reading as evidenced by a steady stream of reprints. Miss Marple first appeared in a novel in 1930, with *Murder at the Vicarage*.[13] The last Marple novel, *Sleeping Murder*, was published in 1976.

Miss Marple is a classic little old lady, even though she is not little physically, being tall and thin. However, she is a bird-watching spinster who spends a great deal of time gardening or knitting fluffy pastel wool, wears sensible, proper clothes, and looks upon gentlemen as creatures from another planet. Jane Marple has a good sense of humor, as the vicar of *Murder in the Vicarage* remarks. Also, her continual linking of suspects or situations with someone or something from the village can be amusing. Some of the statements are startling to strangers because of their disjointedness, as in *The Body in the Library*: "Tommy Bond...and Mrs. Martin, our new schoolmistress. She went to wind up the clock and a frog jumped out"; this statement causes a stranger to ask later, "Is the old lady a bit funny in the head?" (48). However, even though there are amusing aspects to Miss Marple's personality, the comic aspect of the mysteries does not come from Miss Marple herself.

Miss Marple operates within a small circle, the village of St. Mary Mead, and she is quite respected by many who know her as being "sharp as a needle." Among those who look at her without really seeing her, reactions are far different. In *The Mirror Cracked*, after Miss Marple has solved a murder, her nurse scolds Inspector Craddock for discussing the murder: "She's old and frail, and she really must lead a sheltered life. She always has, you know. I'm sure all this talk of murders and gangsters and things like that is very, very bad for her" (216). Miss Marple's nephew, Raymond West, is very fond of her, and generous to her, but he is as blind as Miss Knight, as shown by his description of her in *Sleeping Murder*:

You'll adore my Aunt Jane....She's what I should describe as a perfect Period Piece. Victorian to the core. All her dressing tables have their legs swathed in chintz. She lives in a village, the kind of village where nothing ever happens, exactly like a stagnant pond. (27)

Miss Marple knows, of course, that stagnant ponds are full of activity, including sexual activity. Raymond is always trying to bring Miss Marple up to date on sex by sending her modern novels in which sex is not a sin but a duty. When he mentions that a friend is a homosexual, he is slightly embarrassed, but concludes that "even dear old Aunt Jane must have heard of queers" (*A Caribbean Mystery*, 4-5). In fact, Miss Marple knows the facts of life from happenings in St. Mary Mead, including perversions of all kinds, "Some kinds indeed that even the clever young men from Oxford who wrote books didn't seem to have heard about" (*Caribbean*, 15-16). Miss Knight and Raymond are incapable of seeing Miss Marple as she really is because they see her only as they want to see her. Strangers often simply fail to see her at all after their first glance registers "old lady." In *A Caribbean Mystery* when Miss Marple occasionally joins in a conversation, "everyone was surprised because they had usually forgotten that she was there!" (57).

When Miss Marple comes into contact with a trained observer, however, perceptions change sharply. She has been highly recommended to Deputy Inspector Craddock. When he first meets her in *A Murder Is Announced*, however, she is "heavily enmeshed in fleecy wool" and is so incoherent, flustered, and chattery that Craddock disgustedly thinks that she is "completely gaga" (86). As the discussion of the murder continues, however, Craddock tests her and is surprised by the results: "Craddock caught his breath. She'd got it! She was sharp, after all" (91). Like most other police officers whom she encounters, Craddock comes to respect and enjoy Miss Marple after the shock of their first meeting, the meeting where he observes so much fleecy wool. Miss Marple was manipulating wool, she seemed terribly wooly-headed, she heaped wool around her shoulders, and for a while she certainly pulled the wool over Craddock's eyes. Therein lies the great comedy of the Marple mysteries—the way in which Miss Marple so consistently, deftly, and ever-so-slightly mockingly pulls the wool over the world's eyes.

Of course, Jane Marple is very much what she seems, an old tabby of a certain age and class, content with her garden, her birdwatching, her small round of village social activities. She is all that—and more—but the world at large is not willing to look long enough to see the more.

Conclusion

Miss Marple and Mrs. Pollifax always get the last laugh on the villians because they quietly con those who fail to see them whole, but of the women discussed, only Miss Seeton and Lucy Ramsdale fail to experience the great invisibility that descends upon a woman at a certain age. Miss Seeton's notoriety is satiric, part of Carvic's send-up of elderly lady detectives. Lucy Ramsdale maintains a relatively high visibility because she fights for it and because she doesn't go among strangers. For purposes of the series, she is much more tied to her village of Wingate, Connecticut, than Miss Marple is to St. Mary Mead. Sister Mary Theresa Dempsey usually stays in her study. As for the others, Bertha Cool must convince every client that it is results that count, not gender. Oscar Piper sometimes must convince a colleague to listen to Hildegarde Withers. Further, Hildegarde is considered to be only in the way rather than of any use until she solves the crime. Sister Mary Theresa's friends attempt to dissuade her from meddling in police affairs throughout each of her novels. In *A Caribbean Mystery*, Miss Marple must go to an elderly rich man for help because she knows that people "wouldn't listen to me for a moment. They would say that I was an old lady imagining things" (129). A raffish confederate must get attention for Mrs. Pollifax by saying, "She's okay—she's got the crazy spirit." He also expresses the world's view by adding, "Except wothehell I never expect it from such a person" (*The Amazing Mrs. Pollifax*, 163). He is right in saying that Mrs. Pollifax is one of the crazy ones, and he is expressing society's view accurately by not expecting an older woman to do anything but fade into some quiet genteel corner of the world's consciousness.

We laugh at our comic old lady detectives for varied reasons. Bertha's temper, greed, and cynical attitudes may not seem to have much in common with Lucy's ego, Miss Seeton's fame, Hildegarde Withers' preoccupation with her spinsterhood, or Sister Mary Theresa's devious methods. Yet for all the variety of personality among the women, they all have one thing in common. They are funny because they are unexpected, and they are unexpected because they refuse to stay in their quiet corner. They force the world to realize that they exist. The common core of the humor supplied by little old ladies in comic crime fiction does not rest upon specific eccentricities or upon little versus big, old versus young, or lady versus shady character. It rests upon invisibility. When a woman reaches a certain age, this cloak of invisibility descends so thoroughly that one is inclined to feel sorry for Lamont Cranston, the Shadow, who had to go to the Far East in order to obtain the power to cloud men's minds so that they cannot see him. Our little old ladies can achieve the same effect just by leaving home.

Notes

[1]Francis L. and Roberta B. Fugate, *Secrets of the World's Best-Selling Writer* (New York: William Morrow and Company, Inc., 1980), p. 154.

[2]Fugate, p. 151.

[3]The editions of A.A. Fair's novels appearing in this essay are listed below, preceded by the original date of publication. All quotations will be cited in the text using, where necessary for clarity, the abbreviation given after an entry:

1939 *The Bigger They Come* (New York: Quill, 1984) (Bigger)

1941 *Spill the Jackpot* (New York: Dell Publishing Co., Inc., 1962)

1943 *Cats Prowl at Night* (New York: Dell Publishing Co., Inc., 1968)

1956 *Beware the Curves* (New York: Pocket Books, Inc., 1960)

1957 *Some Slips Don't Show* (New York: Pocket Books, Inc., 1961)

1957 *You Can Die Laughing* (New York: William Morrow & Company, 1957)

1965 *Cut Thin to Win* (New York: William Morrow & Company, 1965)

1970 *All Grass Isn't Green* (New York: William Morrow & Company, 1970)

[4]Fugate, p. 199.

[5]Frank E. Robbins, "The Firm of Cool and Lam," *The Mystery Writer's Art*, edited by Francis M. Nevins, Jr. (Bowling Green: Bowling Green University Popular Press, 1970), p. 139.

[6]The editions of Hildegarde Dolson's novels appearing in this essay are listed below, preceded by the original date of publication. All quotations will be cited in the text using, where necessary for clarity, the abbreviation given after an entry:

1971 *To Spite Her Face* (Philadelphia: J.P. Lippincott, Co., 1971) (Spite)

1973 *A Dying Fall* (Philadelphia: J.B. Lippincott, Co., 1973) (Dying)

1977 *Beauty Sleep* (Philadelphia: J.B. Lippincott, Co., 1977)

[7]The editions of Dorothy Gilman's novels appearing in this essay are listed below, preceded by the original date of publication. All quotations will be cited in the text using, where necessary for clarity, the abbreviation given after an entry:

1966 *The Unexpected Mrs. Pollifax* (Greenwich: Fawcett Publications, Inc., nd) (Unexpected)

1970 *The Amazing Mrs. Pollifax* (Garden City: Doubleday & Company, Inc., 1970)

1971 *The Elusive Mrs. Pollifax* (Garden City: Doubleday & Company, Inc., 1971)

1977 *Mrs. Pollifax on Safari* (Garden City: Doubleday & Company, Inc., 1977)

1983 *Mrs. Pollifax on the China Station* (Garden City: Doubleday & Company, Inc., 1983) (China)

1985 *Mrs. Pollifax and the Hong Kong Buddha* (New York: Doubleday & Company, Inc., 1985)

[8]The editions of Monica Quill's novels appearing in this essay are listed below, preceded by the original date of publication. All quotations will be cited in the text using, where necessary for clarity, the abbreviation given after an entry:

1981 *Not a Blessed Thing* (New York: Vanguard Press, 1981)

1982 *Let Us Prey* (New York: Vanguard Press, 1982)

1983 *Nun of the Above* (New York: Vanguard Press, 1985) (Above)

[9]The editions of Stuart Palmer's novels appearing in this essay are listed below, preceded by the original date of publication. All quotations will be cited in the text using, where necessary for clarity, the abbreviation given after an entry:

1931 *The Penguin Pool Murder* (New York: Brentano's, 1931)

1949 *Four Lost Ladies* (New York: Walter J. Black, 1949) (Ladies)

1950 *Green Ace* (New York: The Mill Co. and William Morrow & Co., 1950) (Ace)

1969 *Hildegarde Withers Makes the Scene* (with Fletcher Flora) (New York: Random House, 1969) (Scene)

[10]Mary Jane Jones, "The Spinster Detective," *Journal of Communication* 25:2 Spring 1975, 106-112.

[11]Heron Carvic, "Little Old Ladies," *Murder Ink,* edited by Dilys Winn (New York: Workman Publishing Co., Inc., 1977), p. 105

[12]The editions of Heron Carvic's novels appearing in this essay are listed below, preceded by the original date of publication. All quotations will be cited in the text using, where necessary for clarity, the abbreviation given after an entry:

1970 *Miss Seeton Draws the Line* (New York: Harper & Row, 1970)

1971 *Witch Miss Seeton* (New York: Harper & Row, 1971)

1973 *Miss Seeton Sings* (New York: Harper & Row, 1973) (Sings)

1975 *Odds on Miss Seeton* (New York: Harper & Row, 1975)

[13]The editions of Agatha Christie's novels appearing in this essay are listed below, preceded by the original date of publication. All quotations will be cited in the text using, where necessary for clarity, the abbreviation given after an entry:

1930 *Murder at the Vicarage* (N.Y.: Berkley Books 1984) (Vicarage)

1942 *The Body in the Library* (N.Y.:Pocket Books, 1965) (Library)

1950 *A Murder Is Announced* (N.Y.: Pocket Books, nd) (Announced)
1962 *The Mirror Cracked* (N.Y.: Dodd, Mead & Co., 1963) (Mirror)
1964 *A Caribbean Mystery* (N.Y.:Pocket Books, 1966) (Caribbean)
1976 *Sleeping Murder* (N.Y.: Bantam Books, Inc., 1981) (Sleeping)

The Comic in the Canon:
What's Funny about
Sherlock Holmes?

Barrie Hayne

"I have a theory that the individual represents in his development the whole procession of his ancestors, and that such a sudden turn to good or evil stands for some strong influence which came into the line of his pedigree. The person becomes, as it were, the epitome of the history of his own family."

"It is surely rather fanciful."

"Well, I don't insist upon it." ("The Empty House," 491)[1]

"A dog reflects the family life. Whoever saw a frisky dog in a gloomy family, or a sad dog in a happy one? Snarling people have snarling dogs, dangerous people have dangerous ones. And their passing moods may reflect the moods of others."

I shook my head. "Surely, Holmes, this is a little farfetched," said I. ("The Creeping Man," 1071)

Sherlock Holmes and Dr. Watson. Don Quixote and Sancho Panza. The intuitive genius, half-mad, and his down-to-earth squire. Two great characters reprised or refracted from the greatest comic novel ever written.

Yet Watson's literal-mindedness is not always a corrective to Holmes's intuitive flights. When Watson's old friend Bob Ferguson puts his own case before the detective as that of someone else, Watson is struck by Ferguson's altruism. Holmes remarks, "I never get your limits, Watson. . . .There are unexplored possibilities about you. . . .We must not let him think that this agency is a home for the weak-minded." ("The Sussex Vampire," 1036). Perhaps most notably—and comically—of all, there is that moment when Professor Presley, subsequently found to be taking the monkey-gland treatment, is seen crawling along a corridor. When Watson diagnoses the man's peculiar gait as lumbago, Holmes rejoins, "Good, Watson! You always keep us flat-footed on the ground." ("The Creeping Man," 1074).

And at the end of what, in the lives of the two characters, is their very last case, when Watson takes literally Holmes's metaphor, "There's an east wind coming," Holmes remarks, "Good old Watson. You are the one fixed point in a changing age." ("His Last Bow," 980).

Fixedness, rigidity, the predictably mechanical—these, as Bergson and others[2] have observed, are of the essence of comedy. Someone who remains mechanically unaltered while circumstances change around him is essentially comic. Yet the fixedness is sometimes Holmes's rather than Watson's, if fixedness suggests feet firmly planted on the ground. There are times when the literal-mindedness is all the detective's, and Holmes, the supreme rationalist, keeps a realistic rein on Watson. Forever after *A Study in Scarlet*, Holmes chides Watson for his introduction of the sensational into the chronicles ("but," says Watson, "the romance was there." *The Sign of Four*, 90). As the saga continues, Holmes complains of Watson's "meretricious," or "sensational," treatment of his cases, which Watson has "degraded," and "embellish[ed]," "tinge[d] with romanticism" what ought to be an exact science. Yet Holmes himself shrugs off his cases in a more literal, realistic way, as "little," "trifling," "simple." When he sits down to tell the tale himself, however, he discovers the necessity of embellishment, romance, concealment, recognizing that Watson "could elevate my simple art, which is but systematized common sense, into a prodigy. When I tell my own story, I have no such aid." ("The Blanched Soldier," 1011)

This disparity of viewpoint when looking at Holmes's deductions, Holmes himself viewing them as commonsense reared into a system, and Watson, unable to see the system, bedazzled by their brilliance, makes for a series of stichomythic exchanges which echo throughout the canon and strike a continuing comic note. Three, beginning with the very first one, will suffice as representative:

"Wonderful!" I ejaculated.
"Commonplace," said Holmes, though I thought from his expression that he was pleased at my evident surprise and admiration. (*A Study in Scarlet*, 26)

"It is wonderful!" I exclaimed.
"It is obvious." ("The Boscombe Valley Mystery," 214)

"Excellent!" I cried.
"Elementary," said he. ("The Crooked Man," 412)

Here is the essence of the comedy of repetition, which Bergson sees as a major device of verbal comedy.[3] Surely "Elementary, my dear Watson," which in that precise form Holmes never actually says, any more than Rick Blaine ever says "Play it again, Sam," takes its place, with all its synonyms, as a comic repetition, alongside Moliere's "Et Tartuffe?...Le pauvre homme!"

Of course there are also those other moments, comic in a different way, showing the fragility and inflation of Holmes's pride, when the detective's explanation elicits a "how absurdly simple" from Watson. Holmes remarks on the first such occasion, and the simile he uses reminds us that his deductions are infused with his egotism, and inextricable from his showmanship (as Watson, with a usually uncredited shrewdness, had noticed in the very first exchange quoted above): "I'm not going to tell you much more of the case, Doctor. You know a conjurer gets no credit when once he has explained his trick" (*A Study in Scarlet*, 33).

The fanciful knight and the literal-minded squire may be less of an apt model than a still more archetypal partnership in which complementary qualities match and sometimes interchange. Watson's fanciful side, his tendency to romanticize in order to interest the reader, is a necessary corrective to Holmes's belief that his cases "should have been a course of lectures" ("The Copper Beeches," 317), something along the lines of "the Fifth proposition of the Book of Euclid" (*The Sign of Four*, 90). But Holmes's fanciful side, the inheritance of the Bi-Part Soul which devolved from Dupin and which is passed on to all the great detectives of fiction, the essential mixture in all of them of the Reason and the Understanding, the intuition and the merely rational powers—this fanciful or intuitive side is held in check by, or more properly tested against, Watson's common-sense. This is perhaps best expressed in Watson's own understanding of his role in the saga:

I was a whetstone for his mind. I stimulated him. He liked to think aloud in my presence. His remarks could hardly be said to be made to me—many of them would have been as appropriately addressed to his bedstead—but none the less, having formed the habit, it had become in some way helpful that I should register and interject. If I irritated him by a certain methodical slowness in my mentality, that irritation served only to make his own flame-like intuitions and impressions flash up the more vividly and swiftly. Such was my humble role in our alliance. ("The Creeping Man," 1071)

Expressed, significantly, in one of the last stories Doyle wrote in the canon, this opinion is clearly endorsed by Doyle; in it there is nothing of Watsonian obtuseness.

That the "alliance" of Holmes and Watson is psychically a marriage needs no insistence here, since it has been taken so long for granted, and reared into the kind of comedy that passes for Baker Street Irregularity by no less a personage than Rex Stout, in the famous "Watson was a Woman," nearly fifty years ago.[4] But it is worth noting that from the marital nature of their alliance arises much of the comedy of the Sherlock Holmes stories, and especially the badinage that goes on between two people who clearly care about one another, but who sometimes feel the irritations of familiarity. Watson's more-than-medical concern about Holmes's use of cocaine, and especially about his apparent fatal illness in "The Dying Detective," or his once-in-a-lifetime faint when Holmes returns from Reichenbach, are matched by Holmes's horror when he has almost killed Watson in "The Devil's Foot" ("I had never seen so much of Holmes's heart before," 965), or when he has caused him to be shot, in "The Three Garridebs" ("For the one and only time I caught a glimpse of a great heart," 1053)—these moments clearly delineate the affection between the couple. The irritation is seen in the many many times Holmes, easily the more testy of the two, derides Watson's abilities, and the occasional crucial thrust, more telling for its rarity, which Watson delivers to Holmes.

One surely does not need to verify the comic qualities of marital tension. Except where such tension extends into tragedy, as in *Othello*, wife-husband bickering has been the stuff of comedy from *Lysistrata* through *A Midsummer Night's Dream* to *Private Lives* and *Who's Afraid of Virginia Woolf* (In *The Odd Couple*, oddly, it takes the pseudo-marital form it has in the Sherlock Holmes stories; emphatically so, and pointing to the universality of Holmes's constitutional untidiness, and Watson's attempts to reform him.) One of the most striking passages illustrating this bickering opens *The Valley of Fear*, the last of the long stories:

"I am inclined to think—" said I.

"I should do so," Sherlock Holmes remarked impatiently.

I believe that I am one of the most long-suffering of mortals, but I'll admit that I was annoyed at the sardonic interruption. "Really, Holmes," said I severely, "you are a little trying at times." (769)

Here is the "impatient" husband, self-absorbed, "trying," and the "long-suffering" wife, who is usually content to let the gibes pass. But a few lines later, the repressed returning, Watson makes one of his rare put-downs of Holmes, and an effectively heavy one it is:

"You have heard me speak of Professor Moriarty?"
"The famous scientific criminal, as famous among crooks as—"
"My blushes, Watson!" Holmes murmured in a deprecating voice.
"I was about to say, as he is unknown to the public."
"A touch! A distinct touch!" cried Holmes. "You are developing a certain unexpected vein of pawky humour, Watson, against which I must learn to guard myself." (769)

The word that Holmes uses, "pawky," is of Scottish origin, and may well be a passing fling at J.M. Barrie, who twenty years before had written a parody of Doyle, which Doyle later acknowledged in his autobiography as the best of many,[5] but the word ignites rather than defuses the bickering between Holmes and Watson, for it connotes an unintentional humour, and in using it Holmes is relegating Watson to the usual uncomprehending role; three times more in the same chapter, with Watson ignoring the gibes, Holmes tries to confirm his partner in that role. As the two discuss the key to the cipher Porlock has sent, and in particular which reference book he has used, Holmes rallies Watson for "that innate cunning which is the delight of your friends," points out that "perhaps there are points which have escaped your Machiavellian intellect," and even, when Watson reaches a correct solution, "you are scintillating this morning," urging him to "one more coruscation."

This exchange, marked by Holmes's ironical depreciation of Watson's reasoning powers, is typical, though lengthier than any other in the canon. Even when Watson is giving Holmes information he does not himself have, the detective either rejects it as not germane to his concerns, as he does with the Solar System ("I shall do my best to forget it," *A Study in Scarlet*, 21; though of course he has made a sophisticated use of it in the case later recorded as "The Musgrave Ritual") or else patronizes it as being on an insignificant topic, as he does with Watson's flow of information about the race track at Shoscombe Old Place ("I seem to have struck a rich vein," 1103; is this double use of the word "vein" a geological metaphor, or yet another gibe—at Watson's profession?). When Holmes examines the Baskerville portraits, he remarks, "Watson won't allow that I know anything of art, but that is mere jealousy because our views upon the subject differ" (749); and this is distinctly an intimate, carping comment of a kind often used by spouses to score off one another, gratuitously. Holmes's famous reaction to Watson's announcement of his engagement to Mary Morstan ("I feared as much,...I really cannot congratulate you," *The Sign of Four*, 157) is scarcely justified by his following statement that "love is an emotional thing...opposed to that true cold reason which I place above all things," for he has hardly demonstrated, even thus far in the canon, much faith in Watson's dedication to cold reason, so that he cannot claim that love is losing him a partner in the rational detection of crime. He sounds much more like a spurned and jealous spouse; and Watson's more sane reply ("laughing,"—"I trust...that my judgment may survive the ordeal,") is both free of jealousy, and self-aware. Holmes's is neither. In one of the very late stories, after some praise of Watson, which is characteristically faint, being more praise of his intellectual failings than of his strengths, Holmes begins his narration with the statement that "the good Watson [itself a patronizing expression] had at that time deserted me for a wife, the only selfish action which I can recall in our association. I was alone" ("The Blanched Soldier," 1000). Any irony here is surely Doyle's, with Holmes the butt; the petulance of the statement again bespeaks the jealous spouse.

Indeed, from the very beginning of the acquaintanceship, Holmes and Watson have looked at each other as prospective mates might do. Surely the scene in *A Study in Scarlet* in which they lay bare their respective failings, and stipulate their demands, calls to mind the "contract" scene in *The Way of the World*, in which Mirabel and Millamant, with obvious affection behind the badinage, rationally lay down the rules for their forthcoming union. Holmes sometimes smokes tobacco, as does Watson. Holmes keeps chemicals about, which Watson will tolerate. Watson has a bull-pup (which we hear nothing more about); Holmes makes no comment, though he might have been remembering his only college chum, Victor Trevor, and how he had used that earlier friendship to lay the foundation of his career, after Trevor's bull terrier had bitten him on the leg. Holmes is given to moods of depression; this suits Watson, who in his present state of nerves wants to avoid noise, from which category Holmes confidently excludes his own violin-playing. The whole basis of the relationship thus entered into—and one need not dwell, so often has it been remarked, on the alacrity with which Watson ups and leaves his various wives at a moment's notice when Holmes signals that the game is afoot—is keynoted in Holmes's remark, "It's just as well for two fellows to know the worst of one another" (19). As Millamant says, "I'll never marry, unless I am first made sure of my will and pleasure." To which Mirabel: "Would you have 'em both before marriage? Or will you be contented with the first now, and stay for the other till after grace?"[6]

In, therefore, the central relationship in the canon, the Holmes-Watson relationship, is recognizably a comic marriage, usually harmonious, but subject to some tensions and jealousies (at least on one side). The long-suffering Watson, as we have seen, largely suffers Holmes's ironies, but responds quite emotionally to gestures of affection. When Holmes shows that unwonted glimpse of his heart in "The Devil's Foot," Watson's loving reaction is followed immediately by Holmes's ironical one. Both reactions are absolutely typical: "You know," Watson says, "that it is my greatest joy and privilege to help you;" whereas Holmes "relapsed at once into that half-humorous, half-cynical vein which was his habitual attitude to those about him" (966). The whole relationship is in conception comic, and, like all elements of comedy, recognizably human.

One reason for its comic quality is indeed that rigid, mechanical element already mentioned that Bergson saw as eliciting our laughter. Again, Watson is not the only fixed point in a changing world and neither even is Holmes. The partnership itself is predictable, as the badinages and tensions of marriage are predictable. In "The Retired Colourman," which, though not written last, Doyle chose to place last, we have a case which deals tragically with marriage; Holmes describes the facts as "the old story...a treacherous friend and a fickle wife." Holmes's view of marriage is always a mordant one ("He never spoke of the softer passions, save with a gibe or a sneer," as we are told in the very first paragraph of the very first short story, "A Scandal in Bohemia," 161). His doubts about the marital relation therefore continue to the end. But this characterization by the detective of one of his last recorded cases follows an extraordinary effusion of emotion by Holmes, from which he is quickly brought back to earth by "the good doctor:" "But is not all life pathetic and futile? Is not his story a microcosm of the whole? We reach, we grasp. And what is left in our hands at the end? A Shadow. Or worse than a shadow—misery" (1113). The depression that Holmes admitted to in his opening "contract" with Watson continues to the end as well, and it is linked with his marital status, or lack of it. The "marriage" of Holmes and Watson may be one of the essential comic elements in the saga, but the rigidity of Holmes the marital sceptic, the misogynist, is no less surely one of the ruling comic qualities in his character. We must take Watson's word for Holmes's idolization of Irene Adler, and his interest in Violet Hunter is primarily Watson's wishful thinking. It is when he reports directly to us of Maud Bellamy in "The Lion's Mane" that we glimpse what he may have missed, being now in his retirement, with the Queen safely segregated: "Women have seldom been an attraction to me, for my brain has always governed my heart, but I could not look upon her perfect clear-cut face, with all the soft freshness of the downlands in her delicate colouring, without realizing that no young man would cross her path unscathed" (1088). This is no country for *old* men, but the danger is still inherent in the sex-relation ("unscathed"). In Watson is a much safer, more long-suffering spouse. The canon certainly bespeaks no "Come back to Baker Street again, John (or James?) honey," for any homo-eroticism is buried in the badinage, but to see two grown men behaving within all the comic conventions of a marriage is to see the centre of the comedy. Neil Simon knew that this was a sure comic recipe for *his* play, and Billy Wilder, who dealt from his first film (*The Major and The Minor*) with disguised and therefore comic sexuality, bringing the theme to its climax in *Some Like It Hot*, gave one more turn to the screw in a later film, *The Private Life of Sherlock Holmes*.[7] The film does not question the sexual normality of the two, any more than the canon raises the question, but Holmes in his dressing gown, Watson always at his beck and call, is an abiding stereotype of comic domesticity.

If we now look at the two characters separately rather than as a pair, it is on the face of things Watson who is the comic character and Holmes the hero of the saga. As Ronald Knox has noted, with his tongue not quite fully in his cheek, "Watson provides what the Holmes drama needs—a chorus...his drabness is accentuated by contrast with the limelight which beats upon the central figure,"[8] Watson's comic qualities reside in his obuseness rather than in his occasional deflations of Holmes. "I saw in the gas-light that Holmes wore an amused smile at this brilliant departure of mine" ("The Resident Patient," 430) sums up his function as obtuse narrator, as well as Holmes's attitude towards him. "There is a delightful freshness about you, Watson, which makes it a pleasure to exercise any small powers which I possess at your expense" (*The Hound of the Baskervilles*, 683) sums up again Holmes's attitude towards Watson, but emphasizes as well his own vanity. As Watson had fixed him for all time at the earliest stage of their acquaintance, "I had already observed that he was as sensitive to flattery on the score of his art as any girl could be of her beauty" (*A Study in Scarlet*, 34).

Dr. Watson and Mr. Holmes, with its no doubt fortuitous recollection of Stevenson's famous novel of dual personality the year before, might well have been Sherrinford Holmes and Ormond Sackler.[9] "Sherrinford" Holmes would have altered little of Sherlock's character, still suggesting his origins in a line of country squires, though perhaps "Sherlock," with its Coleridegean echoes of the person from Porlock (more directly alluded to in *The Valley of Fear*) and the consequent entry into a Xanadu of the Imagination, carries better the suggestions of the Vernet artistic strain. But Ormond Sackler certainly suggests a degree of pomposity and comic rigidity that reminds us again that the ostensible comedy of the stories resides in Watson, and that "John H. Watson, M.D." domesticates, anglicizes and even conceals that comic quality much better than "Ormond Sackler" could have done.

But it is only the *ostensible* comedy that resides in Watson. Sherlock Holmes is above all a character of humours. As Raymond Chandler, with some hyperbole, has said, "Sherlock Holmes after all is mostly an attitude and a few dozen lines of unforgettable dialogue."[10] While Holmes's particular humour, vanity, comes to us more forcibly through the eyes of the eminently ordinary observer who records it, we ought to remember that Watson is not as obtuse as he is often given discredit for being; he is usually apace with his reader rather than several steps behind; and in "The Three Students" his acumen compares favorably with that of a Camford Don's. And as we have just seen, Watson's penetrating gaze sometimes sees through Holmes's veil.

Holmes's vanity appears especially in those *coups de theatre* with which he closes a handful of his cases, an intrinsically comic device, with Holmes appearing as a more or less mock-heroic, practical-joking *Deus ex machina*. Watson several times notes that Holmes "loves to dominate and surprise those who were around him" (*The Hound of the Baskervilles*, 754). In *The Valley of Fear*, the announcement of the murder is "one of those dramatic moments for which my friend existed" (774). In the same novel, Holmes observes: "Watson insists that I am a dramatist in real life" (809). Holmes's *coups* usually serve his vanity as well as dramatizing it, since they score off those who have presumed to doubt his great powers: Colonel Ross, to whom he dramatically introduces Silver Blaze as the murderer of his trainer; the Prime Minister in "The Second Stain," to whom he reveals the dispatch safely in its box; or, especially, Lord Cantlemere, into whose pocket he actually puts the Mazarin Stone. In each of these cases, especially the last, Holmes is in an almost comic-Christly, again mock-heroic, role, staging a miracle which is at once a put-down and a proof for the Doubting Thomas. Poor Percy Phelps has almost given up hope of recovering his Naval Treaty when Holmes reveals it to him under the breakfast cover. When Phelps's shock occasions Watson's customary production of the brandy, which one might be forgiven for thinking is the only prescription he knows, Holmes apologizes: "Watson here will tell you that I never can resist a touch of the dramatic" (466). But no doubt the detective's greatest *coup de theatre* is reserved, appropriately, for Watson, when he throws off the garb of the old bookseller (in context, there is absurd comedy in *The Origin of Tree Worship*, a subject too outre for the hardheaded Watson) and returns to his friend after a two-year absence. It is no less appropriate that Watson submits to Holmes's mastery by fainting for the one time in his life ("The Empty House").

Aside from these grand theatrical gestures, Holmes remains fairly pokerfaced. A.G. Cooper has counted 292 occasions on which the Great Detective either laughs, chuckles, or smiles.[11] But more than once Watson notes the rarity of risibility in his partner: "Holmes seldom laughed, but he got as near to it as his old friend Watson could remember" ("The Mazarin Stone," 1022; this laughter, at the expense of the sceptical Lord Cantlemere, is oddly omitted from Cooper's canvass).

Still, if Holmes rarely laughs, he has a verbal wit which reflects, throughout the chronicles, comedy at the level of the word. Often that wit is sharpened at the expense of Watson and the public officials, the Chorus and the Sophists, in Knox's whimsical terms, characters of fixity. When Watson explains Professor Presley's behaviour in commonsensical terms which do not explain why his dog has attacked him, Holmes comments: "and the wolfhound no doubt disapproved of the financial bargain" ("The Creeping Man," 1075). Just so he had demolished Athelney Jones's reading of the Sholto murder, in a locked room: "on which the dead man very considerately got up and locked the door on the inside" (*The Sign of Four*, 113).

The guying of the police is a game Holmes engages in throughout the stories, beginning with his acceptance of the murder investigation in *A Study in Scarlet* along with Gregson and Lestrade ("However, we may as well go and have a look. I shall work it out on my own hook. I may have a laugh at them, if I have nothing else," 27). Holmes mellows towards his principal police antagonist-coadjutor over the years, and Lestrade towards him, so that in "The Six Napoleons" they become a mutual admiration society for a few moments in which Holmes, by Lestrade's praise (vanity remains his comic sore point), is "more nearly moved by the softer human emotions that I had ever seen him" (595). There is even indulgence in his first remarks to Lestrade after his return from Reichenbach: "you handled the Molesey Mystery with less than your usual—that's to say, you handled it fairly well" (492).

The higher form of comedy in relation to the police, however, draws attention to their failings and professional vanities by distinguishing them directly from Holmes, whose vanity is rarely brought face to face with failure: the method used is dramatic irony, as it is Holmes who solves the case, a fact which we, Watson and the detective know—as do Lestrade and his cohorts, who actually get the credit. This happens so often that quotation is scarcely necessary; it will be enough to not that such an incident occurs for the first time in *A Study in Scarlet* ("The man was apprehended, it appears, in the rooms of a certain Mr. Sherlock Holmes, who has himself, as an amateur, shown some talent in the detective line, and who, with such instructors, may hope in time to attain to a degree of their skill," 86), and for the last time in the story placed last in *The Case-Book*, "The Retired Colourman" ("The remarkable acumen by which Inspector MacKinnon deduced,...the bold deduction,...and the subsequent inquiry...should live in the history of crime as a standing example of the intelligence of our professional detectives," 1122). And so ends the Saga.

Holmes's awareness of his mastery of the rational and intuitive, like Dupin's, is what makes him ultimately superior to the police, who are merely rational, with no spark of genius. The denigration of the official police, however, which began with Dupin's Prefect, and comes to apotheosis with Holmes and the Lestrades and Gregsons, is in the 1890s by no means the commonplace of detective fiction it became over the next fifty or so years. Aside from Dupin, all Holmes's major predecessors *are* official policemen, from Inspector Bucket to the retired Sergeant Cuff to Lecoq. Holmes's famous disparagement of both Dupin and Lecoq (*A Study in Scarlet*, 24-25) plays no favorites between unofficial and official police. But that same awareness on Holmes's part of his mastery of the rational world through means both intellectual and imaginative bears with it the realization that he cannot deal with the powers of supernature. While his opponents several times find his powers "devilish," which suggests both their evil qualities (from the villain's point of view) and their preternatural power, Holmes frequently accepts such characterizations as complimentary: "I believe you are the devil himself." "Not far from him, at any rate" ("The Mazarin Stone, 1021) is both a wry acceptance of those preternatural powers, and a subtle dig at his interlocutor. But in the truly devilish world even Holmes's deductions cannot be valid; and his recognition of his limitation is comic. "In a modest way I have combatted evil," he says in *The Hound of the Baskervilles*, when he seems to be confronted with the very powers of darkness, "but to take on the Father of Evil himself would, perhaps, be too ambitious a task" (681) (We note the "perhaps," as we note the "even" of the Retired

Colourman's consulting, as an act of bravado, "not only the police but even Sherlock Holmes" [1122]). And in "The Sussex Vampire" he looks for the rational explanation of "a Grimm's fairy tale," and reports deadpan his solution of the case in the same dry prose the lawyers used to draw it to his attention: "Referring to your letter of the 19th...the matter has been brought to a satisfactory conclusion. With thanks for your recommendation, I am, sir, faithfully yours." (1044)

Holmes's wit is rarely self-directed, though the guying of the police, and the dramatic irony associated with their having the glory and he the satisfaction ("Populus me sibilat, at mihi plaudo/Ipse domi simul ac nummos contemplar in arca," 86) echoes in those moments when he is in error, and wryly concedes as much, both to Watson and the official police:

"Watson," said he, "if it should ever strike you that I am getting a little overconfident in my powers, or giving less pains to a case than it deserves, kindly whisper 'Norbury' in my ear, and I shall be infinitely obliged to you." ("The Yellow Face," 362)

"Well, well, Inspector, I often ventured to chaff you gentlemen of the police force, but *Cyanea capillata* very nearly avenged Scotland Yard." ("The Lion's Mane," 1095)

Here he has the glory—the second case is very nearly his last—established by fame; but his two principal butts in so many earlier cases have the satisfaction, which he accepts with a gracious wit, of seeing him bested.

There are other times when Holmes's wit approaches self-parody. When he first dazzles a skeptical Watson in *A Study in Scarlet* with his "You mean the retired Sergeant of Marines" (25) on the other side of Baker Street, we are fairly in the realm of pure deduction. But there is both showing-off and self-parody in Holmes's assessment of the red-headed Jabez Wilson: "Beyond the obvious facts that he has at some time done manual labour, that he takes snuff, that he is a Freemason, that he has been in China, and that he has done a considerable amount of writing lately, I can deduce nothing else" (177). Still, we can imagine how Holmes reached each conclusion in the chain. There is even deeper satire of Holmes's methods in his very similar appraisal of the unhappy John Hector McFarlane; "beyond the obvious facts that you are a bachelor, a solicitor, a Freemason, and an asthmatic, I know nothing whatever about you" ("The Norwood Builder," 497). The joke of such statements lies in the fact that most observers (though here Watson follows for us the chain of reasoning, rather than have Holmes explain it) would indeed know nothing about him. The wit is self-aggrandizing as well as, mainly from Doyle's viewpoint, self-satirical.

"Holmes could talk exceedingly well when he chose," Watson says early in their relationship (*The Sign of Four*, 134), and while the foregoing remarks have no doubt borne out Watson's statement, Holmes's wit is reactive and dry rather than epigrammatic. Aphorisms are relatively few, and indeed his observations upon life or the larger topics tend to be fairly prolix, like the famous comparison of crime in the city to that in the country, on the train en route to the Copper Beeches (322-323), or the remarks about unattached women prompted by the disappearance of Lady Frances Carfax (942-943). In the exchange between Holmes and Moriarty in their only meeting before the Reichenbach, there is certainly epigrammatic wit, but Holmes, however witty, is still reacting to Moriarty's verbal agility; it is a fencing with words we are watching; and Moriarty makes the last play:

"If you are clever enough to bring destruction upon me, rest assured that I shall do as much to you."
"You have paid me several compliments, Mr. Moriarty...Let me pay you one in return when I say that if I were assured of the former eventuality I would, in the interests of the public, cheerfully accept the latter."
"I can promise you the one, but not the other," he snarled...
("The Final Problem," 473)

Another characteristic feature of Holmes's wit is insouciance; the exchange I have just quoted follows closely Holmes's remark that "in the pleasure of this conversation I am neglecting business of importance which awaits me elsewhere." The violin or the syringe are tangible examples of Holmes's own brand of sprezzatura, or, more widely, his quality of turning casually away from what is in fact of the utmost importance to him. Once the case is solved, there is always Patti at Covent Garden, a good dinner at Simpson's, or even the pleasures of the cocaine bottle. This is sometimes expressed as verbal witticism: after solving the problem of the Blue Carbuncle by discovering the precious gem in the goose's crop, Holmes ends the story with "If you will have the goodness to touch the bell, Doctor, we will begin another investigation, in which also a bird will be the chief feature" (257).

The particular kind of epigram, however, delphic, often concealing a dramatic irony, which is especially Holmesian is the one Ronald Knox called the Sherlockismus, of which the chief example is the exchange in "Silver Blaze" touching "the curious incident of the dog in the night-time" (347).[12] Another is certainly the closing paragraph of "Charles Augustus Milverton" in which Lestrade, ever the dupe, asks Holmes to investigate the murder of the black-mailer at which Holmes and Watson have been present, and from which they have only just got away from the police. "That's rather vague," says Holmes of the Inspector's description of the less agile of the two escapees. "Why, it might almost be a description of Watson!" Which piece of dramatic irony amuses Lestrade no end.

To the extent, however, that Holmes is a wit at all, his literary context and kinship are inevitably invoked. Critics of detective fiction are a self-regarding lot, as self-regarding as the genre they study, and are much more apt to treat their subjects in isolated relation to that genre. So they find the principal intimations of Holmes in the Dupin and Lecoq he professed to deplore, or even in Sergeant Cuff.[13] There is perhaps here an additional reminder that Holmes may be more profitably placed in the larger context of his immediate time. While all this has been done before, and even in the earlier parts of this paper, here it is once more, with succinctness. Fifty years after Dupin, Holmes is still a romantic, still bringing his intuition to bear on the problem, supplemented by his powers of logic; Watson admires, in "The Speckled Band," "the rapid deductions, as swift as intuitions and yet always founded on a logical basis " (258). He is as much that Bi-part soul, "creative and resolvent," as Poe's detective was. Though Poe deplored Emersonian Transcendentalism and all that Kant (*cant*, or *can't*, as Melville called it), Dupin did bequeath to Holmes that amalgam of Reason and Understanding, imagination and rational thinking. And Holmes, before Thorndyke, was also bringing the ultimate weapons of logic, the scientific tools of the laboratory, to prove his intuitions—we and Watson meet him, as he rushes from the lab full of his latest finding, a scientific test for blood stains. And this meeting takes place the year after Stevenson's strange case of dual personality: in Holmes's spurts of energy alternating with cocaine depressions is yet another reminder of his Bi-part soul. Fully born, at Christmas 1887, is Holmes the dual man, using the methods of the approaching twentieth century to deal with a romantic and mysterious intractability, with which he is at the same time fully in tune.

None of which is especially comic, though there is certainly comedy in the conception overall of a man born out of time who is nonetheless well able to adapt and cope with an alien world. Not the tragic conception of a Matthew Arnold trapped in the monastery of the Grand Chartreuse, but the more comic one of a Hank Morgan who is triumphant in both worlds between which he wanders.

But if Holmes appeared two years before *A Connecticut Yankee*, he also appeared in the same decade as *Patience*, and there is a happy conjunction (and a reminder) in the simultaneous solicitation by Lippincott's of both *The Sign of Four* and *The Picture of Dorian Gray*:[14] though it is odd to find Watson whiling away the time over *La Vie de Boheme*, Holmes certainly is a recognizable bohemian, and belongs to the same aesthetic movement as Wilde. The qualities that Ian Ousby points to in his discussion of this question owe, as he himself admits, as much to Dupin as to the Decadents.[15] But with the title of *A Study in Scarlet* making direct reference to the world of art, and with Holmes himself more insistent than later on his profession as an art, this early Holmes is a figure to be associated with Bunthorne

and Grosvenor, or still more Wilde himself. One could certainly imagine
Holmes, entering the United States, having nothing to declare but his genius,
and his life illustrates Wilde's epigram, that to love oneself is the beginning
of a lifelong romance: Holmes and the Wildean persona (or poseur) share
a common overwhelming egotism with a touch of disarmingly boyish I-
don't-really-mean-it-you-know. Holmes's chief quality of decadence, of
course, is his addiction to cocaine, and even of this there is a broad hint
in Dupin. While this addiction is eventually phased out of the canon, and
is of course deeply tragic in reality, it is presented, despite Watson's air
of reproval, and perhaps because of the very pomposity of that reproval,
as a touch comic. "Why should you, for a mere passing pleasure, risk the
loss of those great powers with which you have been endowed?" sounds
rather like a father uneasily cautioning his son against the evils of
masturbation. And in the treatments of Holmes in legend and parody, the
cocaine addiction has frequently been seized upon as essentially funny. Mr.
Dooley, adopting the persona of the Great Detective, says to friend Hennessy,
"Pass th' dope, Watson."[15] The phrase "Quick, Watson, the needle!" seems
to have acquired an early, jokey currency in newspaper cartoons and
elsewhere, though used nowhere in the stories. It encapsulates the comic
nature of the addiction and is used as late as 1940 as the last line of the
most famous film version of *The Hound of the Baskervilles.* Doyle, however,
had already expressed the comedy of the situation, without foregoing
altogether its poignancy, in the last line of *The Sign of Four,* the novel
which both gives greatest emphasis to the addiction and is closest in spirit
to the Decadent movement: " 'For me,' " said Sherlock Holmes, "'there
still remains the cocaine-bottle.' And he stretched his long white hand up
for it" (158).

There is one final element in Sherlock Holmes himself which links
him with Decadence and Wilde (the long white hand almost suggests Aubrey
Beardsley!) and this is his aversion to women. Again, it is a trait so familiar
as to need no documentation here; Watson discusses it at greatest length
at the beginning of "A Scandal in Bohemia," within the context of the
detective's great respect for Irene Adler: women are the irrational element
which stands in the way of reason, the grit in the sensitive instrument. And
the canon rings with Holmes's depreciation and distrust of that sex which
he allows is Watson's department. "Women are never to be entirely trusted—
not the best of them," he says to a Watson in love in *The Sign of Four,*
a sentiment which Watson finds "atrocious" (129), but which he
characteristically does not try to rebut; again we see the comic fixity of the
two characters, with Holmes's instinctive and unbending misogyny set against
Watson's no less stereotypical conventional reaction.

Inevitably, over the forty years that Doyle (or Watson) annalised Holmes's activities, changes occurred in the character of the detective. The anecdote in Doyle's autobiography concerning Holmes's never being "quite the same man" after the Reichenbach Falls is a familiar one. One insistent note after the return is certainly that of self-parody. "The remarkable narrative" of the previous two years with which Holmes regales Watson is full of Holmesian comic self-aggrandizement, reflecting (no doubt) both Doyle's exasperation with this enforced resurrection and the increasingly comic presentation of Holmes; the tone is very different, obviously, from the one of reverence with which "The Final Problem" ends—"the best and wisest man whom I have ever known." In his own account, Holmes has "passed through Persia," communicating the results of "a short but interesting visit" with the Khalifa at Khartoum to the Foreign Office (There are intimations here of Mycroft, many of whose traits are comic underlinings of Sherlock's). He has spent some months "in a research into the coal-tar derivatives" in a laboratory in Montpelier; and he has "amused" himself with a visit to Lhassa and the head lama (The Sherlockians have spilt ink in querying the spelling: was this a man or an animal?).[17]

But the greatest note of self-parody lies in the references to cases unrecounted. Of some fifteen such references, only four occur before Reichenbach, and these are cited in the service of mystification and the aggrandizement of Holmes rather than of parody: "The new century will have come, however, before the story can safely be told." (447). The one pre-Reichenbach allusion which gives the details of an unreported case does so to highlight the formal problem—"Sherlock Holmes was able, by winding up the dead man's watch, to prove that it had been wound up two hours before, and that therefore the deceased had gone to bed before that time" (218). The later references, to the Giant Rat of Sumatra, "the repulsive story of the red leech" (607), "Wilson, the notorious canary-trainer" (559), and the two Coptic Patriarchs, are on a level of sensationalism and even absurdity which takes them into the realm of the comic. "I have Mr. Holmes's authority for saying," Watson begins "The Veiled Lodger," "that the whole story concerning the politician, the lighthouse, and the trained cormorant will be given to the public" (1095). Another case "worthy of note" begins "Thor Bridge:" "that of Isadora Persano, the well-known journalist and duellist, who was found stark staring mad with a match-box in front of him which contained a remarkable worm said to be unknown to science" (1055). This allusion, indeed, amplifies upon the self-parodic nature of such citations: the victim is, like Holmes himself as well as most of his great antagonists, a double man, leading a life of normality along with one of violence (Moriarty the professor and the Napoleon of crime); he is also well-known, invoking a world of privilege and high politics to which the reader and Watson are only partly privy; the irrational has invaded the everyday world in a seemingly banal way (madness in a match-box); and, once again, as in "The Speckled Band," or later in "The Lion's Mane," nature itself has given us a glimpse of its secrets before which the ultimate twentieth-century defence, science, is powerless. The case of Isadora Persano was one of Holmes's failures, though it is little wonder that these parodic sketches for stories never written have provided points of departure for later pastiches, in *The Exploits of Sherlock Holmes* and elsewhere.[18]

While these untold stories present us with tantalizing and potentially comic situations, in the canon itself there are relatively few cases which actually deliver comedy of situation, and then only momentarily: Holmes is enlisted as a witness at Irene Adler's wedding, Toby the bloodhound loses the creosote trail and returns to his starting point, Watson is caught out while posing as an expert in Chinese pottery. Of the sixty cases recorded, fewer than half—twenty-seven—deal with murder, and Holmes himself points out in "The Copper Beeches," the last story in the first collection, that four of the cases already recorded contained no crime at all (317). "A Case of Identity" and "The Noble Bachelor" are both comic in their conception and form, leading to the discomfiture rather than defeat of the clients, whose short sight or aristocratic hauteur makes them comic butts—the poor girl is defeated of her marital expectations, as the pompous lordling is of his. No murder is present to import a note of tragic seriousness; Holmes all but lays a whip across the shoulders of the wrongdoer in the first case, and lays a quite epicurean little supper for those who wronged Lord St. Simon in the second. In the only two cases in which Holmes loses a client to murder, "The Five Orange Pips" and "The Dancing Men," the elements of comedy and play are there, as both cases, especially the latter, begin with the semblance of a child's game, but are entirely superseded by the seriousness of the unfolding events.

If after Reichenbach, Holmes becomes more self-quizzical, Watson may become more philosophical, and he raises more than once the question of the intrusion of the comic into his records. In the earlier review which begins "The Speckled Band," he surveys the material before him—"many tragic, some comic, a large number merely strange, but none commonplace" (257). He begins the much later case of "The Three Garridebs" with a more sophisticated formulation: "It may have been a comedy, or it may have been a tragedy. It cost one man his reason, it cost me a blood-letting, and it cost yet another man the penalties of the law. Yet there was certainly an element of comedy. Well, you shall judge for yourselves" (1044). This story is a reworking of both "The Red-Headed League" and "The Stockbroker's Clerk:" a man is lured away from a particular place so that crime may be done there. In the first two cases the criminal activity is merely the robbing of a financial institution. In "The Three Garridebs" it is the recovery of a counterfeiter's printing press. While the criminal in the third case is the

most formidable of the three (he almost kills Watson), the situation he sets
up as the basis of his crime is the most comic. Hall Pycroft is lured by
career advancement, Jabez Wilson by the lucrative task—testifying comically
to his stupidity—of copying out the *Encyclopedia Britannica*. But Nathan
Garrideb is a much more absurd butt than either of these, goat-bearded,
peering, cadaverous, an indiscriminate but relentless collector—"Syracusan—
of the best period. . . . They degenerated greatly towards the end" (1048). His
attention to minutiae makes him comic, and we feel little sympathy even
when the loss of the fortune he was foolish enough to believe in sends him
mad at the end. The comic structure of the case—someone looking for a
person with the impossible name of Garrideb—insulates us from any feeling
of tragic apprehension and gives us a comic detachment which is more marked
than in "The Red-Headed League," where the robbery of "one of the principal
London banks" strikes at the heart of the established order, or "The
Stockbroker's clerk," where murder is actually done. Comedy is anarchic,
but the order premised in the canon cannot be endangered; in "The Three
Garridebs," it is not.

On the other hand, one notable story with all the elements of comedy
about it, in which murder does not loom, is given a serious turn by its
raising of the question so often raised in the canon of the irrationality
underlying a precariously stable civilization, the very duality which the
dualities of a Dupin or a Holmes hold in check. "The Creeping Man" is
"one of the very last cases handled by Holmes before his retirement from
practice" (1070-71), and concerns a middle-aged professor's taking of a
monkey gland treatment on the eve of his marriage to a much younger
woman. Pantaloon and Columbine are at least as old as the *commedia dell-
arte*. But Holmes "the dreamer" points the tale in the direction of a moral:
"When one tries to rise above Nature one is liable to fall below it. . . . There
is danger there—a real danger to humanity. . . . It would be the survival of
the least fit. What sort of cesspool may not our poor world become?" (1082-
83). But the moment passes, Holmes "the man of action" springs from his
chair, and he and Watson, with the note of comedy on which so many
of the stories end, and which is a study in itself, confirming the continuity
and the security associated with the pair, are off to tea at the Chequers.
"Cosy peril," the phrase Edmund Wilson attributes to Christopher Morley,[19]
aptly sums up this essentially comic feel of the whole canon.

There are, of the sixty cases, four not narrated by Watson: "His Last
Bow" and "The Mazarin Stone" are told in the third person, and "The
Blanched Soldier" and "The Lion's Mane" are told by Holmes. One of
the minor sources of comedy in the canon arises on those occasions when
Watson is charged by Holmes as his deputy—in "The Solitary Cyclist,"
The Hound of the Baskervilles, "Lady Frances Carfax," and "The Retired
Colourman," and is either allowed to remain unaware that Holmes is also

working on the case (as in *The Hound of the Baskervilles*), or is shown to have failed in his mission (as in "The Solitary Cyclist"). The comedy arises, as we have seen, from Holmes's caustic superiority and Watson's hurt, Holmes's acumen and Watson's obtuseness. But there is another element as well. When Watson disappears as narrator, or even as helper (and he mostly sits "long-suffering" in the chauffeur's seat in "His Last Bow," and plays the part of a messenger in "The Mazarin Stone"), Holmes is seen in the third person as a still more triumphant figure than Watson's customary surprise at this brilliance makes him, or in the first person as a rather less triumphant one. In the two third person stories he brings off *coups de theatre* which confound Von Bork and Count Sylvius; in his own narratives he is defeated by the deadly seaweed or a disease which appears to be leprosy. In either person, however—and none of these four cases gives us a murder, though "The Lion's Mane" gives us death without human agency—the structure of the tale is comic. The least comic of the four is no doubt "The Blanched Soldier," which is at basis about the contest between a man seeking information about his missing friend and the friend's father, who is bent on withholding it; though it raises the spectre of leprosy, it confirms its comic status by bestowing a lesser skin disease on the missing man. "His Last Bow" has the most serious of backdrops ("the most terrible August in the history of the world," 970), but is really concerned, as its somewhat diminishing title-metaphor suggests, with one last performance by these two fixed points in a changing age.

There is also, in these four stories, in the greater aggrandizement and diminution of Holmes, a further dimension to the comedy of his character, either dressed to look like Uncle Sam, or living in retirement with his bees. Lost without his Boswell and his meretricious finales, Holmes comes to be seen in perspective, comically, as both superhumanly powerful and humanly impotent. The one tendency is illustrated in "His Last Bow," as he enumerates the ways in which, since the episode of the King of Bohemia, he has thwarted a series of German designs ("It was I....It was I....It was I...."): "Von Bork sat up in amazement. 'There is only one man,' he cried. 'Exactly,' said Holmes." (979). The other tendency is illustrated in "The Lion's Mane," in his plaint for the missing Watson: "Ah! had he but been with me, how much he might have made of so wonderful a happening and of my eventual triumph against every difficulty!" (1083). In fact, Holmes is "culpably slow" in "The Lion's Mane," and the case is one of his failures, nearly avenging, as he says, Scotland Yard. But these four stories, almost standing outside the canon, and certainly ranking low in any reader's qualitative judgment of the sixty, give us the real Holmes, not triumphing against every difficulty, and not free of a certain amount of posturing ("The Mazarin Stone," as we have seen, ends with one of his theatrical gestures), and in this double view of Holmes is a comedy which, epitomized here, is evident throughout the canon.

Finally, it may be illuminating to look at the stories as representing certain archetypal characteristics of comedy. Northrop Frye has pointed to the game-playing which is intrinsic to detective fiction,[20] which is what saves it, he asserts, from being a *practical* blueprint, as it is already a theoretical one, for the police state. Though Frye is talking of later detective fiction, it seems clear that Holmes, representing established British Victorian order, which Edmund Wilson seems to have seen as his especial value,[21] represents as well, despite his bohemianism and his frequent taking of the law into his own hands, conservative, even conventional, social values. To extend Frye's terms,[22] Holmes is the *eiron* who in most cases is fully aware, fully in control and who puts matters right at the end. But he is also, in some sense, since I have insisted on seeing him as a dual figure, the *alazon*, the pretender: he does know most of what is to be known, he does, not always with total sincerity, deprecate his own performance, and he does aggrandize himself. And no less is Watson a dual figure. He is plainly an *alazon* (coming into our ken from Afghanistan, he might even be seen as a *miles gloriosus*, for a time!), so often the dupe of Holmes and the facts, though not an *alazon* in the sense that Holmes the posturer is. Watson is even an *eiron* in his knowledge of his own limitations, if not in an ultimate Holmesian potency of knowledge. The *eiron and alazon*, of course, are inhabitants of ironic comedy, which is where Frye places detective fiction, and where, too, he places the third character type of the *pharmakos*, or scapegoat. It seems clear that, besides the two central, dual figures, there is a whole succession, within the chronicles, of *alazons* and, more importantly, of *pharmikos*.

The succession of *alazons* is represented in the very first short story by the King of Bohemia, who is indeed (in Holmes's estimation, in a different sense from his own) "on a very different level" from Irene Adler, and whose extended hand Holmes ignores at the end of the story. For Holmes, a classless figure, the King is the first of many in high place whom the detective puts in their proper place, making them the butt of either his wit or his censoriousness. When Lord St. Simon condescends to him by assuming that his clients are rarely of his class, Holmes rejoins, "No, I am descending" (291); when the Duke of Holdernesse is found to be implicated in the kidnapping of his heir from the Priory School, Holmes lectures the proud nobleman in his own hall. It is curious that several of these characters, whose fall from dignity is satisfying to the reader as well as confirmatory of Holmes's power as *eiron* over the *alazons*, show their family likeness in their names: Hohenzollern, Holdernesse, Holdhurst, Holder.

But the villains whom Holmes must face, the Napoleons of crime, are altogether more formidable. As Ronald Knox has said, "they do the cleverest thing a criminal could probably do in the given circumstances," but Holmes is still too clever for them. These villains are not viewed with unequivocal lack of sympathy: like Holmes himself, who says frequently that he could have been a great criminal, they could have turned their great powers to good. Moriarty and Moran, again with the kinship suggested by the similarity of name, are clearly *pharmikos* in the sense of *scoundrel*, but also in the sense of being scapegoats for the society. Yet again we have a point that need hardly be labored: these villains are all doubles, alter egos, of Holmes, the great upholder of the law who might have been a criminal, and his purging of society of these villains is premised on his projection of his dark side on to them. There is, after all, an absolute rightness about the chronicles coming to their appointed end with Holmes and Moriarty, locked in each other's arms, perishing at Reichenbach. And while Von Bork, Charles Augustus Milverton, Baron Gruner and Count Sylvius are, in rough descending order of greatness, lesser beings, they belong to the same family, representing the guilt of a society which Holmes, in purging them, purges of that guilt. In five of the six cases, (Moran being the exception), Holmes levies his own justice on the villain, or else watches while, with pistol or with vitriol bottle, it is done.

If all this sounds less then comic, still less actually funny, it is all part of a corpus of sixty stories which scrutinize ironically, with a good deal of wit, a pervasive sense of the game being afoot, and a large sense of fun, a society reared upon reason but not always proof against the attacks of the irrational. As Edmund Wilson says, "no matter what those queer Greeks do in London, there will always be a British porter and he will always help you to get your train." There are the parameters, and much of the comedy of the chronicles lies in the wry recognition that life goes on, reason prevails, despite strange whistles in the night, or dogs who do not bark, or professors who climb vine-wreathed walls, or mysterious powders which drive sanity from those who inhale them. We may laugh that we have escaped such horrors. But always our guide in escaping them is himself both queer Greek and British railway porter, both dreamer ("We reach. We grasp") and man of action and reason ("Come, Watson, come!... The game is afoot").

A Final Note

At the risk of myself becoming like one of those popular tenors still tempted to make repeated farewell bows before their indulgent audiences, I cannot end this essay without some reference to the remarkable number of parodies, pastiches and homages which the Sherlock Holmes stories have engendered over the years, and which show few signs of diminishing. As I have noted, many of Watson's passing, wry, even "pawky" (the word Christopher Morley aptly applies) allusions to the unreported cases have been used as hints for fuller treatments. And while Holmes has encountered in these treatments almost all his contemporaries, from Freud through Jack

the Ripper to Theodore Roosevelt, he himself, from Robert Barr's Sherlaw
Kombs to Robert L. Fish's Schlock Homes, has been the direct object of
the parody. Writers as diverse as Mark Twain and Agatha Christie[23] have
ridiculed the great detective, with varying degrees of affection, but even in
one of the least sympathetic of his parodists, Mark Twain, there is a glimpse
of the sincerest form of flattery, for *Tom Sawyer, Detective* and, most notably,
Pudd'nhead Wilson belong to the genre which Doyle made one of the most
popular of all time.

Why this flurry of parody and extrapolation? Generally parody seeks
out the serious subject, especially the pompous, and magnifies what it sees
as absurd or self-important, inflates what it sees as trivial. Chaucer's *Sir
Thopas*, Max Beerbobm's impaling of Henry James in "The Mote in the
Middle Distance," John Fowles's guying of the Victorian novel in *The French
Lieutenant's Woman*, all have serious butts. At first sight, comedy is not
the obvious object of parody; and I have written in vain if by now my
reader has not accepted the presence of at least some comedy in the canon.

John Fowles's explanation, coming from a distinguished toyer with
genres, is an enticing one:

> The danger of Conan Doyle's method is caricature, which is properly a weapon
> of humour or satire. That is why Holmes and Watson have been endlessly parodied,
> have been sent up in both senses—into the Pantheon of national archetypes as well
> as by countless teams of professional comedians...it is not just that he Holmes is
> too clever to be true, but rather that he is too true to pure caricature to be "clever"
> by the highest literary standards....In the Sherlock Holmes stories caricature becomes
> the end; it is not related to any significant truth or human folly."[24]

If Holmes and Watson do not belong in the highest literary circles,
we might ask Leslie Fiedler's question, "What Was Literature?,"[25] to discover
why. The Sherlock Holmes chronicles have something of the quality,
something of the life of their own, of *Uncle Tom's Cabin*, a book Fiedler
has sought to redeem from the strictures of those dons who dismiss it as
written for an imperfectly educated mass audience and lacking in the "tragic
ambiguity" of the acknowledged great works of literature. As we have seen
here, however, the Holmes Saga is fundamentally comic rather than tragic,
and the solutions that Holmes imposes dispel, as far as can be, the ambiguities.
But the parodies and the sequels, the sense that Holmes and Watson were
real people, who still receive notes from correspondents seeking advice, testify,
as similar considerations testify to Uncle Tom's, to their humanity. As Fowles
noted, and he might have stopped short at this point, they are both revered
and affectionately rallied. And as Doyle had hoped, they have their less than
humble corner in the same Valhalla where Fielding's beaux, Scott's heroes,
and Dickens's delightful cockneys exist. *That* was Literature.

Notes

[1]The 56 short and four long stories in which Sherlock Holmes and Doctor Watson appear are so well known by title that I do not list them here. But because of that very familiarity, I have also refrained from abbreviating those sacrosanct titles in the text of the essay.

All references to the Saga, the Chronicles, the Sacred Writings, the Canon, the Conan, are to *The Penguin Complete Sherlock Holmes* (reprint of Christopher Morley's edition for Doubleday in 1930), Penguin Books, 1981.

[2]While my formulations in this essay are indebted to a wide variety of commentators on the comic, from Aristotle on, I would cite especially Henri Bergson, *Laughter* (edited by Wylie Sypher for Doubleday Anchor Books, 1956, and bound in with George Meredith's *An Essay on Comedy*); Northrop Frye, *Anatomy of Criticism* (Princeton University Press, 1957); and Elder Olson, *The Theory of Comedy* (Bloomington: Indiana University Press, 1968).

[3]*Laughter*, especially Chapter Two.

[4]This essay is most readily accessible in *Profile by Gaslight* (New York: Simon and Schuster, 1944), ed. Edgar W. Smith, pp. 156-165.

[5]See Arthur Conan Doyle, *Memories and Adventures* (London: Hodder and Stoughton, 1924), pp. 102-106. See also Dorothy Sayers' remarks, quoted in *The Annotated Sherlock Holmes*, 2 vols (New York: Potter, 1967), I, 68.

[6]Act IV, Scene v.

[7]I have heard by reliable word of mouth that this film was originally much longer, and did indeed present Holmes and Watson as a homoerotic couple.

[8]"Studies in Sherlock Holmes," *Essays in Satire* (New York: Dutton, 1930), p. 163.

[9]See *Memories and Adventures*, pp. 74-75, where the first name is given as "*Sherringford* Holmes." The best discussion of the naming of *Sherlock Holmes* is contained in *The Annotated Sherlock Holmes*, I, 9-10.

[10]"The Simple Art of Murder," in *The Simple Art of Murder* (London: Hamish Hamilton, 1950), p. 321.

[11]"Holmesian Humour," *The Sherlock Holmes Journal*, 6, 4 (Spring, 1964), 109-113.

[12]"Studies in Sherlock Holmes," p. 175.

[13]It was the same Lecoq and Dupin who are cited by Doyle himself as the principal fictional models for Holmes (*Memories and Adventures*, p. 74).

[14]*Memories and Adventures*, p. 79.

[15]*The Bloodhounds of Heaven* (Cambridge: Harvard University Press, 1976), p. 142.

[16]See Edward Lauterbach, "Our Heroes in Motley," *The Armchair Detective*, 9.3 (June, 1976), 178-179; also George F. McCleary M.D., "Was Sherlock Holmes a Drug Addict?," in *Profile by Gaslight*, pp. 40-46.

[17] *The Annotated Sherlock Holmes*, II, 320-321. In the words of Ogden Nash: "The one-l lama/ He's a priest./ The two-l llama,/ He's a beast."

[18]*The Exploits*, by John Dickson Carr and Doyle's son Adrian, remains amongst the very best of the pastiches (London: John Murray, 1954).

[19]"Mr. Holmes, They Were the Footprints of a Gigantic Hound!," in *Classics and Commercials* (New York: Farrar, Straus, 1950), p. 273.

[20]*Anatomy of Criticism*, pp. 46-47.

[21]*Classics and Commercials*, p. 273.

[22]*Anatomy of Criticism*, pp. 39-42, and *passim*.

[23]Mark Twain's parody is *A Double-Barrelled Detective Story* (New York: Harper's, 1902). Agatha Christie's parody is Chapter 9, "The Case of the Missing Lady," of *Partners in Crime* (London: Collins, 1929), in which novel Tommy and Tuppence Beresford act out the adventures of most of the prominent detectives of her day and before.

[24]"Afterword," *The Hound of the Baskervilles* (London: Murray and Cape, 1974), pp. 190-191.

[25]*What Was Literature?* (New York: Simon and Schuster, 1982).

The Comic Capers of
Donald Westlake

Michael Dunne

Donald E. Westlake is the author of nearly sixty books published under three names: his own, Tucker Coe, and Richard Stark. Although this impressive publishing output includes, to date, a western, a juvenile, some reportage, and several books unclassifiable except as "just plain novels," Westlake's principal success has been derived from his novels about crime. Reviewers in publications as various as the *New York Times Book Review*, the *New Republic*, and the *National Review* have testified glowingly to Westlake's talent and achievement in these crime novels. The critical consensus has broadened, moreover, in recognizing two, discrete, creative forces in the author. Westlake has been praised at times for his hard-boiled, uncompromising depictions of the corruption and violence that underlie what passes for contemporary American civilization. At other times he has been praised equally as the creator of a comic fictional world energized alternately by irony and farce.

A likely inference might be that Westlake and his career have been "schizophrenic," a suggestion that he considers with mock-seriousness in the autobiographical introduction to *Levine*, a collection of related stories published in 1984. Westlake explains there that the split in his artistic energies arose in the period from 1963 to 1965 when he was producing thrillers under the name Richard Stark for Pocket Books at the same time he was writing comic novels for Random House as Donald E. Westlake. Eventually this paperback enterprise exhausted both itself and Westlake in the early Seventies, an unsurprising development since Westlake also moonlighted during part of that era by producing five serious crime novels for Random House, written under the pseudonym Tucker Coe.

A sampling of titles from all three authorial avatars should suggest Westlake's place in the mainstream of American crime fiction: *Killing Time, Murder Among Children, The Man With the Getaway Face, Butcher's Moon*, and so forth. The earliest of these thrillers earned

Westlake his first literary reputation in the early Sixties as a promising successor to Dashiell Hammett and Raymond Chandler. Westlake's later work in this field won him a place in John Cawelti's *Adventure, Mystery, and Romance* as the representative practitioner of the "enforcer" mode of thriller. The honor is deserved. Westlake's protagonist Parker, the creation of Richard Stark, is so efficient and tough that he doesn't even have a first name. He makes Rambo look like a pussycat.

Other of Westlake's crime novels, all published under his own name, have been called by various reviewers, "criminous farce-comedies," "engaging fancies," and "a Geo. Price cartoon in prose."[1] In the preliminary pages of *Why Me* (1983), Westlake's publisher classifies these books as "Comic Crime Novels," a category recently augmented by *High Adventure* (1985). This listing further distinguishes five of these comedies as belonging to a sub-category, "The Dortmunder Series," a group that Westlake promises to increase with *Good Behavior* in 1986. Surely these books, most particularly the Dortmunder Series, constitute Westlake's chief contribution both to the literature of crime and to the treasury of American humor.[2]

These novels are, first of all, funny because Westlake cannot resist a joke, large or small. For example, in *Help I Am Being Held Prisoner* (1974), the protagonist is named Harry Künt, "with an umlaut," as he futilely protests to his fellow convicts. All his life such linguistically naive folk have mispronounced Harry's last name, bathing him in humiliation and turning him into the sort of misanthropic practical joker who would place an inflatable naked woman atop an abandoned vehicle beside a busy New York freeway just to see what will happen. Because two participants in the ensuing traffic pileup turn out to be Senators joyriding with females other than their wives, Harry Künt ends up in prison where, it is hoped, he will learn his lesson and reform. The warden believes that Harry has persisted in his evil ways, however, because of the activities of another incarcerated practical joker who keeps planting messages saying, "Help, I am being held prisoner!" After many close brushes with violence and assorted farcical misadventures, everything turns out happily for Harry when he and the warden discover who the prankster has been all along: "Butler did it" (270). Although the principal comic effects in this novel depend on the design of a plot involving a secret exit from prison, a complicated bank robbery, and the structural irony of a joker's being victimized by another joker, the small jokes derived from the characters' names testify just as clearly to Westlake's comic vision. Here is an author who will take his jokes where he finds them.

Local effects on the order of these nominal puns function in all of Westlake's crime novels to heighten the comedic impact of his plots. *The Busy Body* (1966) offers a representative instance. The overall design in this novel is as bizarre and macabre as Westlake's epigraph from Charles Lamb portends: "Anything awful makes me laugh. I misbehaved once at a funeral." Without following all the twists of the tale, suffice it to say that the hero, Aloysius Engel, finds himself at one point commanded by mobster Nick Rovito to dig up the body of the late Charlie Brody, a narcotics courier, in hopes of recovering some heroin that may have been concealed in the jacket of the suit in which Charlie was buried. If successful, Engel is then to kill his assistant, Willy Menchik, and bury his body in the same grave. All these complications are necessary to the structure of deception, confusion, and farce that Westlake has planned for his novel, but there is a danger that the immediate effect of these grisly events will be horror rather than amusement. Westlake averts this danger by emphasizing the ordinariness of the protagonist and thereby underscoring the comic disparity between his personality and his current mission. In a particularly effective passage the narrator explains Engel's relief that the heroin is concealed in the corpse's jacket rather than his trousers so that he will not have to stoop to the unseemly act of removing a dead man's pants. The reader is similarly relieved and subsequently amused when the crime boss expresses his shock that Engel could even contemplate such an order. Narcotics traffic and murder may be necessary evils, but Nick Rovito draws the line at indecency, as he explains indignantly to Engel: "Whadaya think, kid? It was going to be something in bad taste, I wouldn't even ask, am I right?" (25). Horror is thus dissipated by laughter. Clearly, such small jokes are not mere ornamentation, but functional elements of Westlake's art.

Jokes of this sort serve still another purpose, related to narrative tone. When Westlake confines his fictional point of view to the consciousness of a single character, as he does in *The Fugitive Pigeon* (1965) and *Two Much* (1975), any humorous observations in the novel serve as elements of characterization, deepening our understanding of Charlie Poole in the earlier novel and Art/Bart Dodge in the latter. That is to say, Charlie appeals to the reader not only in his innocent victimization, but also in his jaunty humor. He is a nice fellow, take it any way around, and so deserves to outwit whoever is trying to kill him. Even the loathesome Dodge is somewhat redeemed by his witty indictments of the beautiful people. The reader concludes that if Dodge can see through social posturing with such incisive humor, he cannot be as bad as his homicidal behavior makes him seem.

On the other hand, when Westlake permits himself to shift his narrative focus from character to character, as he does in *High Adventure* and *Nobody's Perfect* (1977), the impact of local comic effects is subtly different. In the case of the more recent novel, the reader decides, on the basis of their wry perceptions, that Kirby Galway and Innocent St. Michael are witty and appealing characters. It is inevitable, however, that the reader will decide further that the voice containing and absorbing their voices is more witty still. Thus, while Westlake's ventriloquial narrative generously distributes the jokes among two or three characters, the reader recognizes back there somewhere the stronger accent of the author and the comic vision that gives it life.

Two examples from *Nobody's Perfect* will clarify this point. In the first, Ian Macdough, a scheming Scottish laird, recalls that his benefactress, Aunt Fiona, died "as mad as an African general and as incontinent as Atlantis" (173). Macdough's venality and lack of familial piety emerge clearly in this reflection, but the reader cannot fail to detect also the note of authorial humor. The joke, that is, may be consistent with Macdough's character, but it is, in another sense, too good for him. The same is true of another and better piece of local humor. Earlier in the novel, an equally corrupt character named Arnold Chauncey reflects on the many despicable means by which he has financed his sybaritic life. One scam was to steal all the royalties of Heavy Leather, a rock band he once managed. Chauncey recalls, "He hadn't *wanted* to steal those benighted Glaswegians' money, but at the time it had seemed that his need was greater than theirs; certainly his arithmetic was" (52-3). Once again the reader will accept the financial dishonesty and moral rationalization apparent in the reflection to be perfectly suited to Chauncey's character, but once again the reader will also assume the hand of the master behind it all. Chauncey is simply not as funny as this remark is. Through local comic effects of this sort, Westlake simultaneously develops his characters and legitimizes his authorial voice. Initiated by the jokes liberally bestowed on hero and villain alike, the reader quickly recognizes that Westlake's fundamental intention in these novels is comic and, thus reassured, may sit back in smiling anticipation of ultimately happy events to come.

Nowhere is Westlake's authorial voice more consistently and richly comic than in the series of novels dealing with the Dortmunder gang. The members of this amorphous group, at one time or another, are John Archibald Dortmunder, the mastermind responsible for the gang's intricate capers; his chain-smoking paramour May, who doubles as a checker at a Bohack's supermarket; Andy Kelp, an incurable optimist who prefers to steal only doctors' cars because they are so luxuriously appointed, but who is considered an incurable jinx by Dortmunder; Stan

Murch, an inspired getaway-car driver, whose only topic of conversation is the quickest way to get from point A to point B and every road involved in getting there; Murch's Mom, a bitter, unillusioned New York taxi driver; Roger Chefwick, a mousy lock man and safe cracker whose hobby, playing with trains, is more nearly a manic compulsion; and Tiny Bulcher, sometimes called "the beast from forty fathoms," a monster leg-breaker and strong-arm man whose favorite cocktail is vodka and red wine. Throughout a series of incredibly varied, ingeniously devised robberies and one kidnapping—Byzantine in its complexity—these miscreants succeed at crime only to fail, fail only to succeed, and illustrate along the way the depth and brilliance of Westlake's comic imagination.

First of all, the texture of these novels is richly laced with small comic elements testifying to Westlake's satiric perceptions of contemporary life. (Let us recall that Westlake first perceived whatever Art/Bart Dodge later observes.) In *Jimmy the Kid* (1974), for example, Dortmunder's self-concept is shaken because the gang's plan to kidnap a rich child named Jimmy Harrington has been derived from *Child Heist*, a thriller written by Richard Stark, rather than from Dortmunder's teeming brain. May tries to restore his image by summarizing a magazine article she read about French film directors. Even though the script might come from Stark's book, she argues, it would be Dortmunder's fine-tuning that would distinguish the caper from an ordinary crime: "The point was, you could be the aw-tour on the kidnapping idea. Like a movie director" (40). May's rationale pacifies Dortmunder, as if he were a character in a Woody Allen movie rather than in a crime novel.

Another trendy topic arises as the gang discusses each member's role in the upcoming caper. Murch's Mom objects to the plan in a speech worthy of Phil Donahue: "I suppose you'd want May and me to take care of this brat, like the women in the book....That's very sexist....Wanting May and me to take care of the kid. Role-assumption. It's sexist." Murch responds, "Goddamit, Mom,...you've been off with those consciousness-raising ladies again" (33). The reader gathers with amusement that even criminals are afflicted by the faddishness and psychobabble clogging the popular media.

It is unsurprising that the vocabulary of the "glossy mags" has corrupted even the Murches, since in the Dortmunder novels the fabric of American culture is continually revealed as shot through with mindless sloganeering better suited to hiding the truth than to revealing it. In *Nobody's Perfect*, for example, Westlake exploits the plot device of a news item's appearing in the New York *Post* to make a satiric point. His narrator observes that the item is printed "in the section that in the unenlightened past was known as the Woman's Page, but which today operates under a discreet anonymity, offering Fashion, Society

Notes, and Recipes to an audience presumably no more than fifty-two percent female" (65). Small satiric barbs of this sort are evenhandedly distributed along gender lines in Westlake's fiction, and so to balance the scales one might consider the narrator's reflection about jolly times at the Officers' Club in *Help I Am Being Held Prisoner:* "There's nothing like a joke about homosexuality to make men rub each other's shoulders" (119). The view of society determining such narrative commentary, within and without the Dortmunder series, is satiric in its identification of intellectual and sexual foolishness, but it is basically comic also in that it allows all manner of harmless absurdities to proliferate for the reader's amusement. Thus, as in the case of the local elements discussed earlier, Westlake can at the same time develop his comedic relation with the reader while advancing his plot or elaborating his setting.

That Westlake is more a benevolent humorist than a bitter satirist is evident in the fact that he is willing to make fun of himself as well as of societal dysfunctions. Recall that in *Jimmy the Kid* Westlake makes his alter ego Richard Stark the author of *Child Heist*, a thriller that Andy Kelp stumbles across while in jail upstate. Through this device Westlake suggests that Stark's fiction is most likely to appeal to a lamebrain like Kelp. This self-reflexive irony is compounded when Kelp explains the book's attractions to Murch. He says that the novel is about "a crook named Parker. He'll remind you of Dortmunder" (22). As is probable in an absurd analogy, the tough, two-fisted, always competent Parker is demoted toward the ridiculous as much as Dortmunder is elevated toward the heroic. In the process, the conventions of the thriller are challenged for the reader's amusement. Westlake even writes chapters 7, 12, and 21 of *Jimmy* in the style of Richard Stark. Finally, in a coda to Westlake's novel, Stark is informed by his lawyer that he cannot sue Jimmy Harrington for producing *Kid Stuff*, a wildly successful film based on his experiences as the kidnap victim. The self-allusive joke grows very complex indeed.

Another form of self-reference is Westlake's practice of subtly alluding to his other novels through the use of recurring devices. For example, in novel after novel the narrator explains that although May is a chain-smoker, she cannot light one cigarette from another because she always smokes them down to a stub too small to handle. The detail in itself is no more than mildly amusing. Repetition from book to book increases the humor incrementally, however—very likely because it can draw increasingly on the experienced reader's anticipation.

The same is true for Westlake's descriptions of the O.J. Bar and Grill on Amsterdam Avenue, the usual setting for the gang's business meetings. For one thing, the regular patrons of the O. J. are always deeply engaged in some form of barroom philosophy as Dortmunder enters: the etymology of the word "spic" for example, or the relative merits of public and private schools, or the proper first aid for nosebleed. When farcical fisticuffs follow, as they usually do, the criminals never participate, only the law-abiding customers. Rollo the bartender, who breaks up these fights, never remembers his customers by name, only by drink preference. Murch is always "the beer with salt;" Tiny, "the vodka with red wine;" Dortmunder, "the bourbon." Even this drink is a source of incremental humor, always the same rotgut, "Amsterdam Liquor Store Bourbon," and Westlake always notes the slogan on the label: "Our Own Brand." These drinks are always served in the back room, at a table overhung by a naked light, in a small clear space surrounded by liquor boxes piled up to the ceiling. The path to this back room always takes Dortmunder past the restrooms labeled "Pointers" and "Setters."

The unvarying repetition of these devices might be seen to illustrate the intersection of the mechanical and the human that Henri Bergson proposed as the source of humor. Such regularity suggests also the humours and ruling passions that governed comic characterization in classical and neo-classical literature. May's constant smoking, Kelp's incurable optimism, Murch's compulsive recounting of routes, detours, minutes, and miles clearly derive from the tradition of characterization practiced by Plautus, Terence, Ben Jonson, and Alexander Pope. The practice should not be confused with mere stereotyping. It is more properly a mode of symbolic characterization in which a salient habit or attitude serves as a short-hand representation of the whole character and his function.

In *Nobody's Perfect*, for example, Westlake brilliantly encapsulates the personality of Kelp's nephew Victor when Dortmunder recalls why Victor is no longer an FBI agent: "They threw him out...because he kept putting a suggestion in the FBI suggestion box that they oughta have a secret hand-shake, so they'd be able to recognize each other at parties" (103). It is unsurprising, in the light of this habit, that Victor is responsible for introducing Dortmunder and Kelp to Griswold Porculey, the art forger, a man equally in thrall to his compulsions. We see another example of Westlake's comically acute characterization when Kelp recounts Porculey's previous criminal experience as the handpainter of counterfeit twenty-dollar bills. Kelp explains that "it turned out he was spending five hours just to do one side of one bill. You know, those twenties, they're all full of tricky little stuff" (104). Even Kelp perceives that two dollars per hour is poor recompense for such devoted counterfeiting. Dortmunder agrees: "Crime doesn't pay....I'm gradually coming to that conclusion" (105). By thus embedding these humours and ruling passions in his characters, Westlake practices a mode of comedy long sanctioned by literary tradition.

Dortmunder's melancholy reflection that crime does not pay illustrates another of Westlake's comic devices, the domestication of his criminals. These felons, especially in the Dortmunder series, are not Little Caesars or Scarfaces reveling in gross and luxurious debauchery. Usually they are just scraping by, realizing not much more financial return on their investment of dishonest energy than the hapless Porculey. Dortmunder agrees to the kidnapping of Jimmy Harrington, for example, because they have been living for months solely on May's salary from Bohack's, and he feels he has not been pulling his weight. In *Nobody's Perfect*, Dortmunder is shocked to learn while Christmas shopping that a bottle of perfume for May will cost $27.50, but he is willing to shell out this substantial portion of his dwindling resources because he thinks that it is wrong to "boost" a Christmas present. In a more extended illustration, as May nervously awaits Dortmunder's return from a b. & e. (breaking and entering) at 3:45 a.m., she is the epitome of proletarian domesticity:

May had put together a special dinner, all of Dortmunder's favorites: Salisbury steak, steamed green beans, whipped potatoes from a mix, enriched white bread, beer in the can, and boysenberry Jell-O for dessert. On the table were lined up the ketchup, the A-1 sauce, the Worcestershire sauce, the salt and pepper and sugar, the margarine, and the can of evaporated milk. (*Jimmy*, 35)

Such details operate, as Aloysius Engel's squeamishness does in *The Busy Body*, to ally the reader with the "perpetrators" rather than the pillars of society. Along the same line, Kelp has a soft spot in his heart for his unsuccessful nephew Victor and tries to get him started in the crime business. Murch and his Mom spend many happy evenings together by the stereo listening to recordings of the Indianapolis 500 auto race. Chefwick's wife is usually baking a fattening dessert in the kitchen while he is down in the basement, playing with his trains and plotting how to gain entrance to a bank vault. In such domestic circumstances, the reader's imagination can closely approach the condition of these criminals. In consequence, Westlake produces the smiling comedy of recognition as effectively as the laughing comedy of social satire.

That this should be so is, of course, another irony. Westlake's characters outside the law appeal to us because they are fumbling mortals, recognizably like ourselves. They therefore challenge and ultimately overturn our social and moral assumptions about the sorts of persons who commit crimes. The surprise thus occasioned by overturned assumptions is one of the most effective of all sources of humor, as we have known since Aristotle connected humor and incongruity in the *Poetics*. This last form of humor is also the most fundamental to Westlake's Dortmunder series since it inheres not merely in the novels' local texture or characterizations but in the plots and in Westlake's overall intentions.

All the novels of the Dortmunder series—and several others such as *Who Stole Sassi Manoon?* (1968)—are structurally based on elaborate capers. Westlake's criminals accept these enterprises as necessary conditions of felonious existence. Dortmunder and Kelp, for example, consistently call crimes as unlike as kidnapping and jewel theft "capers." When Harry Künt goes on a double-date during one of his vacations from prison, the foursome quite naturally attend a "caper movie" (*Help*, 100). For the non-criminal classes, however, it might be helpful to consult John Cawelti's *Adventure, Mystery, and Romance* for a definition of this phenomenon. Cawelti writes, "The caper is a special sort of action in which an individual or a group undertakes a particularly difficult feat that can only be accomplished through a stratagem of considerable subtlety and complexity."[3] Cawelti proposes Homer as the creator of the first caper: convincing the Trojans to admit a wooden horse crammed with enemy soldiers into their supposedly impregnable fortress. He suggests further that in modern times the caper seems particularly well suited to presentation through the visual media. Readers of a certain age will surely respond to this suggestion with pleasant memories of the Impossible Mission Force consuming costly minutes of prime-time television to show us a socket wrench slowly and silently turning a chrome nut. The pleasure there, and in all capers, surely derives first from the viewer's or reader's rapt contemplation of the minutiae of the design and then from his accustomed anticipation that the plan and its execution will dovetail with happy congruence.

Surely Dortmunder, the criminal mastermind, would applaud Cawelti's phrase, "stratagem of considerable subtlety and complexity." In fact, he does so in *Nobody's Perfect* while the gang celebrates the completion of a particularly sophisticated caper: successfully arranging for a bogus robbery to steal $100,000 and a counterfeit painting from Arnold Chauncey, the unprincipled villain who hired the gang to steal the real painting from him in order to defraud his insurance company. Dortmunder is unusually mellow on this occasion: "All Dortmunder could say was, it was the best worked-out goddam plan *he'd* ever seen in his life" (151). In this caper, everything works as perfectly as it might have done on *Mission Impossible*. Dortmunder and the reader are therefore surprised—and only the reader is amused—when Chauncey and Leo Zane, a hired killer, show up in the next chapter, eventually forcing Dortmunder and Kelp to accompany them to London to resteal the real painting or possibly a forgery—from the best-guarded auction house in the world. In such turns of event lies the key to Westlake's success and the motivation to preface the term "caper" with "comic" when applying it to his works. Westlake's ingenious design in these books is to have his characters develop an incredibly complex caper, to execute it conscientiously, and then to watch helplessly as it all goes to pieces. Westlake's reader is equally frustrated and can only respond with amazed laughter as all his expectations of logical consequences are replaced by comic incongruities.

The meticulous care with which Westlake builds these logical expectations surely accounts for much of his comic success. An extended example from *Help I Am Being Held Prisoner* should serve to clarify the point. In these paragraphs, Harry Künt contemplates the double bank robbery caper that he and his fellow prisoners hope to pull off during one of their elopements from jail:

> There were so many elements to the thing. Either some way had to be found to borrow a truck from Twin Cities Typewriter on the afternoon of the robbery, or some other Ford Econoline van would have to be stolen and stored and repainted with Twin Cities' name and colors. A uniform had to be found for Eddie Troyn to match the uniforms worn by the bank guards. The names and addresses and home phone numbers of the late-staying bank employees had to be learned, to cut down the possibility of a doublecross—a teller, for instance, phoning police headquarters rather than his wife. A typewriter had to be picked up somewhere for delivery to the bank, and it had to be the same color and make as all the other typewriters used there.
>
> Then there was the laser. That was another entire robbery in itself, as major in its own way as the bank job. And, in fact, even more frightening; forcing entry into a bank began to seem like kid stuff in comparison with breaking into an Army storage depot patrolled by rifle-toting soldiers. So Camp Quattatunk had to be cased, more uniforms had to be obtained, the specific location of the laser had to be determined, a getaway vehicle had to be provided for, and a complete game plan had to be organized. (106)

Incredibly enough, each of the difficulties is surmounted, the Army camp is robbed, the equipment is secured, the necessary precautions are taken, and the bank robberies go forward. Of course, not everything turns out exactly as planned, but the complexity of the operation must impress us even so.

In *Who Stole Sassi Manoon?* Robby Creswel comments on a caper that displays similar ingenuity: "We want to kidnap Sassi Manoon, right? So what do we do? We steal a car. Then we bounce a forged check. Then we kidnap two men and steal their truck. We steal a Persian carpet. Before this is over, about the only thing we won't have done is spit on the sidewalk" (90). The note of irritation creeping into Creswel's meditation is occasioned by his feeling that some capers are just too clever for his, or anyone's, good. The aggravating circumstance in this case is the fact that a computer called STARNAP has designed the caper, thus supposedly eliminating the chance of human error and the frustrations that bedevil Künt and his associates. The master of the computer is Kelly Bram Nichols IV, about whom we read, shortly after Creswel's pout, "He felt good. Starnap had worked everything out, everything down to the smallest detail, with the kind of precision and attention to minutiae that only a machine could give to the task. And the precision paid off" (101). In this passage Westlake seems at first to have allowed STARNAP's design to reach its logical and inhuman fulfillment. The reader soon learns, however, that the brilliant caper has succeeded in kidnapping not the gorgeous and wealthy starlet, Sassi Manoon, but rather Adelaide Ashby, an elderly British crook.

All the capers in the Dortmunder series involve similarly egregious mismatches of cause and effect, planning and execution. In *Jimmy the Kid*, for example, after the gang ingeniously hijacks the limousine carrying their kidnap victim, they discover that it is too wide to drive into the back of the truck they have stolen for just that purpose. Later they get lost while sensibly trying to lay a confusing trail for the police. One of the many art thefts in *Nobody's Perfect* is necessitated because the rolled up Veenbes painting, *Folly Leads Man to Ruin*, gets mislaid during a riot created by a mob of kilted Scotsmen overexcited by a concert of bagpipe music. In *The Hot Rock* (1970), the gang must break into the city jail, after breaking into the state prison, because Alan Greenwood cleverly concealed a stolen emerald in the jail while awaiting transport to the big house; however, he neglected to tell any of the other gang members about his cleverness. Since the emerald turns out not to be in the jail cell after all, the gang must then break into an insane asylum. And so it goes in caper after caper.

In *Nobody's Perfect*, Westlake's narrator puts his finger on the problem when he observes, "Dortmunder always planned well, nobody could argue that, but things never worked out the way they were supposed to" (152). In that novel, all the finely crafted art thefts are aimed at stealing the same painting or its flawless counterfeit. In *The Hot Rock*, the gang tries over and over to steal the same priceless emerald. In both novels, and in Dortmunder's career generally, meticulous planning brings frustration rather than fulfillment. Over the many centuries since Homer invented the genre, readers of caper literature have grown accustomed to seeing such careful planning logically rewarded. The astonishment provoked by having their reasonable expectations overturned surely accounts for much of Westlake's comic success with these readers.

A plot summary of *The Hot Rock* should confirm how this comic transaction takes place. The gang—augmented by an insatiable womanizer named Alan Greenwood—is hired by Major Patrick Iko, minister of the African nation of Talabwo, to steal the legendary Balabomo Emerald, now the property of the rival African nation of Akinzi and on display at the New York Coliseum. The gang almost pulls the heist off perfectly, thanks to Dortmunder's brilliant plan involving phony uniforms, picked locks, bombs, a diversionary car crash, and so forth. Unfortunately, Greenwood's sweaty palms cause him to drop a glass case, triggering an alarm and bringing guards running. Everyone escapes but Greenwood, who secretly swallows the emerald. The gang must then break into prison in order to help Greenwood and the emerald break out, an ironic reversal moving Dortmunder to many sad reflections on the ways of the world. The plan is perfect. Greenwood is freed. It turns out, however, that he concealed the emerald in a city jail cell before being transferred to the big house. Breaking into the city jail requires Dortmunder to develop an even more bizarre plan involving, among other things, the use of a helicopter, thereby providing a transcendent experience for Murch, who has never driven one before. Again everything goes off without a hitch, and again the emerald is missing, stolen by Greenwood's dishonest attorney, E. Andrew Prosker, who has meanwhile had himself committed to an insane asylum to escape the gang's wrath. Breaking into the asylum poses an even greater challenge, and Dortmunder rises to it through the use of a Tom Thumb locomotive. This time, Chefwick is in heaven. Once again they succeed brilliantly. Once again they fail to secure the emerald, which Prosker has stashed in a safety deposit box hedged 'round with so many fail-safe security measures that even Prosker can't get at it. To steal the emerald once and for all, Dortmunder employs more uniforms, a bank robbery, split-second timing, impersonations, and hypnotism. The caper is gloriously successful. Then Major Iko and Prosker join forces to double-cross everyone and get away with the emerald. Dortmunder finally gets it back at the airport and turns it over to the rightful owner, the government of Akinzi, in exchange for a copy he intends to sell to Major Iko for $200,000. The book ends portending bad times for the bad men and good times for the good, namely the Dortmunder gang.

This prosperous ending of *The Hot Rock* is atypical of the series. The gang members are usually as near to broke at the end of the novel as they were at the outset. The plot is otherwise typical, however, in its adherence to a larger pattern. The gang members plan flawlessly, they follow their plan studiously, often with considerable flair, and—like the kidnappers of Sassi Manoon and most of Westlake's other comic crooks—they end up with something other than what they set out for.

In this respect, Westlake's characters more nearly resemble finite human beings buffeted by the vagaries of quotidian life than the perfect personifications of an author's logical, but wishful, thinking. Their attraction for readers is, in this light, unsurprising. It is the attraction of like for like. Major Iko comes very close to articulating this appeal when he says consolingly to Dortmunder, "It was a good plan, and you did run into bad luck, but I'm pleased to see you don't waste time justifying yourself" (23).

The reader rejoices that Dortmunder and Westlake's other comic characters spunkily refuse to be subdued by circumstances. Though their excellent designs are twisted and often ruined by music-maddened Scots, by cases of mistaken identity, by gems that turn up in the wrong places, by foreign cars that have their gear shifts where the turn signals ought to be, by traffic jams, by snowstorms, they maintain their comic resilience. As a result, the reader may accept with smiling good grace Westlake's more serious concern in these novels: the disparity between intention and execution, desire and achievement, the ideal and the real. By exploring these insights through devices varying from small jokes to structural incongruities, Westlake is able to deal with profound truth in comic forms. He thereby allows his readers to laugh rather than to cry at perhaps the most depressing truth of the human condition, the fact that Nobody's Perfect.

Notes

[1]For these reviews and a sampling of other opinions, see Phyllis C. Mendelson and Dedria Bryfonski, eds., *Contemporary Literary Criticism*, 33 vols. to date (Detroit: Gale, 1973-), 7: 528-9.

[2]The ten novels by Donald Westlake treated in this essay were all published in New York. They are listed below with their publishers and dates; further references to the novels will be noted parenthetically in the text:

The Fugitive Pigeon, Random House, 1965.

The Busy Body, Random House, 1966.

Who Stole Sassi Manoon? Random House, 1968.

The Hot Rock, Simon & Schuster, 1970.

Help I Am Being Held Prisoner, M. Evans, 1974.

Jimmy the Kid, M. Evans, 1974.

Two Much, M. Evans, 1975.

Nobody's Perfect, M. Evans, 1977.

Why Me, Viking, 1983.

High Adventure, Mysterious Press, 1985.

[3]John G. Cawelti, *Adventure, Mystery, and Romance: Formula Stories as Art and Popular Culture* (Chicago: Univ. of Chicago Press, 1976), p. 74.

Is It Or Isn't It?: The Duality of Parodic Detective Fiction

Lizabeth Paravisini and Carlos Yorio

Writers of detective fiction discovered long ago that every genre begets its parody and that parody can be the vehicle for genre renovation and transformation. Contrary to other genres (like the pastoral novel and the tale of chivalry) for which parody signaled their end as viable means of literary expression, detective fiction has incorporated its parody and, through it, humor into the tradition. The genre, which already involved the reader as an active participant (a "puzzle-solver"), has added a new dimension to reader participation by forcing a decision as to whether the work is to be read as a "straight" novel or as a parody. Parody has been one of the principal strategies used by writers in the renovation of detective fiction—that is, parody has led to the development of the genre; parody has brought humor to what was in its origins a predominantly humorless genre; and parody has been incorporated into the genre in such a way as to be often unrecognizable as parody.

Parody has not always been highly regarded as a form of literary expression. Definitions of it have ranged from that of the *Oxford English Dictionary*, which defines it as a "burlesque poem or song," to Gilbert Highet's definition in *The Anatomy of Satire* as "imitation which, through distortion and exaggeration, evokes amusement, derision, and sometimes scorn."[1] More recent studies on parody downplay its satiric (negative) aspects and emphasize the avenues it opens for the revitalization of genres.

In her book *Parody/Meta Fiction: An Analysis of Parody as a Critical Mirror to the Writing and Reception of Literature*,[2] Margaret Rose argues that when the formal possibilities of a specific genre appear to have lost their function—i.e. when techniques and structures have grown stale—the genre can gain new life by parodying the older forms and stretching them beyond their former limits. With this function in mind, Rose defines parody as "in its specific form, the critical quotation of preformed literary language with comic effect, and, in its general form, the meta-fictional mirror to the process of composing and receiving literary texts" (p. 59).

It follows from this definition that the distinctive literary role of parody is that of offering two texts within one: the parody itself and the parodied or target text: both present within the new text in a dialogical relationship. Parody is, above all else, dialogical; in parody we find two languages crossed with each other, two styles, two linguistic points of view—in short, two speaking subjects. And although only one of these languages (the one being parodied) is present in its own right, it is the other language (the parodic one) which guides the reader to a new way of perceiving the original.[3]

Because of its "dialogic" nature, parody is "ambivalently critical and sympathetic towards its target" (Rose, p. 34). Parody satirizes its target while being dependent on it for its own materials and structures. The difference between the parody and the target can be used as a weapon against the latter while simultaneously refunctioning the target text for new purposes. Thus parody represents the creation of an alternative form which allows writers to supersede and reorient older traditions. Parody, which is self-reflexive in that it mirrors the process of writing and examines the aims and nature of fiction, is renovating in that it leads to the development of new, if self-conscious, literary forms.

Since parody is self-conscious, it follows that its aims and methods will be different from those of non-parodic works. Non-parodic texts, since their aim is to convince the reader of their truth and reality, strive to blur the reader's awareness of the presence of the literary medium by concealing the literary devices used in the creation of the text. Parody, however, is only effective when the reader's awareness is at its peak. Therefore, since it aims at sharpening the reader's awareness of the presence of the literary medium, parody will focus on the distinctive devices of the original, "laying them bare."[4] The reception of parody by the reader depends on his ability to recognize this "laying bare of the device."

Because parody focuses on the distinctive features of a genre, the ideal reader reaction occurs when the reader recognizes the discrepancy between the parody and its target, while also enjoying the recognition of the hidden irony involved in the highlighting of certain elements. The recognition of the discrepancy by the reader is vital to the effectiveness of parody because the reader's function is to redecode the parody (a work that has resulted from the decoding of the original by the parodist who encoded it again in a "distorted" form). The reader of parody is challenged to the task of interpretation by the evocation of his expectations for a certain text, genre, style or literary world, before these expectations are disappointed. These expectations, however, can be of use to the parodist; they can either inhibit the reader's understanding of the new work or provide him with a familiar framework that could place the new work within the limits of his experience.

It is undeniable that contemporary detective fiction is to a large degree parodic. From its beginning as a genre, detective fiction contained within it the seed of its own metamorphosis: it was a genre which adhered rigidly to a formula, offering a familiar combination of characters and settings, and prototypical detective figures. The development of the hard-boiled detective story in the United States, although widening the possible variations of crime fiction, basically provided an alternative formula. The formulaic nature of the genre, however, is the basis of its appeal. Tzvetan Todorov, in his essay "The Typology of Detective Fiction" writes about the need to work within—not outside—the formula if one wants to write detective fiction:

As a rule, the literary masterpiece does not enter any genre except perhaps its own; but the masterpiece of popular literature is precisely the book that best fits its genre. Detective fiction has its norms, to develop them is to disappoint them: to "improve upon" detective fiction is to write "literature," not detective fiction.[5]

If we accept Todorov's assertion that to transcend the formula is to abandon the genre, then we must conclude that the one avenue left for developing the genre from within is to parody the elements that constitute the formula in order to stretch them beyond their former limits. Hence the innovative changes in the contemporary detective novel which can only be explained as parodic and which create a new bond between writer and reader as two who are "in the know" and can recognize and enjoy the presence of familiar elements in new and often humorous forms. The appeal of parody is at the basis of the popularity of writers such as Robert Barnard, Colin Watson and Robert Parker. We will concern ourselves with one of them, L.A. Morse.

Larry Morse has published four novels to date: *The Old Dick*, (1981, a 1982 Edgar Award winner), *The Big Enchilada* (published in 1982 but written before *The Old Dick*), *An Old-Fashioned Mystery* (1983), and *Sleaze* (1985).[6] All four novels are clearly parodic, and their particular interest in our context rests on the fact that as parodies they run the gamut of parodic forms and styles to be found in contemporary detective fiction.

Morse's works are remarkable for having elicited widely divergent responses from critics and readers alike, responses clearly connected to the recognition (or lack of it) of the parodic aspects of the texts. The following are quotations from some of those responses, taken from reviews of *The Big Enchilada*, the first book written by Morse:

There is sex and/or violence on every tenth page, but it's all romp. The coupling is adolescent fantasy, the blood merely catsup, and the wit doesn't detract from the seriousness of the message. *The Big Enchilada* sends up every canon of private eye from Raymond Chandler to Mickey Spillane. In a genre that is already a parody of machismo, Morse has done the near impossible. He has created a parody of parodies.[7]

I found *The Big Enchilada* a truly vile book, one of the worst I've read in a long time. The main character is a pig and a lout. The violence and sex are gratuitous. The plot is a melange of incredible coincidences. If the book is a parody, it's a complete failure. If it's serious, it's worse.[8]

How tough is Sam Hunter? Remember Dirty Harry? . . . Next to Sam Hunter, Dirty Harry looks like Mother Theresa. In fact, *The Big Enchilada* requires a body count, rather than a review. . . .
    The plot: What plot?
    L.A. Morse has written either the best West Coast detective novel or the best West Coast detective novel parody in years. Either way, its great fun.[9]

These reader responses to *The Big Enchilada* reveal four important elements evident in readings of detective fiction: (1) that readers are often unsure as to whether what they are reading is a parody or a "straight" work; (2) that parody has been so readily accepted into detective fiction that it often doesn't matter to the reader whether the work is parodic or not; (3) that if you are a naive reader—one unable to distinguish between parody and its original—you can miss the point entirely; and that (4) if the work is humorous, it probably is a parody.

The Big Enchilada introduces Sam Hunter, a tough, wise-cracking private eye in the Philip Marlowe mold—only more so. What the book offers is precisely more of everything; it is a parody-by-exaggeration which succeeds by humorously heightening the elements commonly found in hard-boiled detective novels. As the critic quoted above suggests, the novel indeed requires a body count. A firm believer that nothing succeeds like excess, Morse presents us with seven corpses, more than sixteen maimed, castrated, mutilated or merely beaten up bodies, and at least twelve offers of sex (not all of them accepted). The excess alone could mark the book as a parody; but what Morse has in mind is a more systematic, tongue-in-cheek send-up of the genre.

The narrative follows the well-established pattern of the hard-boiled genre: first person narration, every chapter opening with Hunter's comments on Los Angeles (that "work of fiction") prior to facing violence, sex and mayhem, and closing with Hunter's wise-cracking, cynical remarks prior to moving on. Chapter One establishes the narrative pattern that will be followed in the following chapters. It opens with Hunter looking out his office window, business being slow, and considering a vacation to Mexico:

It was another stifling summer day. A sulphurous yellow haze hung over most of Los Angeles. From my window I could see the cars backed up about two miles at one of the freeway interchanges. Down below the winos were shuffling around looking for some patch of shade where they could escape the sun. Even the packs of kids that would usually be breaking windshields or ripping antennas off of parked cars were not on the streets today. It was that hot. (7)

This is followed quickly by the abrupt entrance of a hulk who trashes Hunter about, warning him to stay off Domingo, and leaving him to calm his scantily-clad secretary's fear with a brief and rough bout of sex:

When I was through I let her down slowly. She slid down the wall until she was sitting on the floor, skirt above her waist, legs spread apart, totally spent.
I zipped up my pants and left the office.
I wanted to get something to eat.
I also wanted some information. About Domingo. Whoever or whatever that was.
My vacation would have to wait. Until I found Domingo.
At the very least, Domingo owed me a new desk. (11)

The brief chapter accomplishes two goals. On the one hand, it sets the pace for the chapters to follow, which will open with amusingly cynical remarks about Los Angeles, followed by quick bouts of violence and/or sex, and end with Hunter on the move, commenting wrily on the mess left behind. On the other hand, it affectionately recreates for the reader the elements we have come to associate with the hard-boiled genre: the steaming city of Los Angeles, the dusty office in a dilapidated building, the absence of clients (until a case comes looking for him), the sexy secretary (a dark, voluptuous Mexican) with whom the detective has a friendly, no-strings-attached sexual relationship, the provocation of his thirst for vengeance by an act of unjustified and unexplained violence.

The pattern accounts for the quickness of the pace and explains the staggering amount of bodies Hunter leaves scattered around Los Angeles. It also allows for the introduction of almost every conceivable character associated with the genre: the corrupt cop, the teenage porn star, the gruff cop who helps Hunter reluctantly, the all-powerful nymphomaniac gossip columnist, the grotesquely fat former star turned dope-dealer, and the monosyllabic hulk of a bodyguard, to mention just a few.

The accumulation of elements and characters, presented without derision, but with a speed and frequency not found in non-parodic examples of the genre, is the chief source of humor in the book. This "humor by accumulation" is helped along by Hunter's wry and amusingly detached commentary, as shown in the following examples.

Hunter on women:

I stuck my head around the shower curtain and saw that it could have been a lot worse...it was only the daughter of the woman who manages the apartment building. Her name was Candi or Cindi or Bambi or one of those goddam dumb names that were dropped on kids by parents who were terminally warped by the Mickey Mouse Club.... She was blonde and pretty in a slutty sort of way that exactly suited her name, Suzi or Sherri or whatever it was. (50-51)

Hunter on sex:

She pulled away the towel. "Oh, Sam!" She fell on me like she was dying of hunger and I was the Christmas turkey.
What the hell. I had a couple of hours before my appointment. (137)

Hunter on food:

I had some time to kill so I went to the Krakatoa Restaurant.... Honoring its name, they served a huge cone-shaped pile of noodles that was volcanically hot. The side dish of chile sambal that I poured onto the noodles was nearly strong enough to dissolve the bowl it was in. The delicate, sarong-clad girl who served me couldn't believe what I was doing. She called the rest of the staff out and they stood at a discreet distance away as I worked through the heap. They politely applauded when I finished and returned to their respective jobs. (186)

Morse's humorous style (described by one critic as crackling with "witty toughness"[10] and praised by another for his "superb Chandleresque descriptions of our fair city and its denizens and a gusto so 'macho' it almost creates an acceptable context for his graceless hero"[11]) has been the only aspect of the book to be universally celebrated. The same two critics, for example, reach widely different conclusions regarding the book. While the first finds it to be full of fun, the second one asks:

Who's more despicable in *The Big Enchilada*...the slimy porn-smack czars whom shamus Sam Hunter tracks down or Hunter himself? He throws his steak on a restaurant floor, pulls a Roscoe on a guy playing his car radio too loud, kicks down a door rather than look for the key and leaves poisonous snakes slithering through Beverly Hills.
Hunter may speak to the anger in us all, but I'd rather cross the street to avoid speaking to him.

The two are characteristic of the responses elicited by *The Big Enchilada*, which range from enjoyment of the book *as a parody* to complete rejection of its sex and violence by readers not able to recognize which elements of detective fiction it parodied. The responses are interesting because very few of them fell on the middle ground between acceptance and rejection. That was not the case, however, with *The Old Dick*, a book which received almost unanimous praise from readers and critics, and which was not readily identified by readers as a parody. It is our contention that *The Old Dick* is Morse's best parody (in that it offers the most creative re-elaboration of the formula), as well as being the most representative of the fine line between parody and the "straight" genre that characterizes the contemporary detective novel.

The Old Dick has been described as a "sly send-up of the hard-boiled detective (starring) Jake Spanner, the world's oldest gumshoe, leading a host of geriatric avengers culled from L.A. rest homes."[12] We could add to that apt description that the novel is also a parody nested within the parody of a parody.

The novel opens with a typical scene from a Spillane-type hard-boiled detective novel:

Duke Pachinko lay propped against the wall, a dripping red sponge where his face used to be. He wouldn't bother anyone again.... The blonde looked at the body, and then she looked at me. Her eyes narrowed and her lips parted.... She slowly raised my hands and placed them on her breasts.... Her breath was coming in deep shuddering gasps. I put my hands at the neck of her dress. A quick pull, and the silk tore apart with slithery ripping sound. She stepped out of the remnants of her dress and walked across to me moving like she was hypnotized, her eyes fastened on the bulge in my trousers.... (9-10)

But (alas!) a page and a half later we discover that this is not *our* novel but the parody of a hard-boiled detective novel that our septuagenarian hero Jake Spanner is reading: "I closed the book (he tells us) and put it down on the bench outside. I really didn't need to read stuff like that." (10) From the opening pages of *our* novel, Jake establishes himself as a reader of detective fiction; a reader, moreover, who having been one of the original private eyes in his youth, is ready to reject the parodic world of contemporary detective fiction:

And fifty years later he was lying on an unbelievably ugly couch, reading about a guy named Al Tracker who could shatter other guy's jaws without ever hurting his own hand, and who had beautiful women lining up to give him blow jobs. Tempus fugit.
Forty pages into the book, there had been a garroting, a defenestration, a dismemberment, and a gang rape. Al was out for vengeance (red, I supposed) and a malignant dwarf with a steel hand was out to rip Al's balls off. I dozed off. (33)

Throughout the novel Jake will remain a reader of the adventures of Al Tracker[13] (his reading of that novel parallels our reading of his own adventure), and he will constantly compare the details of his case to those of Al's tale. If, as a parody of the original private eye (a parody of Jake's original self), Al Tracker is found wanting, Jake (also a parody of his original self because he is a very old man) will constantly compare the parody that he is against the parody that Al represents.

There are actually three versions of the private eye present in the novel: (1) Spanner's former self, that of the prototypical private eye as exemplified by Sam Spade; (2) Al Tracker, a parody of the original private eye who bores Spanner the reader because his adventures are too far-fetched and unrecognizable; and (3) Jake Spanner as an old man, constantly comparing himself at seventy-eight to the original Jake Spanner of fifty years before. These three versions of Spanner are constantly present in the text, but only the young Spanner is present in his own literary right; Al Tracker and the current Jake Spanner are copies trying desperately to emulate the original.

The first of these copies, Al Tracker, is bound to fail because he is too much of a caricature. And it is Jake himself as a reader who repudiates him throughout the novel:

Since it didn't look like there was anything I could do until the next day, I smoked myself to the point where the adventures of Al Tracker would seem amusing, if not intelligible. Somewhere between Al wiping out a witches coven and being beaten to a bloody pulp by a gang of Oriental men with bamboo sticks, I got a call from Sal.... Just as Al was about to sink himself into the lubricious body of his client's wife, I gratefully sank into deep, dark, dreamless sleep. (84)

But Al Tracker is also a figure which must be transcended if Jake is to come close to recreating his former self. Jake's existence as a parody, we must remember, is only validated to the degree that he is a "distorted" version of the original. And surely enough, as the plot of Jake's own case thickens, Jake leaves Al behind:

I got into bed and picked up the adventures of Al Tracker. He was hanging by his fingers from a freeway overpass. How did he get there? I didn't care. After recent events, Al's exploits seemed all too tame and plausible. (177)

What Jake cannot succeed in leaving behind is his present self, subject as he is to the indignities of being a 30-year-old private eye in a 78-year-old body. And this incongruity between what a tough private eye *should* do and what the old Jake Spanner *can* do is the source of most of the humor in what is, after all, a very funny book.

Incongruity has long been offered as an explanation for the creation of humor. Quintilian, in his *Institutio Oratoria*, links humor to the disappointment of expectations, a view echoed by Kant, for whom humor was "an affectation arising from the sudden transformation of a strained expectation into nothing."[14] This concept of humor is particularly apt to describe humor in *The Old Dick* since it arises, for the most part, from the disappointment of our expectations as Jake's attempts to act fail miserably *because* he is an old man.

Interestingly enough, however, the novel is not a satire of old age although the work has a fair share of satiric elements.[15] Unlike parody, satire is not necessarily limited to the imitation, distortion or quotation of other literary texts, and the humor in *The Old Dick* is indeed restricted to the incongruity—not between youth and old age—but between two literary figures: the old dick (Jake at 78) and the even older dick which is his former self. (Notice that the title itself, *The Old Dick*, is semantically ambiguous.) The hard-boiled detective is obviously the target of this parody and the elements of the prototype are always present as the sub-text which makes humor possible.

This constant presence of sub-text and text in a dialogical relationship is indeed what makes the work a parody, since parody requires literary self-consciousness, awareness of the need to "lay bare the device." Larry Morse is aware of the need for writers working in the genre to highlight the fact that detective fiction has become a self-conscious genre:

I started writing detective fiction because I knew the genre very well, and enjoyed it. While I never set out to "satirize" it, the genre is by now so formulaic that it's impossible to write about private detectives without some acknowledgment or awareness of what's gone on before. What I do is admit that you can't take this stuff as deadly earnest and serious.[16]

And indeed, most parodies of detective fiction, *The Old Dick* included, do more than just establish a dialogue between parody and target, they also subvert from within those elements that characterize the genre. *The Old Dick*, for example, ends with Jake, who at 78 had faced abject poverty, running off with the crook Sal Piccolo and his million dollars to Tunisia, thereby subverting the prototypical moral stand of the hard-boiled detective. In doing so, Jake has broken the professional code that is such an intrinsic part of the model.

Jake's subversion of the rules points to the need to liberate the genre from strict adherence to the original formula. That is, after all, the recurring theme in the book. Jake, at 78, is as old as the hard-boiled genre, and could be seen to stand as its representation. By accepting the 78 year-old Jake as a private eye, we, as readers, have already subverted our own expectations of what detective fiction should be and in the process, we have allowed for the stretching of the formula beyond its former limits.

A different kind of subversion takes place in *An Old-Fashioned Mystery*, where Morse tries his hand at a truly satiric parody. The clear satiric intent— the use of laughter as a weapon against the classic mystery genre—sets this book apart from Morse's other work. In his preface to the book, Morse refers to *An Old-Fashioned Mystery* as "the mystery to end all mysteries," as "the eschatology of the mystery,"; and indeed, here the classic mystery becomes the object of satiric ridicule in a way not found in those works in which he parodies the hard-boiled detective novel. To judge by the parodic treatment of the two types of mystery fiction in Morse's work, it is not hard to see which type he finds to be alive and well (and likely to be renovated through parody), and which type is dead and gone.

The target text in this parody is obviously the classic mystery in general and Agatha Christie's *Ten Little Indians* (also published as *And Then There Were None*) in particular. The book's premise will be familiar even to casual readers of murder mysteries: ten people gathered together in an isolated manor on one of the Lawrence River Thousand Islands (no boat, no phone, no way out) where it is soon obvious that a killer is loose.

The characters are just as easily recognizable behind their *Clue* masks: Rosa Sill, the nowhere-to-be-found hostess, brand-new heiress, and perfect murder victim; the apoplectic Col. Nigel Dijon who hides God knows what bizarre secrets from his military service in the Asian colonies; Beatrice (Aunt Budgie) Dijon, seemingly harmless wife for whom Rosa's millions could bring freedom from the Colonel's sado-masochistic tendencies; Mr. Eustace Drupe, executor of the will, whose briefcase suspiciously reveals a one-way ticket to South America; Derrick Costain, society beau and Rosa's fiance; Cerise Redford, Rosa's secretary-companion, soon to be unmasked as her illegitimate sister; Mrs. Hook, the housekeeper and potential mass poisoner; Mr. Ching, the cook and erstwhile spy, present to disprove the notion that no Chinaman can figure in a detective story; the plainly loony Mrs. Cassandra Argus, possibly the murderess of Rosa's mother; and eye-shadowed society fop Sebastian Cornichon, smart-alecky twin brother of Society-Girl Detective Violet Cornichon. The latter is set on solving the mystery and ready to entertain bids on the manuscript. The only problem is that as soon as she builds her case and identifies the culprit, her suspect is either poisoned, defenestrated, chopped, drowned, strangled or bludgeoned.

The technique used by Morse in the structuring of *An Old-Fashioned Mystery* is remarkably similar to that used in *The Big Enchilada*: a pattern is established early in the novel and then repeated in a fast-paced narrative that lends itself to the humorous accumulation of familiar elements in parodic excess. Violet's case against Mrs. Hook is just one of the many examples of the burlesque imitation of the quintessential classic detective story:

So, Sis, you're saying that this Hacker killed Mrs. Hook and took her identity. But all the time Mrs. Hook was not Mrs. Hook, but was really Helga Milch. And thus it turned out that Hacker, who is a convicted murderer, is posing as a woman who was herself playing a part to hide the fact that she's an acquitted murderer. What a delicious irony! (154)

But Mrs. Hook is to be found moments later nearly cut in half with a cleaver:

> "Wrong again, Violet," Sebastian said after a moment, flashing his sister a friendly grin.
> Cerise began to sob hysterically, her body shaking with each new burst.
> Sebastian moved to comfort her. "Take it easy," he said. "No use crying over split Milch"....
> "I say! What's that?" Derrick pointed to the ground next to the body.
> "Golly, you're right!" Sebastian said. "Look, Sis. It's the footprints of a giant duck!" (156)

As this and many other examples could show, every cliche found in the classic mystery is employed here, the book being after all a highly elaborate literary joke. The intended audience for this novel is clearly the inveterate reader of classic mysteries, since the deepening layers of humor can only be appreciated by those who are "in the know." The humor arises primarily from the recognition of the multiple "quotations" from other novels found in the book:

> The text is reminiscent of those sequences of fast-flashed photographs that show the events of an era in the space of a minute. Situations, characters, phrases, and dialogue zoom past, evoking elusive images of other books; often the source stays tantalizingly out of reach, just below the surface of memory....After a few pages the reader will "know" that a Christie classic is the basis for the book, and, as the situation unfolds, will be amused and amazed by its simplicity.[17]

The "insider's joke"[18] is obvious both in Morse's manifest intention of parodying Christie, and in his commitment to breaking every single one of Father Ronald Knox's Ten Commandments of Detection (which the reader of *An Old-Fashioned Mystery* will find in a footnote on page 217). This commitment results in a major "transgression" of the rules of detective fiction (or so it has seemed to readers and critics):

> This all would be very thrilling and suspenseful except that Ms. Fairleigh chooses to end with a twist that leaves the reader feeling nothing but betrayal. (Indeed I wanted to throw the book across the room.) This gimmick is low-class, unartistic, unnecessary and it violates the very reason for reading any crime fiction-to try and deduce who the criminal is before it is revealed at the end of the novel. This is impossible in *An Old-Fashioned Mystery*. The ultimate result is disappointment.[19]

The "gimmick" of course is Morse's breaking of Knox's First Commandment, which clearly states that "The criminal must be someone mentioned in the early part of the story, but must not be anyone whose thoughts the reader has been allowed to follow." By making the author the guilty party, Morse fails to satisfy the reader's need for a logical explanation, thereby crossing the imaginary line between what some readers are willing and unwilling to accept in parodies of detective fiction. It is worth noting that the majority of critics commenting on *An Old-Fashioned Mystery* professed to like the novel very much "up until the deus ex machina."

The "transgression" brings us back to Todorov's contention that in order to write detective fiction we must work within the formula, since "to develop the norms is to disappoint them." A review of readers' responses to Morse's books reveals the enthusiastic acceptance of the parodying of the elements of detective fiction, as long as the parody does not transcend the essential rules that govern the genre. The parodist, they seem to tell us, can break the Fifth Commandment ("No Chinaman must figure in the story") with impunity; but he must not break commandments that transcend essential rules (i.e., "All supernatural or preternatural agencies are ruled out as a matter of course"). And whereas Chinamen in detective fiction can turn out to be pretty funny, reunions in heaven apparently are not.

The choice of humor as the imaginary line that separates successful from unsuccessful parodies is not inappropriate when applied to detective fiction in general and Morse's works in particular. His most successful parody, *The Old Dick*, is both the book that remains closest to its model and his funniest one by far. This connection between humor and "success" in parody is underscored by the critics' reactions to Larry Morse's work. The further he strays from the conventions of the genre, the greater the diversity in the responses to his work and the greater the number of readers who do not recognize the humor in the text.

The Old Dick and *The Big Enchilada* succeed precisely because they can be wildly funny books, even while poking fun at the conventional formulas of detective fiction. They offer clear evidence (the pun *is* intended) of the possibilities parody opens for the revitalization of detective fiction. That the genre has been able to incorporate its parody into the tradition assures us of many more detectives stories to come.[20]

Notes

[1](Princeton: Princeton University Press, 1962), p. 69.

[2](London: Croom Helm Ltd., 1979)

[3]Mikhail Bakhtin, *The Dialogic Imagination*, translated by Caryl Emerson and Michael Holquist, (Austin: University of Texas Press, 1981), p. 79.

[4]Tuvia Shlonsky, "Literary Parody: Remarks on Its Method and Function," in *Proceedings of the 4th Congress of the International Comparative Literature Association*, Vol. 2, 1966, p. 800.

[5]*The Poetics of Prose* (Ithaca: Cornell University Press, 1977), p. 43.

[6]The editions of Morse's works discussed in this essay are listed below, preceded by the original date of publication. All quotations will be cited in the text using, where necessary for clarity, the abbreviation given after the entry:

1981   *The Old Dick* (New York: Avon, 1981). (TOD)
1982   *The Big Enchilada* (New York: Avon, 1982). (TBE)
1983   *An Old-Fashioned Mystery* (Toronto: Lester & Orpen Dennys, 1983). (OFM)

We will omit *Sleaze* (New York: Avon, 1985) from the discussion since our analysis of *The Big Enchilada* holds true for the parodic elements to be found in *Sleaze.*

[7]Margaret Cannon, "Gritty Antidotes to Bucolic Boredom," *MacLean's*, 14 June 1982, p. 53.

[8]Bill Crider, quoted by Walter Albert in "The Big Controversy," *The Not So Private Eye*, Issue 11 1/2 (1984), [s.p.]

[9]Michael Neill, "Mystery Roundup,"*NY Daily News*, 1 February 1982, [s.p.].

[10]Richard Labonte, *"The Big Enchilada," Ottawa Citizen*, 12 March 1982, [s.p.].

[11]*"The Big Enchilada," Los Angeles Times*, 14 March 1982.

[12]*Cannon*, p. 53.

[13]There is a parodic link—a very funny private joke—concerning *Red Vengeance*, the book that relates Al Tracker's adventures. It parallels, and parodies, Sam Hunter's first adventure, *The Big Enchilada* (which must be remembered, was written before *The Old Dick*). In an amusing case of intertextuality, this is what Hunter (Tracker?) has to say: "I would extract vengeance, red vengeance...Vengeance! I could taste it in my mouth. A red haze dropped before my eyes, and I saw vengeance, red vengeance. It would be mine. It would be good." (TBE, 139-140)

[14]*Institutio Oratoria*, Book 6:3 (Cambridge: Harvard University Press, 1960), p. 17. Kant's remarks are quoted in *The Psychology of Humor*, J. Goldstein and P. McGhee (eds.) (New York: Academic Press, 1972), p. 8.

[15]*An Old-Fashioned Mystery*, as we will see later, is Morse's true satiric parody.

[16]Morse's correspondence, 3 January 1986. He adds the following: "The writer's job is to engage the reader, to entertain, to keep the reader turning pages; humor is one effective method of achieving this, and because I enjoy it myself, I try to put a lot of humor in my books. Looking at Fowler's Humor Chart, I probably use all of the approaches that are mentioned. If nothing else, humor is a good way of avoiding solemnity, pomposity and arrogance self-importance, three of the deadliest sins that can afflict a writer...."

[17]John North, *"An Old-Fashioned Mystery," Quill & Quire*, March 1984, [s.p.].

[18]There is, of course, an additional "insider's joke" in the Runa Fairleigh hoax. Fairleigh is the reclusive author whose disappearance—leaving behind the manuscript "found" and "edited" by Morse—is as mysterious as the novel she has written.

[19]Kelly Devries, "Low Class Gimmick Ending Spoils The Mystery in Otherwise Good *An Old Fashioned Mystery*," *The Newspaper*, 1 February 1984, [s.p.].

[20]Our heartfelt thanks to Larry Morse for giving us access to his reviews and correspondence and answering our many questions.

Contributors

Earl F. Bargainnier was Fuller E. Callaway Professor of English at Wesleyan College. A former President of the Popular Culture Association, he was the author of more than sixty articles and *The Gentle Art of Murder: The Detective Fiction of Agatha Christie.* He has previously edited *Ten Women of Mystery* and *Twelve Englishmen of Mystery* and co-edited *Cops and Constables.* Professor Bargainnier died January 3, 1987.

Jane S. Bakerman, Professor of English at Indiana State University, has served as advisor-contributor to *Twentieth Century Crime and Mystery Writers,* editions I and II. Her essay, "Ruth Rendell," appeared in *Ten Women of Mystery,* and "Daphne du Maurier" appeared in *And Then There Were Nine...More Women of Mystery,* which she edited. She is also co-editor of *Adolescent Female Portraits in the American Novel: 1961-1981; An Annotated Bibliography.*

Elaine Bander is a member of the Department of English at Dawson College in Montreal, where she teaches a course on detection and literature. She has published a number of articles on aspects of detective fiction, especially on Dorothy L. Sayers, as well as others on Jane Austen.

Neysa Chouteau is senior editor in the Webster Division of McGraw-Hill Book Company, and **Martha Alderson** is editor there. Alone and together, they have contributed to *And Then There Were Nine, Cops and Constables, Twentieth Century Crime and Mystery Writers, The Mystery Fancier,* and *Ellery Queen's Mystery Magazine.* Both contributed to *Portraits of the Adolescent Female in the American Novel.* Neysa Chouteau has also published in other fields and is co-author of a series of arithmetic books for special education students.

Wister Cook is Associate Professor of English at the Georgia Institute of Technology. She has published articles on Joan Didion, Alexandra Roudybush, and John D. MacDonald, has presented papers on comedy at meetings of the Popular Culture Association in the South, and is currently writing an essay on the Roman Catholic priest as detective.

Mary Jean DeMarr is Professor of English at Indiana State University. Her articles on detective fiction have appeared in *Clues* and *The Mystery Fancier.* She has recently co-edited *Adolescent Female Portraits in the American Novel: 1961-1981; An Annotated Bibliography.* She is American

Editor of the Modern Humanities Research Association's *Annual Bibliography of English Language and Literature*.

Michael Dunne, Professor of English at Middle Tennessee State University, has previously written extensively about both American literature and popular culture. He is co-author of *Main Themes in American Literature* and is editor of *Border States*, the journal of the Kentucky/Tennessee American Studies Association.

Barrie Hayne is Professor of English at the University of Toronto. An Australian specializing in American literature and film, he has contributed essays to various journals and books, including *Ten Women of Mystery*, *Twelve Englishmen of Mystery*, *Cops and Constables* and *Twentieth Century Crime and Mystery Writers*.

Frederick Isaac is Librarian at the University of Santa Clara in California. His numerous articles have appeared in library journals and such mystery oriented magazines as *Clues, The Mystery Fancier*, and *The Armchair Detective*. He also regularly contributes mystery reviews to the San Francisco *Chronicle*.

H.R.F. Keating is the distinguished British novelist and short-story writer, creator of Inspector Ghote of the Bombay CID. Among his awards are the Crime Writers Association Gold Dagger in 1964 and 1981, a special Edgar Allan Poe award in 1965, and Ellery Queen's Mystery Magazine Prize for short story in 1970. He was for fifteen years crime fiction reviewer for *The Times*, London. His studies of crime fiction include *Murder Must Appetize*, and *Writing Crime Fiction*.

Lizabeth Paravisini is Chair of the Puerto Rican Studies Department and Director of the Bilingual Program at Lehman College of the City University of New York. Her publications include articles, reviews and translations of contemporary Caribbean and popular literature, and she is editor of a forthcoming volume of essays on Puerto Rican women writers. Her co-author **Carlos Yorio** is Professor of Linguistics at Lehman College and the Graduate Center of CUNY. He has published numerous articles on reading, language errors, and applied neurolinguistics, and is co-author of *Who Done Did It?*, a "crime reader for students of English," published by Prentice-Hall.